Retro Style

Retro Style

Class, Gender and Design in the Home

Sarah Elsie Baker

B L O O M S B U R Y

LONDON • NEW DELHI • NEW YORK • SYDNEY

Bloomsbury Academic

An imprint of Bloomsbury Publishing Plc

50 Bedford Square	175 Fifth Avenue
London	New York
WC1B 3DP	NY 10010
UK	USA

www.bloomsbury.com

First published 2013

British Library Cataloguing-in-Publication Data
A catalogue record for this book is available from the British Library.

ISBN:	HB:	978-0-8578-5107-9
	PB:	978-0-8578-5108-6
	ePub:	978-0-8578-5109-3

Library of Congress Cataloging-in-Publication Data
A catalog record for this book is available from the Library of Congress.

Typeset by Apex CoVantage, LLC, Madison, WI, USA.
Printed and bound in India

Contents

List of Tables and Illustrations

Tables

Figures

Acknowledgments

Knowingly, and sometimes unknowingly, many people have helped me write this book. I am most grateful to everyone who took part in my ethnographic research. Without your generosity this project would definitely not have been possible. I would also like to thank Bev Skeggs, Joanne Hollows, Mica Nava, Jackie Botterill, Helen Powell and Rosalind Edwards for inspiring me and offering extremely helpful comments along the way. I want to thank Ben Pitcher, Karen Cross, Rebecca Bramall, Jorge Camacho and Jamie Hakim for listening to me talk about retro for what must have seemed like forever, and my colleagues at Middlesex University—in particular James Graham, Ginnie Crisp and Ben Little—for taking the strain while I was on research leave. I would like to thank my new colleagues at Victoria University for asking great questions and for getting me to think about design in new ways. Special thanks go to my parents for not only putting up with but encouraging my continual analysis of people and their things. Most of all, I would like to thank Dom for his support and belief in my abilities, as well as for his patience with my ongoing desire to "do up" the house.

Introduction

On Saturday, May 26, 2007, the *Guardian Weekend* magazine published a special retro issue consisting of articles about retro food, cars, fashion, gardens and homes. The style section of the magazine featured enthusiasts in their living rooms surrounded by retro objects from various decades including 1970s patterned wallpaper, 1960s pineapple ice buckets and 1950s fabrics. Almost every week since, the magazine has included domestic interiors that are described as retro, vintage or mid-century modern.

This is just one of the many examples that illustrate the proliferation of objects and styles that are described as retro. Retro is global as well as local. It can be found in popular media and on high streets, in fanzines, on the Internet and on market stalls. As the example above demonstrates, *retro* is used to describe clothing, music, food and events, as well as decorative objects, furniture and interiors. Despite its prevalence and cultural familiarity, popular and academic definitions of the style are hard to come by, and the production and consumption of retro objects, furniture and interiors have never been the sole focus of academic research. This book aims to address this lacuna with an ethnographic study of the production, consumption and representation of domestic retro style in Britain. It considers what retro means and why it is valued, who is involved in its production and consumption and how retro style manifests itself in the domestic interior.

My approach to these questions, and my motivations for exploring them, comes partly from an observation of the domestic interiors of my family and of the changes in value of one object in particular: flying ducks. Flying ducks are ceramic wall plaques that are often bought and sold in sets of three (Figure 1.1). Originally mass-produced in the 1930s, the ducks were sold as "fancies" and were hung on the walls of many suburban homes (Oliver *et al.*, 1981:190). In the 1950s the production and consumption of ducks increased, and cheaper sets made of plaster were produced. These flying ducks were available to those with lower incomes, and the objects became "more readily associated with working-class homes" (Gillilan, 2003:32). It was in 1951 that my grandparents received a set of plaster flying ducks as a wedding present. The ducks were displayed above the stairs in the tied cottage they lived in as part of my grandfather's employment as a farm laborer.

Figure 1.1   Flying ducks on the back wall of a 1940s/1950s front room (2010). © Clive Morgan 1st Choice Images.

When my grandparents moved in 1965, the ducks moved with them and found a new location on the wall above the sideboard.

Flying ducks were associated with bad taste by journalists, architects, designers and cultural critics in the 1930s partly because they were a part of the "Tudobethan" aesthetic that mixed antique styles and modern materials (Ryan, 1995). The frivolous fancies were also viewed as inappropriate in modernist domestic interiors and were part of the gendering of mass culture that has been well documented (Huyssen, 1986; Oliver *et al.*, 1981; Ryan, 1995). This association intensified in the 1950s, 1960s and 1970s. In the early 1960s the ducks appeared as part of the working-class interiors on the long-running British soap opera *Coronation Street*. Most notably, the ducks were written into the storyline of the soap in the 1970s, when Hilda Ogden, a character who worked as a cleaner, redecorated her home. The ducks, her serving hatch and her "muriel" (as she called it, instead of "mural") represented her aspirations for a better life. However, Hilda's taste was a subject of ridicule by the other characters on the street and by the audience. From this point on, flying ducks became more widely thought of as tasteless, and they decreased in value. In 1979 Michael Thompson noted that "despite the demand created by the practitioners of high camp, there is little if any, market in second-hand Tretchikoffs, cocktail bar requisites, plaster ducks and garden gnomes" (1979:19). This does not mean, however,

Figure 1.2   Flying ducks in a 1990s retro room (2006). © Dave Young.

that the value of the ducks decreased for my grandparents, who continued to display their set until my grandmother broke one of them while cleaning in the early 1990s.

Thompson was also unaware of the revaluation of flying ducks that was around the corner. From the early 1980s onwards, a different type of consumer was buying flying ducks to recreate 1950s retro interiors (Figure 1.2). The ducks were valued precisely because of their previous associations with bad taste and the working classes. As one retro retailer I spoke to put it, flying ducks are

> the icon of the fifties and of working-class chic...they were bad taste, but to my customers that's good. (Helen, retailer, 2006)

In the beginning this increase in value was marginal enough not to affect their price. However, as part of the prevalence of retro style already referred to, original sets of ceramic flying ducks have sold for more than £100 on eBay in recent years. Flying ducks have also become common in branding and advertising as symbols of domesticity.[1]

In my family I was the person who seemed most aware of the renewed value of my grandparents' taste, and I was most likely to think it desirable.

Even in comparison to family members of a similar age, my taste was, and is, markedly different. These differences are a product of my own biography: a combination of moving to a more middle-class area when I was young as a result of my parents' social mobility, of being the first one to get a degree, of studying advertising and working in arts marketing, of living in London, of studying for a PhD and of writing this book. These experiences distance me both temporally and spatially from the tastes of my grandparents. My identity allows me, if so inclined, to display flying ducks without being marked as old-fashioned or tasteless.

It is the process by which the value of retro objects and styles is made and unmade, and the positions and perspectives that allow this to take place, that I will argue is lacking in many previous discussions of retro style. This brief narrative of the changes in value of flying ducks illustrates that the classification of an object as retro is more than an acknowledgment of material characteristics. It is also a cultural, social and aesthetic judgment of value and a process of revaluation that relies on knowledge of the past cultural associations of objects and styles. The naming of an object as retro also marks its movement from one context to another. Symbolically, and often materially, flying ducks move from spaces such as my grandparents' front room, to retro boutiques, to the pages of lifestyle magazines and to the walls of designer apartments.

In this book I have set myself the task of detailing, analyzing and theorizing this process. I consider how the value of domestic retro style is made and unmade through the cultural practices of production, consumption and representation in three spaces: retail, the media and the home. To do this I draw on textual and ethnographic data gathered between 2006 and 2010. This includes interviews conducted with six retro retailers, four tastemakers and twelve retro enthusiasts over a six-month period in 2006/2007. As such, the ethnographic material in the book records a specific moment in the history of retro style and the home.

The story of flying ducks that I have documented here is specific to Britain. So, too, are many of the other examples I include in the book. This means that for the international reader the analysis may appear culturally specific. However, because (re)valuation hinges on position and perspective, detailed contextual analysis is essential, and this could not have been achieved by thinking about the global meanings of retro. In any case, it is the process (rather than the story of specific cultural products) that has wider relevance. While class, gender and race manifest themselves in different ways according to where you are in the world, the narratives of cultural appropriation of old material objects associated with "trailer trash" in the United States (airstream trailers, flowery curtains and leatherette seats), the urban working class in Mexico (film posters, basketware and religious artifacts), communist orkers in China (water flasks and utilitarian furniture) and Kiwiana in New Zealand (tiki glasses and decorative objects made of paua shells) raise similar issues to those explored here. Although the items in question are unique, the value to be derived from appropriating objects and styles associated with working-class culture seems ubiquitous.

An approach to retro style that focuses on cultural practice and uses ethnographic methods is not unprecedented. Over twenty years ago, Angela McRobbie (1989) argued that an analysis of production and consumption practices could produce richer accounts of retro that questioned theorizations of the style as nostalgic or superficial. More recently, as part of ethnographic research on secondhand cultures, Nicky Gregson and Louise Crewe (2003) interviewed a number of retro retailers and consumers. They argued that the historical, geographical and symbolic biographies of goods were particularly important to the production and consumption of retro. Both these studies also documented a number of pivotal moments in the development of the style. In my approach and the discussion of my findings I am deeply indebted to this research.

However, when I read these texts, a number of areas did not fit with my experience. In the research of Gregson and Crewe there were references to individuality, difference and cultural capital but no substantial discussion of the class positions of retro retailers or enthusiasts. This seemed strange considering that my own background, education and employment had been so influential in shaping my taste and differentiating it from that of my extended family. Gregson and Crewe's analysis also suggested that men were more likely to fantasize about past identities than women (Gregson and Crewe, 2003:52). Considering the number of lifestyle television programs that had used the practices, objects and identities associated with the mid-century housewife as a resource (see Hollows, 2003), I was not sure how accurate this was.

In McRobbie's work the discussion of class and gender was more overt, but I still felt that part of her argument needed to be explored. In a revised version of "Second-Hand Dresses and the Role of the Rag Market" McRobbie suggested that "increasing fluidity across old class lines," the mass production of retro styles and the role of the media in circulating tastes meant that the constituency for retro style had grown and was increasingly diverse (McRobbie, 1994:138). McRobbie's argument implied that the relationship between taste and class was less direct than it once had been and that the production and consumption of retro style had partly contributed to this change. The article also suggested that new fashions and styles increasingly came "from below" and that there was a case for the "death of the designer" (McRobbie, 1994:153). McRobbie wrote that women and young girls were central to this process and that retro style played with the "expectations of femininity, post-feminism" (1994:148). She celebrated these changes and looked positively on the new "freedoms" of postmodernity.

My own feelings about the relationship between retro style and class were less optimistic. From my experience selling retro jewelry at a market in North London, the style seemed to be a middle-class interest. Part of the value of retro objects derived from ideas about authenticity and connoisseurship: qualities that have long been associated with high culture and high levels of cultural capital. More generally, I felt that taste and aesthetic disposition continued to shape, and be shaped by, class and gender identity.

I embarked on this project, therefore, to explore the disparity between previous theorizations of retro style and my own observations. To do this I have examined the aesthetic choices, practices and identities of retro retailers and enthusiasts. I ask whether mass production, retro retailing and the media have created larger and more diverse constituencies for retro style and whether these changes have contributed to the dislocation of the relationship between taste, class and gender. I document the history of retro style for the home and consider whether the difference between my own observations and those of previous theorists is a product of the development of retro style over time, indicative of differences between retro fashion and retro interiors, or whether retro style has an alternative history that is linked to cultural distinction. I also consider how the consumption and production of retro reflect and contribute to gender norms and ask what an analysis of the style can offer a feminist politics.

By exploring these questions, this research engages not only with academic discussions of retro but also with wider discourses of the radical potential of the style. Throughout the book I document, and often question, the ways in which retro styles are represented as available to all, as less hierarchical forms of consumption and as necessarily less commercial and harmful to the environment. At the same time, consuming retro style can also be less dependent on economic resources, often involves reuse and seems to represent a form of disaffection with the status quo. Thus, I take into account both the limits and the potential of the production and consumption of retro style as socially and environmentally progressive practices.

By recognizing and discussing these complexities, the book engages with a number of wider debates. Methodologically the book feeds into the increasing body of work focused on the social, cultural and political significance of everyday domestic experiences, technologies and design (e.g., Briganti and Mezei, 2012). The research responds to discussions regarding the relevance of class analysis to contemporary British society and draws on theorizations that suggest culture has become central to the making of class (Savage, 2000; Skeggs, 2004a). Through discussions of consumer culture and family life the book also engages with theories of gender power and womens empowerment in a postfeminist context. By focusing on the positions and perspectives from which retro style is made and unmade, I also consider the ways in which certain individuals accumulate capital and appropriate the objects, styles, feelings and affects of others to enhance their own status. In this regard, the book is in dialogue with ideas about the commodification of experiences, bodies and identities considered central to neoliberal culture and flexible capitalism (e.g., Aronczyk and Powers, 2010; Gilbert, 2008; Skeggs, 2004d; Wernick, 1991). At the same time, this project engages with the body of work that has identified an increasing disaffection with commodified relations among some consumers (Binkley and Littler, 2008; Lewis and Potter, 2011; Soper, 2008). Thus, while this research is centered on exploring the cultural practices that make and unmake the value of retro style, it also provides a useful route into some of the political, social and cultural issues at stake in contemporary consumer culture.

OUTLINE OF THE BOOK

In Chapter 2 I continue the discussion of the theoretical and methodological approaches introduced here. As I have suggested, previous theorizations of retro style influence my approach, and I begin chapter 2 by considering how the style has been defined. I explore the difference between retro, vintage and mid-century modern. From a critical review of the literature and analysis of various examples, I set out my own definition of retro style as a cultural, social and aesthetic judgment of value. Drawing on theories that suggest authenticity has become an important quality in contemporary European societies, I argue that categorizing objects as retro often bestows them with high cultural value (Appadurai, 1986; Clifford, 1988; Lash and Lury, 2007; Lury, 1996). I propose that the definition of an object as retro is not available to all but depends on the appropriate knowledge, identity and context, all of which are contingent on high levels of cultural capital.

I suggest that movement from one context to another is central to the making and unmaking of the value of retro style and that methodological approaches that focus on object biographies are particularly useful to explore this movement (Appadurai, 1986; du Gay et al., 1997; Hebdige, 1988; Kopytoff, 1986). I argue that these approaches are advantageous because they recognize that the processes of production, consumption and representation contribute to the making of meaning and value in complex and interrelated ways. I also identify some of the limits of circuit of culture type models, including the problems inherent in predefining the activities that go on in certain spaces, for example, associating the home with consumption rather than production. This leads me to propose an approach to retro style that focuses on specific spaces (retail, the media and the home) and all the cultural practices (consumption, production and representation) that take place within them. To do this I draw on ethnographic and textual data, and the chapter goes on to discuss the politics of representing domestic cultures and the everyday. I also consider my role as a researcher and as a selector of sources. I argue that reflections on the research process are as important as the content and analysis of the research product itself. This is especially significant because of the emphasis I place on position and perspective in the making and unmaking of retro style.

Chapter 3 includes a more detailed discussion of the aestheticization of everyday life, and I explore how the value of authenticity and the emergence of lifestyle reflect, and emerge from, the concept of the "possessive individual" as an ideal. This leads me to consider the extent to which aesthetic values (as defined by the art-culture system) are available or attractive to all. To explore this question I turn to sociological debates about the pertinence of class in light of the charge that it is losing its credibility in contemporary consumer society (Beck, 1992; Chaney, 1996; Giddens, 1991). Drawing on the work of Pierre Bourdieu, Mike Savage and Beverley Skeggs, I argue for the salience of class as a concept and for its relevance to the analysis of retro style. In the second half of the chapter I go on to discuss the problems with a Bourdieusian model when analyzing gender and materiality. This leads me to explore studies of consumption that have been influenced by actor-network theory and theories of affect. I document how these approaches attempt to go beyond symbolism and the accrual of capital, and I outline how these perspectives have influenced the ethnographic methods I have used. Finally, I set out the approach to class and gender that I adopt in the book.

In Chapter 4 I document a history of the retro aesthetic. I begin the chapter by suggesting that a new way of consuming the past emerged in the 1960s that was different from the consumption of secondhand, antique and revival that went before it. I argue that retro style built on these traditions but placed more emphasis on eclecticism and individuality. I go on to document how retro style developed from the mid-1960s to the 1990s. I argue that what once had been associated with youth and counterculture in the 1960s had become thoroughly popularized by the 1980s and 1990s. To conclude the chapter I briefly explore the use of retro aesthetics in more recent cultural products, and this frames a discussion of the politics of the popularization of retro style.

In Chapter 5 I continue the discussion of the consequences of the popularization outlined in Chapter 4 by exploring retro retailing in its various forms. I begin the chapter by suggesting that as retro styles are mass-produced, other modes of acquisition (where and how objects are purchased) become more valuable to retro retailers and enthusiasts. Thus, although the popularization of retro style may mean more objects are available, distinctions are made that narrow the definition of retro styles that are in good taste. I go on to explore how this process is evident in the practices of retro retailers. Focusing on retro retailing in boutiques and market stalls I explore the role of retailers in the processes of urban and aesthetic gentrification. The chapter considers the gender and class identity of retro retailers in relation to theorizations of other cultural intermediaries; I find that most retailers have different identities from their customers. This argument is made more complex, however, by the discussion of informal retail networks such as jumble sales and eBay. These sites allow individuals or small groups to become retro retailers without establishing themselves as businesses. Thus, I explore the extent to which these alternative spaces give individuals agency, in terms of both allowing more democratic relations of exchange and enabling anticonsumerist practices.

In Chapter 6 I discuss the role of lifestyle media in popularizing tastes for domestic retro style. Drawing on recent theorizations of lifestyle media and class, I consider the power relations that are played out on screen and in magazine pages. I suggest that because of their high levels of cultural capital, retro enthusiasts and collectors can disrupt the normative distributions of power between expert and participant. I also argue that there is a hierarchy of different types of retro tastes and that three related values (eclecticism, individuality and effort) emerge as important to the success of a retro interior. I consider how enthusiasts' and collectors' knowledge can deviate from that which is considered desirable in the mainstream media. Through analysis of micro and niche media aimed at retro enthusiasts and collectors, the differences in the values and practices of these groups are highlighted.

In Chapter 7 I begin to analyze the ethnographic research I conducted with retro enthusiasts in their homes. I document the type of interiors that enthusiasts create. I explore how retro enthusiasts discuss their objects in terms of originality, quality and individuality and analyze their visions of ideal interiors. This allows me to consider the similarities between my findings and other studies focused on domestic space, taste and class. I also examine the appropriation of old working-class objects and identities by retro enthusiasts and discuss these findings in relation to theorizations of the practices of the new middle class. I find that the majority of retro enthusiasts are from middle-class backgrounds. A minority come from working-class backgrounds; in the second half of the chapter I consider the practices and tastes of these individuals in more detail.

The discussion of the homes and practices in Chapter 7 points to a number of interesting issues in terms of the gender. Thus, in Chapter 8 I focus specifically on retro femininities and consider McRobbie's theorization that retro style allows women to play with gender norms. I begin by briefly outlining the gendering of modernist discourse because retro enthusiasts often take inspiration from modernist interiors. I explore whether there has been a neutralization of modernist design in terms of gender. I go on to document retro enthusiasts' homemaking practices, specifically DIY (do-it-yourself) and shopping, and consider the extent to which these practices produce normative gender roles. In the second part of the chapter I explore the visions of past lives that often accompany the production of a retro interior. Focusing specifically on fantasies of domestic life, I explore the differences between enthusiasts' lifestyles and practices and those of the mid-twentieth century housewives that they fantasize about. I argue that the glamour associated with past objects and identities is part of their appeal. To conclude the chapter I consider what these findings can offer a feminist politics.

Finally, in the Conclusion to the book, I draw together the arguments of each chapter and discuss my findings in relation to previous theorizations of retro style. This discussion leads me to consider the radical potential of retro style in terms of equality and sustainability. I also highlight a number of areas for future research.

The Definitions and Distinctions of Retro Style

I don't understand what retro means. Is it stuff that is pretending to be old or something, you know like a '60s lamp that was made in the year 2005, is that retro? Or is it old bits of crap, old bits of toot, what is it?...I don't know what retro means, but I'd better because everyone knows what it is.

—Tommy, retailer and entrepreneur (2005)

Retro is a term that is familiar to most people and is usually used to describe the revival of past styles. However, in practice its meaning is ambiguous. As the quote above demonstrates, even a retailer and entrepreneur who is considered one of the founders of retro retailing in Britain (although he would not define himself in those terms) does not know what it means. This ambiguity is partly because objects described as retro in one context may be described as vintage, mid-century, secondhand, kitsch or antique in others. Thus, I begin this chapter by exploring previous theorizations of retro style and by introducing and defining some of its qualities in relation to debates around postmodernism. I go on to develop my own definition of retro style and describe how this definition influences, and is influenced by, a methodological perspective inspired by work on object biographies. I conclude the chapter by reflecting on the specificities of researching domestic cultures and by outlining my approach to the empirical research used in the book.

DEFINING RETRO STYLE

The use of the term *retro* to describe cultural products and material objects is said to have occurred first in France in the early 1970s. It emerged as a way to characterize the growing interest in styles from the recent past in French avant-garde cinema, at Parisian fashion houses and in street markets (Guffey, 2006:14; Samuel, 1994:85). The term was adopted in Britain, and a shop bearing the name "retro" appeared in London in 1974 (Samuel, 1994:85).

However, it was not until much later that references to retro appeared in academic research (Baudrillard, 1994; Franklin, 2002; Gregson and Crewe, 2003; Guffey, 2006; Jameson, 1985; Jenß, 2004; McRobbie, 1989, 1994; Samuel, 1994; Thorne, 2003). Although recent discussion of retro and nostalgia has emerged from literary studies (e.g., Boym, 2001; Thorne, 2003), attempts to define the qualities of retro objects are most explicit in work from, or within, the context of design and art history (e.g., Franklin, 2002; Guffey, 2006). In my view, however, these theorizations are inadequate because they adopt an approach that is focused on the classification of objects into existing style categories.

In his paper "Consuming Design: Consuming Retro" Adrian Franklin suggests that *retro* is the term given by consumers and producers to the consumption of secondhand goods originally mass-produced in the 1950s to 1980s (2002:98). Even though the majority of retro goods are from this period, this definition is limiting. It attempts to contain retro within an established notion of style that has specific material characteristics and can "be named and dated" (Auslander, 1996:1). Defining *retro* in this way, Franklin conveniently ignores the flexibility of retro as a style category. For example, both newly produced objects, such as reproduction 1950s-style fridges (Figure 2.1), and

Figure 2.1   1950s-style fridge (2010). © Vorm in Bleed, Shutterstock.com.

objects produced before the 1950s, such as 1940s sofas (Figure 2.2), have been defined as retro. Indeed, retro is interesting precisely because of its flexibility.

While terms like *vintage* and *mid-century modern* have also been used to describe reproduction items in recent years, they more commonly describe original items. In Britain at least, furniture and decorative objects described as vintage tend to have more of a granny-chic aesthetic and show obvious signs of wear. This includes items such as 1930s wooden tables and chairs, floral fabrics and mirrors with beveled edges. The term *mid-century modern* alludes to the designs of the 1950s and 1960s and tends to include higher-price items designed by, or in the style of, famous modernist designers. Furniture such as teak cabinets, rattan and wire chairs and atomic-style fabrics are commonly found within this category. Even though certain objects are frequently associated with these definitions, the categories are relatively interchangeable: a teak sideboard could be described as vintage in one context, mid-century modern in the next and retro in another. However, because retro is more likely to include both reproduction and original items, it is the most flexible. Thus, by using the term *retro* in this book, rather than *vintage* or *mid-century modern,* I can explore a range of ideas about authenticity and value.

In *Retro: The Culture of Revival,* Elizabeth E. Guffey also explores the meaning of retro style from a design-history perspective. Her definition of *retro* is

Figure 2.2   1940s sofa (2010).

more complex than Franklin's because she acknowledges that *retro* is "a word with many meanings" (2006:9). She points out that *retro* has been used to define objects that are technologically obsolete, in addition to those that are considered design classics; and to describe original objects as well as reproductions (2006:9–10). She also recognizes that the term can convey a backward outlook on life, as well as representing a questioning of the positive progressivism of the modernist era.

However, in the rest of her book, in which she discusses the retro revival of four styles (art deco, art nouveau, the 1950s and futurism), these complexities are less apparent. By analyzing retro through the revival of other distinct styles, which are easier to define, Guffey implies that the development of retro style was linear. She suggests that a retro interest in art nouveau was superseded by a retro interest in art deco. Although the style is subject to trends, I would argue that Guffey's analysis pays insufficient attention to its eclecticism. For example, the shop interior of the late 1960s fashion retailer Biba, which Guffey (2006:87) uses as an example of the revival of art deco style, was at the same time also fitted with Victorian and art nouveau objects. Therefore, much like Franklin, Guffey reverts to a discussion of retro style as a number of specific design movements that can be named and dated.

Approaching retro in this way allows Guffey to argue that the style is a speeded-up version of revival. She observes that the time it takes for an out-of-date object or style to become fashionable has changed from 160 years in the 1930s to 15 years in the 1980s (Guffey, 2006:161). I agree in part with Guffey's observation, particularly in light of the many material objects made in the 1980s, 1990s and even 2000s that are now being defined as retro. The increase in the speed of revival is one of the characteristics that distinguishes retro objects from antiques, which according to the official definition should not be less than 100 years old (Hearnden and Norfolk, 2006).

Yet in practice this distinction is far from clear-cut. For example, at Kensington Antiques Fair in London, a traditional and relatively exclusive antiques fair, dealers are starting to sell retro objects and furniture alongside antiques. This is evidence of the wider desirability of retro in comparison to antiques, and of the crisis in the antiques market more generally (Jenkinson, 2010). Indeed, in some respects retro style could be thought of as the "new antique." Like the definition of an object as antique, retro is less transient than changing fashions for specific items or styles. For example, 1950s atomic coat racks became popular with retro enthusiasts in the 1980s and are now considered a classic piece of twentieth-century design. As long as retro style is associated with classic status, recognized as good taste and not overtaken by categories such as vintage and mid-century modern, objects defined as retro retain positive connotations and decrease in value relatively slowly. This characteristic further demonstrates the limitations of Guffey's account of retro as simply a product of an increase in the speed of fashion cycles.

There is one other problem with Guffey's analysis of retro style. In her exposition she examines the history of retro style from a production-led perspective that concentrates on artists, designers, producers and their cultural products, but does not consider consumers or more informal retail networks such as market stalls. This is a rather one-sided account of the development of retro, and it means that Guffey reproduces some of the earlier conclusions regarding the emergence of the style in the context of postmodernism (Baudrillard, 1994; Jameson, 1985). Like Frederic Jameson and Jean Baudrillard, Guffey suggests that retro style gratifies a nostalgic desire that is characteristic of postmodernism and a product of "mediated imagery and temporal rupture" (2006:22). Just as Jameson argued that retro aesthetics were illustrative of the cultural dominance of pastiche and the reduction of history to aesthetic styles, Guffrey also suggests that retro represents "a view of the past that removes, rather than invests, meaning" (Guffey, 2006:28; see also Jameson, 1991:20).

For Jameson, the pillaging of history, exemplified by retro cultural products, was evidence of a schizophrenic subject unable to "retain its own past" (1985:125). He suggested that postmodernism, or the logic of late capitalism, involved the waning of affect and that schizophrenic experience was "an experience of isolated, disconnected, discontinuous material signifiers which fail to link up into a coherent sequence" (1985:119). This argument assumed a loss of identity, which, in Jameson's opinion as a Marxist, was previously formed through class consciousness. Jameson considered this loss, and the nostalgic or retro styles associated with it, to be negative and called for a return to the ideals of modernism.

Taking a slightly less pessimistic position, Guffey suggests that retro style can lay bare the "arbitrariness of historical memory" (2006:163). Thus, she seems a little more positive than Jameson about the challenge that retro mounts to modernist progressive cheerleading. At the same time, however, she argues that retro is "unconcerned with the sanctity of tradition or reinforcing social values" and "pillages history with little regard for moral imperatives or nuanced implications" (Guffey, 2006:11, 163). Like Jameson and Baudrillard, Guffey warns that "as entire periods of the recent past are introduced into the popular historical consciousness through retro's accelerated chronological blur, we risk incorporating its values as well" (2006:163). Thus, by limiting the discussion to the production of retro items and their "accurate or inaccurate" depiction of history, theoretically Guffey does little but rehearse old debates and reiterate their conclusions: that retro style is evidence of the draining of meaning characteristic of late capitalism.

These are conclusions that have been contested (Gregson and Crewe, 2003; Jenß, 2004; McRobbie, 1994; Samuel, 1994; Thorne, 2003). In one of the most recent direct engagements with Jameson's discussion of retro, Christian Thorne argues that "retro takes a hundred different forms" (2003:102). Thorne goes on to suggest that there is a second way of understanding certain facets of retro culture in addition to Jameson's apocalyptic vision. Drawing on the ideas of Walter Benjamin regarding the radical potential of the outmoded, Thorne suggests that retro can represent a desire for a world in which commodity culture is less pervasive, "in which objects have been handed down for our care" (2003:112).

The critique of the dystopian visions of postmodern theorists such as Jameson is also evident in earlier discussions of retro. One of the most direct engagements is by Angela McRobbie in her book *Postmodernism and Popular Culture* (1994), in which she republished the article "Second-Hand Dresses and the Role of the Rag Market." In this book McRobbie is positive about some of the interventions by theorists such as Baudrillard, Jameson and Jean-François Lyotard. She recognizes the usefulness of Baudrillard's discussion of hyperreality and Jameson's discussion of the prevalence of the visual image. She also finds Lyotard's questioning of the narratives of progress implicit within capitalism and Marxism immensely valuable.

However, McRobbie is rightly critical of some of the assumptions of theories of postmodernism, many of which are reproduced in the discussions of retro style above. She argues that the superficial does not necessarily represent a decline into depthlessness and that focusing on practices of production and consumption can produce better understandings of the making of meaning and value (McRobbie, 1994:4). McRobbie also questions Jameson's theorizations of the schizophrenic subject and its association with postmodernism. She doubts whether full subjectivity ever existed and argues that if it did it was only ever available to a privileged few whose identities had been fully inscribed in history and culture. She proposes that Jameson's feelings of loss may be a result of the disempowerment of white middle-class masculinity as the "broken voices" of Others are more able to speak (1994:29). For McRobbie, the expression of fragmented identities can be linked to a politics of empowerment, "with finding a way of mounting a challenge" (1994:29).

Although the original version of "Second-Hand Dresses and the Role of Rag Market" was written significantly earlier, these arguments about postmodernism are rehearsed in McRobbie's discussion of retro style. In contrast to Jameson, McRobbie argues that it is problematic to view retro style as nostalgic and depthless if it is placed within the context of postwar subcultures. Using examples of Teddy Boy jackets, the Laura Ashley tea dress, Peter Blake's sleeve for the Beatles' *Sgt. Pepper* album, and punk DIY (do-it-yourself) fashion, McRobbie suggests that retro involves imaginative recreation as well as pastiche and fleeting nostalgia. For example, she writes that rather than being sterile and meaningless, retro styles play with "the norms, conventions and expectations of femininity" (1994:148).

Like Raphael Samuel (1994), and anticipating later empirical studies of retro (Gregson and Crewe, 2003; Jenß, 2004; Thorne, 2003), McRobbie also suggests that the production and consumption of the style involve learning about the past and include the appropriation of secondhand retro items as well as reproduction ones. This observation moves the discussion away from focusing solely on capitalist forms of production and exchange. Retro style involves the buying, selling and swapping of secondhand goods at jumble sales, at markets and on the Internet, as well the consumption of reproduction objects and aesthetics offered by large corporations.

This wider view of the typology of retro style, and examination of all cultural practices involved in its production and consumption, also shapes McRobbie's second line of argument. In a critique of the male bias of research on youth subcultures, she suggests that girls and young women play a major role in appropriating, creating and selling subcultural styles. McRobbie argues that retro styles are central to the "internal, unofficial job market" within subcultures and that the appropriation of subcultural styles by wider audiences has allowed young women to take part in, and influence, fashion (1994:153).

Although McRobbie recognizes that cultural capital is essential to the production and consumption of retro, she suggests that the working classes are able to participate in retro fashions. Critical of views that suggest the style is an "act of unintended class condescension" (Carter, 1983; Wolfe, 1974), she argues that retro style "marks the increasing fluidity across old class lines which previously distinguished 'working-class' from 'middle-class' youth" (1994:152). She suggests this fluidity is due to shifts in access to education, particularly in art schools; the increased circulation of retro styles by the media; and the blurring of the boundaries between the high street and the marketplace, making retro styles easier to obtain. Unlike Jameson, McRobbie does not view the "do-it-yourself plundering of culture" or "fluidity across old class lines" as illustrative of the death of the politics or as the logic of late capitalism. She argues that it is evidence of young people condemning the "adult social order with the politics of their adolescent identities" (1994:3).

The optimism of McRobbie's account is echoed by Samuel's chapter on retro style in *Theatres of Memory*, published in the same year. Samuel argues that retro chic began as antifashion and that it showed "irreverence towards the pretensions of high art...by ignoring the conventional boundaries of sex or class" (1994:91). He concludes that retro chic may have "prepared the way for a whole new family of alternative histories," as camp and kitsch did for the sexual revolution in the 1960s (1994:112). Therefore, both McRobbie and

Samuel argue that because retro style celebrates the everyday, it reflects and contributes to the breakdown of class boundaries and gender norms.

McRobbie's and Samuel's arguments are partly a consequence of the wide range of retro objects they include in their accounts. While I would argue that Samuel takes this too far by including reproduction antiques and new age crystals, he and McRobbie manage to avoid some of the problems encountered by the other theorists discussed above. They do not try to name and date retro style as Franklin and Guffey do. Nor do they limit retro to a discussion of reproduction or pastiche as Jameson or Baudrillard do. Samuel and McRobbie also recognize that value and meaning are created through processes of consumption as well as production. By doing this, their expositions reflect the diverse number of objects categorized as retro and the wide range of practices involved in the making and unmaking of these items' value.

However, in relation to my own experiences, the discussions of both Samuel and McRobbie overly emphasize and celebrate the democratic potential of retro style. Although Samuel recognizes that cultural capital is necessary for the production and consumption of retro style, he does not consider the position from which the naming of an object as retro takes place. While McRobbie discusses the identities of retro retailers and consumers, she does not base this on any empirical evidence. Nor does she explore the process by which old-fashioned objects are changed into retro ones. These factors seem crucial when defining retro and gauging whether the style represents an "increasing fluidity across old class lines" or "plays with the norms, conventions and expectations of femininity" (McRobbie, 1994:148–152).

RETRO STYLE AS A CULTURAL, SOCIAL AND AESTHETIC JUDGMENT OF VALUE

From past literature and my own observations it is clear that retro objects and styles have many different characteristics. As Edward, a writer and enthusiast, told me,

> There is often a lot of confusion or ambiguity about the term retro, between the consumption of, and interest in, original artefacts, or an interest in, or design of, reproductions, and I've had some quite heated discussions with people who really thought it meant only one of those. (Edward, writer and retro enthusiast, 2006)

Like Edward, I consider retro to include original secondhand objects produced in the past and newly manufactured items designed in past styles. Unlike secondhand, retro style does not specify its origin, and this makes the style more

Figure 2.3   Reproduction Roberts radio (2010). © Roberts Radio Ltd.

ambiguous. For example, an original 1950s Roberts radio and a reproduction are both described as retro (Figure 2.3).

The ambiguity of retro as a style category is intensified by the absence of specific material characteristics by which the style can be identified. Objects as disparate as a 1930s enamel colander and a 1980s stereo system are described as retro. This led Nicky Gregson, Louise Crewe and Kate Brooks to argue that "attempting to define what constitutes retro in any meaningful way is not just an impossibility but a misplaced endeavour" (2003:62). They suggest that what "gets identified and sold as retro depends fundamentally on the complex intersections of who is doing the selecting and selling with where that someone is at the time, as well as their own biographies" (2003:63).

Although I am warier of ignoring the materiality of retro objects than Gregson, Crewe and Brooks (2003) are, the emphasis they place on the practices involved in the creation of retro is instructive. If it were only the objectified historical connotations of objects that defined the style, then almost any item from the past 100 years could be categorized as retro. Even a large proportion of newly produced items could be described as retro because designers use past styles as source material. As one designer I spoke to suggested,

There are only so many shapes, colours and styles that you can use...you know, things have to go around. (Wayne, designer, 2006)

Moreover, the intrinsic value of goods is called into question when the physical features of objects and styles are unchanged in their transformation from old-fashioned to retro. Thus, it is a combination of the characteristics of the material objects themselves; the practices of consumers, retailers and intermediaries; and their contexts that make the style.

As Gregson, Crewe and Brooks (2003) acknowledge, the practices of consumers, retailers and intermediaries are particularly central to the definition of retro style. As such, these practices are cultural, social and aesthetic judgments of value. For example, when a retailer chooses a piece of furniture to go in a shop window, when a consumer buys a decorative object at a jumble sale to put in his or her lounge, and when a journalist writes about an interior in a lifestyle magazine, they are all judging items as desirable and, to varying extents, are changing the wider value of objects and styles in the process. Frequently, these practices mark a shift in the perceived value of an item from rubbish or junk to retro or design classic. For example, in Figure 2.4 the homeowner sits in his house decorated in the style of lower-middle-class décor of the 1930s. The items shown in his front room are not those commonly associated with good taste. At the same time, his choice of décor and the

Figure 2.4   Retro enthusiast in his home (2005). © Annie Collinge.

inclusion of his interior in the style section of the *Guardian Weekend* magazine increase the visibility and value of 1930s items. The image and accompanying article about his home emphasize the cultural knowledge, authenticity and individuality symbolized by retro styles. These are qualities that are highly valuable in the cultural economy, a point I return to below.

The framing of this interior as desirable rather than old-fashioned is partly contingent on the identity of the owner. The contrast between his home and his appearance emphasizes that he has made a conscious style decision. The range of objects, the lack of clutter and the way the pieces are displayed also communicate definite style choices. Of course, the image is an extreme example of a retro home. Yet these factors also influence the categorization of objects and styles as retro in more eclectic interiors. For example, as I argued earlier, the meaning and value of a set of flying ducks change depending on whether they are owned by an elderly working-class women who displays them in her front room surrounded by furniture and decorative objects collected over a lifetime, or by a young middle-class couple who hang them on the wall of their designer apartment juxtaposed with newly produced design classics. An elderly working-class women exhibiting old objects and styles would be more likely to be labeled as old-fashioned.

However, the contexts and identities of previous owners do not prevent objects and styles from being categorized as retro and appropriated by others. As I argued in the Introduction, the previous life of flying ducks adds to their value. Thus, in contrast to Jameson, who suggests that retro style is evidence of the past becoming a series of decontextualized and unrelated signs with no sense of the shape of history, retro style involves recontextualization. By this, I mean that as objects and styles are appropriated, their histories are imagined and new meanings are made through the practices of production, consumption and representation. For example, it is clear from the article accompanying the image in Figure 2.4 that the owner of the 1930s interior has historical knowledge of the period and also imagines the lives of those who lived through it. In some ways, this is no different from other engagements with history because historical contexts are always interventions constituted textually through narrative and spoken from certain perspectives (Jenkins, 1995; White, 1989).

At the same time, however, retro style can be less detailed than other historical encounters. As a style category, retro is evidence of the cultural value of "pastness" in general. For example, Edward told me that most people

> make that mental move once and everything else follows. It doesn't mean that once [they]...fall in love with 1950s things [they]...are only ever going to love 1950s things. For most people it opens the door to recognising that they can have the whole lot. (Edward, writer and retro enthusiast, 2006)

The ability to "have the whole lot," or to appropriate widely from the past, depends on cultural knowledge. The revaluation of an old-fashioned object, and the naming of it as retro, is a classification based on knowledge of past styles and current fashion trends. As Skeggs argues, the classifier knows of the prior "signification and association of the object, a position that can be seen to give it authentic value" (2004a:108). Thus, rather than satisfying "deep nostalgic desire," the production and consumption of retro are more concerned with "difference, taste and individuality" (Gregson and Crewe, 2003:11). The act of appropriating and defining a material object as retro associates it with originality, singularity, connoisseurship and the arts. Therefore, by recognizing and valuing retro objects, individuals attempt to create different and authentic selves (Jenß, 2004).

This process of revaluation is partially depicted by the art-culture system devised by James Clifford (1988) (Figure 2.5). Clifford (1988:19) argues that cultural artifacts are assigned value relative to one another and that this establishes hierarchies. He observes that authenticity is highly valuable in the West. For example, the original is generally considered more authentic and thus superior to the reproduction. Clifford also suggests that the art-culture system "establishes the contexts in which [cultural products] properly belong and between which they circulate" (1988:223). Art as singular and original is contextualized by the art world and connoisseurship (zone 1) as opposed to

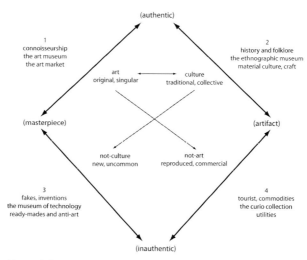

THE ART-CULTURE SYSTEM
A Machine for Making Authenticity

(authentic)

1
connoisseurship
the art museum
the art market

2
history and folklore
the ethnographic museum
material culture, craft

art
original, singular

culture
traditional, collective

(masterpiece)

(artifact)

not-culture
new, uncommon

not-art
reproduced, commercial

3
fakes, inventions
the museum of technology
ready-mades and anti-art

4
tourist, commodities
the curio collection
utilities

(inauthentic)

Figure 2.5   The art-culture system (Clifford, 1988).

reproductions and commodities contextualized by the market (zone 4). These zones could be compared to the divide between high and popular culture. However, Clifford's approach is more interesting than this simple dichotomy because he argues that movement is central to the system. He writes that it is the circulation of artifacts between zones that generates new, more authentic and more valuable objects. Thus, Clifford names the art-culture system "a machine for making authenticity" (1988:224).

This model of the making of value seems particularly relevant to retro style, whereby mass-produced commodities, rubbish and junk are revalued and recontextualized. For example, Homemaker china originally mass-produced by Woolworths in the 1950s is now sold as a retro classic and displayed next to modern art in the collection of the Manchester Art Gallery in Britain. Thus, while Samuel observed that the consumption of retro style showed "irreverence towards the pretensions of high art" (1994:91), retro is now part of a change in the values of the art world rather than a move beyond them. As Clifford's discussion of the art-culture system makes clear, it is recontextualization that generates authenticity and that has high cultural value in the field of arts and culture. Consequentially, the ability to appreciate and appropriate retro objects reflects and produces high levels of cultural capital.

However, for some retailers, consumers and journalists, the term *retro* has been devalued by the many reproductions sold on the high street and the prevalence of the style in the media. For example, many retailers prefer to use *vintage* or *mid-century modern* to describe their products because these terms connote originality. This is one of the reasons Tommy, a retro retailer and entrepreneur, makes a derogatory comment about retro in the quote at the beginning of this chapter. This move away from retro could be interpreted as a decrease in the value of the style altogether. However, those objects described as vintage or mid-century modern are often the same as those previously described as retro. Thus, rather than being attributed to specific material objects, value is derived from searching for, appropriating and naming new and more authentic qualities. This observation reinforces arguments made about the aesthetic economy that suggest that it is the taking on and off of cultural resources, or cultural prostheses, that creates value (Lury, 1998). I return to discuss these ideas in Chapter 7.

This analysis also exemplifies the movement central to the art-culture system. Indeed, although Clifford devised the art-culture system in a discussion of collecting and the valuation of tribal artifacts by Western museums, other theorists have suggested that its values have become central to consumer culture (e.g., Featherstone, 1991; Holt, 1998; Lury, 1996). These arguments are particularly relevant to the discussion in this book and are explored in more detail in Chapter 3.

The emphasis on movement in the model of the art-culture system also resonates with methodological approaches that recognize the role of both production and consumption in the creation of meaning and value. One of these approaches focuses on object biographies, which is particularly useful for exploring the value of retro style. This is the perspective I now outline.

OBJECT BIOGRAPHIES, COMMODITIES AND STYLE

The biographical approach to cultural artifacts was first discussed in detail within anthropology and is most famously associated with the work of Arjun Appadurai and Igor Kopytoff in *The Social Life of Things* (1986). In the book Appadurai and Kopytoff argue for a methodology that analyses "things in motion" and that focuses on all stages in an object's life. They suggest that object biographies can illuminate "a tangled mass of aesthetic, historical and even political judgements, and of convictions and values that shape our attitudes to objects" (Kopytoff, 1986:67). While I do not agree with the part of Appadurai's argument that suggests that "exchange is the source of value" (my reasons for this are outlined in Chapter 3), following objects can be fruitful to understand how use and exchange value are established across time and space (1986:4). Through observation of the changes and the continuities in the meaning and value of material objects, the social relationships that make, maintain and sever exchange value can be explored. For example, as Peter Stallybrass (1998) argued in his discussion of commodity fetishism, it was the biography of Marx's coat going back and forth to the pawnshop that helped Marx think about the relationship between use and exchange value. Thus, a biographical approach to retro objects and styles makes it possible to explore the aesthetic, social, cultural and political judgments that make and unmake their value.

Although the approach in *The Social Life of Things* influences the methodology in this book, the majority of the discussions in the collection are limited because they view the trajectory of objects as linear. For example, in the introduction, Appadurai suggests that object biographies should focus on "production, through exchange/distribution to consumption" (1986:13). From previous studies of secondhand consumption and the earlier discussion of retro style in this chapter, it is clear that the value of objects is certainly not used up through use. As Gregson and Crewe argue, "Use and exchange-value extend well beyond the first cycle of consumption," and value is not something inherent to commodities but is "open to constant relational and active negotiation" (2003:2). Thus, circular or network models of the relations between production and consumption are preferable to those that are linear.

One of these models is the "circuit of culture" outlined by Richard Johnson (1986) and developed by Paul du Gay and colleagues in *Doing Cultural Studies: The Story of the Sony Walkman* (1997). The circuit of culture is an approach that explores the meaning of cultural artifacts through an analysis of the processes of production, representation, identity, regulation and consumption. This biographical model breaks with conventional linear readings of the links between production and consumption and emphasizes the flows and connections that exist between these contexts and the actors within them. Du Gay and colleagues suggest that linkages and power relations between cultural processes are not "determined, absolute or essential for all time" but are located in the "contingencies of circumstance" (1997:3). In addition, the circuit of culture emphasizes movement and circulation, a point that Scott Lash and Celia Lury (2007:5) argue has become more important in the contemporary culture industry. Lash and Lury suggest that products no longer circulate as identical objects determined by the intentions of their producers but "spin out of control of their makers. In circulation they move and change through transposition, translation and transformation" (2007:5).

However, as Lawrence Grossberg (1997) has suggested, the circuit of culture is not without its problems. By focusing on the cultural processes in which meaning and value is created, the materiality of the objects themselves is often neglected. In addition, singling out and locating the distinct sites of production, representation and consumption can be overly reductive because it predefines those domains and their contents. For example, when du Gay and colleagues (1997) focus on the production part of the circuit, they explore the history and organizational structure of Sony. While this is a valid approach, if reproduced it could miss the important work of production in other contexts. For example, a significant amount of activity that happens in domestic contexts could be framed as production as well as consumption. Furthermore, in relation to retro style, practices such as renovation and selling from home complicate the idea that there are distinct sites of production, representation and consumption.

Therefore, to avoid these problems, in this book I investigate all the cultural practices that go on within specific contexts rather than predefining spaces and activities in terms of production, consumption and representation. I focus on retailing, the media and the home because these are the most significant contexts in the making and unmaking of the value of domestic retro style. By concentrating on these specific spaces, the approach also goes some way to tackling the second problem that Grossberg highlights: the neglect of materiality. This is because, as Elizabeth Shove, Matt Watson and colleagues (2007) have argued, concentrating on cultural practice encourages the study of the dynamic relationships between people and their things.

Focusing on style also encourages a discussion of materiality. As Nigel Thrift argues, style is not a frivolous add-on. It "can be counted as an agent in its own right in that it defines what is at issue in the world" (2008:14). As well as being a symbolic way of categorizing, defining and valuing, style is an objectification of meaning and value that is always-already the outcome of complex sets of power relations. Thus, style creates the need for a methodological perspective that recognizes that both the material and social worlds are as much constitutive of culture as constituted by it: a nonreductive view of culture as continually made by practice. I return to consider this theoretical and methodological perspective in the next chapter.

DOMESTIC CULTURES AND ACCESSING RETRO KNOWLEDGE

By exploring the practices that go on in retail space, in the media and in the home I am concerned with everyday domesticities. As Elizabeth Silva (2010:32) has suggested, the home is "made out of practices that always stretch beyond the boundaries of the home as location," and this is why retailing and the media are incorporated into the book. As suggested above, past discussions of retro style have focused on art, clothing and film rather than decorative objects, furniture and interiors. This is partly a result of the inconspicuous nature of domestic retro style. Old or old-looking furniture and decorative objects have always been present in homes, whether unchanged since their original production, purchased secondhand or bought as revival pieces. For this reason domestic retro style was less obvious in its early manifestations in comparison to retro in its other forms. For example, those individuals who purposefully wore retro clothes in the 1950s and 1960s were distinctive because secondhand or old-looking clothing had become largely undesirable (A. Palmer and Clark, 2005:173).

The domestic interior is also a space that is less visible to academics and social commentators than the cinema, gallery or street. New blockbuster films and art exhibitions are largely in the public eye, while people's domestic practices and interiors are not so accessible. This does not mean, however, that studying domestic space is less important. On the contrary, social, cultural, economic and political changes are played out and made in the spaces of the home. Ironically, it is this ordinariness that has meant that until relatively recently domestic cultures have not been the focus of academic research, especially within cultural studies. As Joanne Hollows argues, "Cultural studies has frequently remained preoccupied with the spectacular and transgressive dimensions of cultural life and ignored seemingly mundane cultural practices" (2008:5). Hollows goes on to suggest that the marginalization of domestic space within cultural studies is partly due to "the assumptions that have underpinned wider theories of modernity and the ways in which these theories are gendered" (2008:5). Although feminists have worked to try to dismantle these assumptions, investment in domestic life, like consumption, has often been thought of as a trivial preoccupation with little real political consequence. By neglecting the practices of production and consumption that go on in domestic spaces, some of the theorizations of retro style explored above reproduce these assumptions (e.g. Guffey, 2006; Jameson, 1985). Thus, while these accounts provide a useful starting point, by only focusing on production and public space they give inaccurate definitions of retro style and dubious theorizations of its development and its consequences.

However, academic discussions of domestic cultures and the home have increased in recent years (see Hollows, 2008; Briganti and Mezei, 2012). Influenced by material cultures research as well as science and technology studies, interest in material objects and spaces has grown in a range of disciplines. Some have called this the material turn (Bennett and Joyce, 2010). The increased interest in the domestic is also a product of the recent fascination with the home in contemporary art and lifestyle media. By highlighting the domestic, artists and the media make the home more visible to audiences (including academics) and in the process make mundane spaces and objects spectacular. Consumers are also involved in this work, and although I have emphasized the ordinariness of domestic cultures here, the activities of those involved in domestic retro style are also often highly conspicuous. For example, putting a set of flying ducks on a wall with 200 others is a very definite style statement. Thus, in the research I adopt an "ordinary" approach to the spectacular and consider how mundane objects are made distinctive through everyday practices.

In seeking to understand the cultural practices involved in the making and unmaking of the value of retro style, I am concerned with the lived experiences of retro retailers, enthusiasts and tastemakers. To explore these experiences I have used ethnographic methods. I began the research process by visiting and taking photographs of retro shops and interviewing four tastemakers involved in retro style. Over a period of six months in 2006 I then observed and interviewed six retro retailers and twelve retro enthusiasts. I have continued to keep in contact with some of the participants and have observed, albeit informally, how enthusiasts' homes and practices have changed.

Although this study draws on a relatively small sample, the aim of the project is to explore the making of meaning and value in specific contexts rather than to produce a large database of empirical data. Although some may suggest that this limits the extent to which my findings can be generalized, I would not have been able to explore the practices of retailers and enthusiasts in such detail with a larger sample. In any case, whether an analysis is based on a small or large sample, there are always problems involved in claiming to represent the experiences of others (Ramazanoğlu, 2002).

ETHNOGRAPHY AND ACCESSING RETRO KNOWLEDGE

The legacy of poststructuralism and standpoint epistemologies has led researchers across a variety of disciplines to question their truth claims. "The critique of objectivity and emphasis on the significance of social position and lived experience has, in particular, always been a central theme of feminist epistemology" (Darling-Wolf, 2004:32).[1] Feminist scholars have argued that all researchers take positions that are shaped by an experience of being (Haraway, 1988; Harding, 1987). This epistemology, often referred to as feminist standpoint theory, questions the ways of "disowning responsibility" and renouncing accountability for research that are common in positivist methods (Stanley, 1990). It argues that experience and social position can be a source of knowledge and that this can challenge "the structures of oppression operating in the dominant social order" (Darling-Wolf, 2004:33). Most commonly in this approach, the experiences of women have been used to question the hegemonic position of masculine theory and knowledge.

Although feminist standpoint theory made advances in the academic arena by acknowledging experience as a form of knowledge, this methodology has been problematized in more recent approaches to ethnography (Gray, 2003). Ann Gray (2003:183) notes that feminist standpoint theory can often lean toward essentialism. She argues that it assumes individuals possess an identity before experience and continues the positivist project because it claims that experience can produce better "truths." She also suggests that it privileges certain types of experience. For example, a standpoint position can imply that a female academic could produce a more authentic and realistic account of gender inequality than a male academic. This is clearly problematic and potentially paralyzing, particularly in relation to class. As Fabienne Darling-Wolf asks, "How can issues of class, in particular, ever be adequately addressed by highly educated middle-class intellectuals—the kind of people who may have the means to publish their works?" (2004:35).

The way that Skeggs conceptualizes experience addresses this problem. She argues that rather than viewing experience as "a foundation for knowledge," based on a fixed notion of what it is to be a woman or working class, experience should be thought of as informing the take-up of positions that are continually in production (1997:28). For example, my experience of conducting this research, as well as my background, influences my analysis of retro style. As such, rather than being a reflection of reality, all academic research is an intervention, and all academics speak from specific positions that are continually made through practice.

Yet, if all academic research is constructed, why should it be based on "lived cultures" or empirical methods at all? After all, purely theoretical work can be just as valuable as performative political intervention, in the sense that it is seeking to produce the effect that it names. However, as the discussion above highlights, culture is ordinary and material. It is "not a free floating set of ideas or beliefs"; it is materialized in institutions, texts and the practices of everyday life (Gray, 2003). The everyday cannot be fully understood, as Pierre Bourdieu argues, "unless 'culture', in the restricted, normative sense of ordinary usage, is brought back to 'culture' in the anthropological sense" (2005 [1979]:1). In addition, good ethnographic research can challenge "theoretical reductionism" (Hall *et al.,* 1980:74). Therefore, there is merit in attempting to make sense of how culture is produced and lived in everyday life, as long as we are aware that these will only ever be attempts. As Gray notes, "We can never capture the 'whole truth' of the social and the cultural, rather we can, from our specific vantage points, produce a version of the truth, but one which we present modestly for others to consider" (2003:21). This approach problematizes research methods that claim to represent true experience, while also suggesting that ethnographic research is of value in creating knowledge.

In recognition of the complexities involved in representing the experience of others I have adopted a "reflexive practice" that acknowledges the social, cultural and political position of the researcher. Reflexivity, as Skeggs (2004a) acknowledges, is more than simply telling of the self or writing a paragraph about yourself at the beginning of a book. It is sometimes assumed that by making these gestures the problems of power, perspective and privilege are dissolved (Skeggs, 2004a:128). Rather, Skeggs argues, truly reflexive work is about practice. In this regard, she is greatly influenced by Bourdieu, who, she argues when discussing reflexivity, did not mean direct self-examination. He meant an exploration of "the relationship between the properties of discourses, the properties of the person who pronounces them, and the properties of the institution which authorizes him to pronounce them" (Skeggs, 2004a:129).[2] By implication, the process of conducting research and reflections on the process are as important as the content and analysis of the product of the research itself.[3] Informed by this perspective, I have questioned the extent to which this project is simply an exercise of my own taste. This is particularly important if, as I suggested earlier in the chapter, the categorization of a material object as retro is based on an aesthetic, cultural and social judgment of value. As Bourdieu argues, "Nothing classifies somebody more than the way he or she classifies" (2005 [1979]:19).

The material objects, texts and individuals I discuss in the book have partly identified themselves. The archival materials, including the images I have used, have usually been contextualized by text defining them as retro. The four tastemakers and six retailers I spoke to defined themselves as selling or interested in retro, vintage or mid-century modern. The twelve enthusiasts also all identified themselves as interested in retro, vintage or past popular culture.[4]

However, I am the person who has identified retro as an important area of study; I have chosen specific examples of the style; and I have classified the retailers and enthusiasts involved in its production and consumption. In recognition of this, throughout the research I have remained aware of the knowledge needed to access retro cultures. The exclusivities of this knowledge are emphasized by the journey I had to undertake to complete my ethnographic research.

I was only on the periphery of retro cultures when I started this project, and I did not know many people who were interested in retro style for the home. Thus, I decided to conduct a number of in-depth interviews with key tastemakers in order to access participants.[5] As Bourdieu (2005 [1979]) argues, tastemakers are the arbiters and creators of the rules within a particular field, and because of this they usually have valuable cultural knowledge and contacts. The interviews with tastemakers taught me what was at stake in retro culture, its history and my participants' feelings about its future. In Bourdieu's (1992) terms, they made it possible for me to get a "feel for the game." They also helped me to formulate the definition of retro style I outlined above.

It was necessary for me to learn about retro not only because I wanted to define its characteristics but also because I found that I could not get interviews without making references to my own knowledge of the style. Potential interviewees, especially tastemakers and retailers, would ask me "what era I was into" and who I had interviewed so far. In some cases I felt that only by giving the right sort of answers would I be allowed to continue. In this regard tastemakers and retailers were guarding their knowledge. This is unsurprising because it is this retro knowledge that generates their income, and gatekeeping prevents dissemination and potential devaluation.

The exclusivities of retro cultures made posing as an "unknowing outsider" impossible. This position is usually advised for conducting interviews in order to elicit more detailed information (Silverman, 2004). In their study of retro retailing, Gregson, Crewe and Brooks (2003) adopted this approach. They note that the "positionality we adopted as interviewers was as 'unknowing outsiders' keen to learn what our respondents would tell us about their work and lifestyles" (2003:79). There are numerous circumstantial reasons that may have produced this difference. It may have been due to consumers and producers of retro style being more difficult to access in the southeast of England

(Gregson and colleagues' study was conducted in the north of England). It could have been that in the eyes of the potential participants I had to compensate for my relatively young age with knowledge of retro style. Or it may have been that since Gregson and colleagues' study in 2003, retro style has become more exclusive.

Aside from these circumstantial differences, however, I would argue that the position of outsider that Gregson, Crewe and Brooks (2003) adopted is difficult to take up in any ethnographic research, especially in an environment where interviewees possess high levels of cultural capital. In retro cultures, as Gregson and Crewe (2003) argue elsewhere, cultural capital is essential. Therefore, perhaps Gregson and colleagues underestimated the knowledge they needed to access the field and were not as unknowing as they suggested.

Although I was not an unknowing outsider, I was certainly not an insider either. This is a position that is impossible to adopt as a researcher who is influenced by the conventions and interests of academia. My identity as an academic was also constantly highlighted by my tape recorder, camera or camcorder. Therefore, the position I took was that of a semi-outsider, a researcher with some knowledge of retro style but a researcher nonetheless. My ability to take on this role was undoubtedly aided by my class, age, race, gender and appearance. My identity as a middle-class white female in my late twenties (at the time) with an "arty" style of dress enabled me to access the field. As a female, I was at an advantage because I was viewed as nonthreatening and was therefore more likely to be asked into participants' homes. In addition, the discrepancy between my age and the age of my participants (I was often ten or more years younger than interviewees) meant I was able to elicit more information. Many participants adopted a pedagogical approach in the interview and wanted to train me to appreciate retro styles and to produce retro interiors. One of the interviewees even gave me a book on retro design at the end of the interview. This was a kind gesture that acknowledged our similar interests and also displayed superior knowledge of the style.

Other differences in my identity made the research difficult. Although I am from a similar background to most of the enthusiasts I interviewed, they had more status. Participants had significantly more economic capital, were older than me and usually had more knowledge of design. The combination of these differences made me feel as though I was "researching up." This sometimes made the interview process tricky. Interviewees tried to ask probing questions about the research and occasionally turned the tables on the interview. They would also mention past designers and manufacturers whom they assumed I knew. I felt I had to pretend to know who they were to maintain the authority of an interviewer. As Gray (2003:51–52) notes, researchers often experience difficulties accessing participants and negotiating the power relations between the interviewee and the interviewer when researching more powerful groups. She considers this to be one of the reasons why "crucially important groups—cultural producers, enthusiasts of middle or so called 'high' culture, policy makers—who in different ways shape and form the cultural landscape, have been under-researched in cultural studies" (2003:51).

While interviewees would happily talk about gender, I found them to be wary of the subject of class. As Skeggs (2004a) notes, for many individuals, particularly the middle classes, the subject of class has become irrelevant and distasteful. This was made obvious in the first tastemaker interview I conducted. I found that when I told the participant that my research was focused on class he became defensive. Subsequently, I told interviewees I was researching retro style and revealed my interest in class only if they questioned me further. This strategy was necessary both to get enough participants to interview and to have them be open when discussing their taste. Although in most cases I did not reveal the class angle of my research, I did ask interviewees about the subject. Some questioned the relevance of class to modern life. Some also considered themselves working class, when I felt they were middle class. These points are discussed in much more detail in Chapter 7.

While writing this book I have been careful not to erase the exclusivities of retro style that I have begun to describe here. I have done my best not to succumb to the "democratic impulse" to celebrate the "community" I was studying, which was certainly tempting considering how grateful I am to my participants (Gray, 2003:51). I have also tried to be critical of my own involvement in these taste cultures. At the same time, I have also found spaces of resistance and relationships that go beyond capital accumulation in the practices involved in the production and consumption of retro style. This perspective is, of course, a product of my own position: as someone who speaks as both a consumer of retro and a cultural theorist critical of ideas about the democratic potential of the style.

CONCLUSION

I began this chapter by exploring previous theorizations of retro style. In a discussion of this body of work, I have highlighted the problems with accounts of retro style that focus only on production and the material qualities of objects. In agreement with McRobbie and Samuel, I have suggested that the value of retro style is made through consumption as well as production, representation and materiality. In contrast to Jameson, who considered retro objects and styles to be a series of decontextualized signs, I have argued that retro involves recontextualization. The naming of an object or style as retro is often part of its transformation from old-fashioned junk to design classic. As such, it is a cultural, social and aesthetic judgment of value. I have proposed that this process is partly depicted by the art-culture system, a model drawn up by Clifford to show the creation of value within the arts. Like the relocation of tribal artifacts in Western museums, past everyday objects are recontextualized and valued because of their authentic connotations. As in Clifford's model, the transformation of everyday objects is not available to all. Judgments of retro style are contingent on the knowledge of the person making the categorization, the appropriate identity of the owner and the appropriate context. These factors all depend on high levels of cultural capital.

To explore the contextual movement depicted by the art-culture system, I have argued that a method focused on object biographies is most appropriate. This approach moves away from one-sided accounts of production or consumption because it explores all the elements in the cultural circuit. It locates objects in specific contexts, which is particularly important in light of my proposed definition of retro style. Most importantly, it allows for an exploration of the processes of valuation and legitimation.

An approach that focuses on valuation and legitimation must also consider the role of academic research and the position of the researcher in this process. I argued that reflections on the process of conducting research are as important as the content and analysis of the product of the research itself. I found that tastemakers, retro retailers and enthusiasts often questioned my authority as a researcher. I proposed that this was a product of their high levels of cultural capital and class backgrounds. This finding is explored in more detail in Chapter 7.

Retro Style and the Cultural Politics of Everyday Life

Two of the central questions asked in this book are whether domestic retro style represents an uncoupling of the relationship between class and taste, and whether the production and consumption of the style allow individuals to challenge and play with gender norms. In this chapter I discuss the theoretical frameworks that set up the discussion of my ethnographic work. I begin by exploring the history and the legacy of discourses of possessive individualism. I consider the role of authenticity in consumer culture and the salience of ideas around the aestheticization of everyday life. I go on to consider debates around the disintegration of class and outline the ways in which the Bourdieusian concept of capital has been utilized to counter these theorizations. While I argue that metaphors of capital are useful to explain class distinctions in a context that continues to be structured by individualism, I describe a number of problems with Pierre Bourdieu's ideas in relation to gender and materiality. Drawing on work from consumption studies that has been influenced by actor-network theory and theories of affect I explore approaches to social life that go beyond symbolism and capital. I conclude by offering a theoretical module that attempts to synthesize these seemingly opposing perspectives in order to detail, analyze and theorize the production and consumption of domestic retro style. In the spirit of Luc Boltanski (2011) this position attempts to reconcile critical and pragmatic theoretical paradigms.

CONSUMER CULTURE AND THE AESTHETIC ECONOMY

A number of accounts of consumer culture have suggested that the processes and values identified by James Clifford in the art-culture system have become central to production and consumption in postmodernity (e.g., Featherstone, 1991; Holt, 1998; Lury, 1996). For example, in her seminal discussion of consumer culture, Celia Lury writes that the art-culture system has increasingly influenced the production, consumption and representation of all consumer goods, "particularly following the rapid growth in the so-called culture industry in the twentieth century" (1996:52). Building on the work of Mike Featherstone (1991), she suggests that the art-culture system has provided a context within which an aestheticised mode of involvement with objects has been adopted by many consumers, a mode within which the objects of material culture are related not simply to social relationships but also to specifically symbolic or cultural values, especially authenticity. (Lury, 1996:54)

Lury calls this aestheticized mode of involvement the stylization of consumption. She argues that the value of goods in consumer culture derives partly from the legacy of complex ideas relating to artistic genius and the artwork's transcendence of everyday life that were prevalent in the eighteenth, nineteenth and early twentieth centuries in Euro-American societies. Lury goes on to suggest that these developments contributed to the intensification of the concept of the "possessive individual" as an ideal (1996:57).

The individual as "possessive," or as the "proprietor of his or her own person or capacities, owing nothing to society for them," was first consolidated in the writing of Enlightenment thinkers such as Thomas Hobbes and John Locke (Macpherson, 2007 [1962]:3). As Crawford Brough Macpherson (2007 [1962]) emphasizes, possessive individualism is a market society's version of the self in which selfhood becomes aligned with exchange value, circulation and competition. In discourses of possessive individualism the terms of individuality depend not only on the possession of a unique body but also on the continuity of consciousness and memory (Lury, 1998:7). Rather than being defined by the ownership of objects, individuality is dependent on the ownership of oneself: on the articulation of a plausible history (Abercrombie et al., 1986:33; Pateman, 1988). As such, it is the capacity to stand outside of the body and relate to the self as property that defines the individual. A possessive self is "a self who is judged in terms of the accumulation of possessions and for whom identity itself is a kind of wealth (of objects, knowledge, memories and experience)" and for whom authentic culture becomes valuable (Lury, 1996:57).

The intensification of the possessive self as an ideal in the eighteenth and nineteenth centuries in Britain and the United States reflected and contributed to the increasing separation between the public and private spheres. For example, in her discussion of nineteenth-century U.S. literature, Gillian Brown (1992) argues that the rise of domesticity and its associated values of interiority and privacy are part of the history of the development of individualism. She observes that as women were removed from the public sphere of production, the home became increasingly thought of as a stable, timeless and traditional retreat outside of modern public life. At the same time, however, nineteenth-century domestic culture was distinctly new, modern and inflected with ideas around property and exchange. Brown argues that the role of discourses of domesticity and middle-class modes of femininity in shaping the development of possessive individualism often goes unrecognized.

The gendered division of labor that contributed to the separation of the public and private spheres meant that women were more likely to be involved in, and associated with, consumption. As Don Slater argues, when consumer culture and commodification gathered pace in the twentieth century, "women's responsibility for domestic reproduction [was] increasingly defined . . . as a responsibility to manage consumption" (1997:56). In this process, the female consumer became associated with passivity, irrationality and frivolity (Slater, 1997:57). Slater argues that this was because women had not had full access to the terms of subjectivity central to the model of the possessive self that formed the basis of the conceptualization of the consumer (Abercrombie *et al.,* 1986; Cronin, 2000; Slater 1997). I return to this argument below.

It has been suggested that the idea of the "self as project" continues to structure recent consumer culture and is a continuation of the notion of the possessive self as an ideal (Cronin, 2000:274). For example, Anne Cronin documents how in advertisements for Nike the self is represented "as a project to be aimed at" as well as a "projecting forward of an already-established identity" (2000:276). As in earlier discourses of possessive individualism, individuality is defined as the capacity to relate to self as property and to articulate a plausible history. Investment in the self is also fundamental to ideas regarding the change from way of life to lifestyle. As Lisa Taylor notes, "Lifestyles are performed improvisations in which authenticity is conceived as an entity which one can manufacture" through symbolic repertoires (2008:83). In light of these arguments, the popularity of retro objects and styles may be a product of the greater importance placed on the symbolic dimensions of domestic life and of the increase in value of authenticity in contemporary consumer culture.

Since Featherstone's (1991) and Lury's (1996) discussions of the aestheticization of everyday life, it has been argued that aesthetics and affective experience have become even more essential in generating economic value in the global economy (e.g., Andrejevic, 2011; Lash and Lury, 2007; Thrift, 2008). The creativity that is integral to design supplies the new commodities and markets on which capitalism relies (Gilbert, 2008:109).[1] Innovative products and new consumers have become increasingly difficult to find in the saturated markets of developed economies, and thus the value of creativity has increased. In recent years the creation and design of new technologies have become particularly valuable to organizations (Boyle, 2003:273). It has been suggested that the constant stream of new and updated technologies in the workplace and home is unsettling for some consumers (Boyle, 2003:261). Thus, the growth in the consumption and production of retro style for the home may also reflect a desire for familiarity and timelessness in a society imagined to be fast-paced and impersonal.

Organizations and marketing departments are well aware of these feelings; goods and services appear to resist commodification through association with past styles, creativity and the arts. As Fred Myers argues, "[T]he valorization of "art" and material culture in the West has often been based on the object's resistance to, or transcendence of, global processes involving commodification, markets, money and mass culture" (2001:4). In Samuel Binkley's (2008:600) terms, the "fetishized defetishization of commodities" is highly valuable in a market saturated with goods and becomes a common selling strategy. For example, as I explore in Chapter 5, high street producers and retailers often attempt to disassociate themselves from markets, money and mass culture in order to make their products more attractive. Therefore, it could be argued that the authentic and its associated values of originality, singularity and connoisseurship have become synonymous with the fashionable. This may be one of the reasons retro objects and styles are often in fashion.

Despite the relevance of theories of the aesthetic economy to retro style, the extent to which aesthetics have become central to all consumption and production practices has been questioned. For example, Alan Warde (2002:192) is doubtful whether the logic of cultural goods can be extended to other types of items. He writes that the production and consumption of a screwdriver are likely to be "practical, mundane and ordinary, rather than driven by aesthetic considerations" (2002:193). Warde is also skeptical of the extent to which everyday life is aestheticized, arguing that, in the end, his "guess would be that most people prefer a comfortable to a beautiful life" (2002:194). He suggests that aesthetic considerations may be important only to certain sections of the population, most notably youth subcultures and fractions of the middle class. Therefore, while the prevalence of retro style may be a symptom of the increase in importance of aesthetic values in consumer culture, its consumption and production may be limited to these specific groups.

LIFESTYLE, CULTURAL CAPITAL AND CLASS

So far in this book I have proposed that the definition of retro style is dependent on cultural knowledge and that this is valuable capital in the symbolic economy. I have argued that previous studies of retro have failed to focus on the perspectives and processes involved in the making of the style, even those studies to which I am otherwise indebted (Gregson and Crewe, 2003; McRobbie, 1994; Samuel, 1994). I have also suggested that it is partly because of this omission that Angela McRobbie and Raphael Samuel are able to argue that the consumption and production of the style have contributed to a blurring of class boundaries. This is an argument with which I feel more than a little uneasy because making old-fashioned objects and styles into retro ones depends on the possession of specific preexisting identities and contexts. In order to explore the disparity between my perspective and theirs in more detail, I now consider recent sociological debates about the relevance of class to everyday life.

In the early 1990s a number of social theories emerged that argue that class has become less relevant in late modernity or postmodernity (Beck, 1992; Giddens, 1991). Ulrich Beck (1992) and Anthony Giddens (1991) suggest that the emergence of new "consumer freedoms," driven by changes such as globalization, economic restructuring and shifts from Fordist to post-Fordist modes of production, had blurred previously established class boundaries and driven a change to lifestyle-based consumption patterns. They both argue that in a consumer society individuals reflexively constructed their identities. In *Risk Society: Towards a New Modernity,* Beck suggests that "class society only remains useful as an image of the past" and that it has lost its "subcultural basis and is no longer experienced" (1992:91). He argues that individuals, although influenced by structural forces, can choose which lifestyles to acknowledge and take up and which ones to ignore. In *Modernity and Self Identity,* Giddens similarly writes that "the signposts are now blank," meaning that the choices consumers make are now their own rather than inherited (1991:82). He suggests that the self becomes a reflexive project to be worked on. Giddens theorizes that "individuals are forced to negotiate lifestyle choices" rather than having decisions be determined by class, race or gender (1991:5). In his view, even those "under severe material constraint" make lifestyle choices (1991:6).

Zygmunt Bauman (2000) and Michel Maffesoli (1988) have also theorized the decline of class cultures. However, they argue that consumers are not detached from group affiliation: they are grouped in neotribes. *Neotribes* are transitory, affective and emotional groups formed on the basis of shared lifestyles and consumption patterns. Bauman suggests that this "spawns communities as fragile and short lived as scattered and wandering emotions, shifting erratically from one target to another" (2000:34).

This view of the decline in relevance of social class has been adopted in discussions of consumption. For example, in "Identity, Commodification and Consumer Culture" Robert G. Dunn writes that the "democratizing tendencies inherent in consumption have been rapidly accelerated in the post-war period" (2000:123). Based on an exposition of the conditions of postmodernity (including the blurring of the boundaries between high and popular culture, the aestheticization of everyday life and the "historical transition from production to consumption"), he argues that there has been an ideological shift from occupational to consumer roles and a weakening of class consciousness (2000:123). Thus, Dunn suggests that "lifestyle consumption" has overtaken "socially delineated statuses" (2000:116).

These ideas about class, lifestyle and consumption echo some of the theorizations of retro style discussed above. While having a decidedly different politics from theorists such as Giddens, in their discussions of retro style McRobbie and Samuel both suggest that class distinctions are less marked than they once were. McRobbie and Samuel write as if those who are interested in retro style are linked by lifestyle choice and not by their class identity. For example, in the earlier version of "Second-Hand Dresses and the Role of the Rag Market" McRobbie (1989) contests Bourdieu's (2005 [1979]) theorizations regarding the correlation between lifestyle and social class. She writes that Bourdieu thought that students and bohemians could "risk looking poor and unkempt while their black and working-class counterparts dress up to counter the assumption of low status" (1989:27). McRobbie argues against this because she believed that the relationship between class and taste had changed since Bourdieu first published *Distinction* in 1979.

More recently, however, a number of sociologists and cultural theorists have returned to Bourdieu's ideas in their discussions of class and taste (e.g., Savage, 2000; Skeggs, 2004a; Southerton, 2001a; Taylor, 2008). They have questioned concepts of more mobile identities formed through consumption, especially the conclusions of Beck and Giddens. Before I discuss these debates in detail, it is necessary to outline Bourdieu's conceptual framework.

In *Distinction: A Social Critique of the Judgement of Taste,* Bourdieu (2005 [1979]) argues that consumption is one of the principal ways in which class-based distinctions are reproduced. He suggests that class is a relational process, or mode of differentiation. In a later discussion of *Distinction,* Bourdieu writes that "to exist within a social space, to occupy a different point or to be an individual within a social space, is to differ, to be different" (1998:9). He suggests that individuals occupy social space through accumulating resources (capitals) that can be converted into status (symbolic capital). He identifies four types of capital: economic, social, cultural and symbolic. Economic capital consists of an individual's financial resources. Social capital is formed of the social networks that can bring advantage. Cultural capital exists in three forms: as objectified in cultural objects, in an embodied state (implicit knowledge and practices) and as institutionalized through educational qualifications. Capitals function differently according to their context, or in what Bourdieu (2005 [1979]) calls "semi-autonomous social fields" (for example, the fields of politics or of the arts).

Bourdieu (2005 [1979]) suggests that cultural capital, as objectified in material objects, partly defines the power or status of that object within social space. He argues that the symbolic power of objects is a reflection of the cultural capital needed to consume them. In *Distinction* he suggests that as "distance from necessity" grows, stylization of life increases and material objects that represent a "taste for reflection" become more attractive.

For example, he argues that the difficulty in appreciating a picture of an object "socially designated as meaningless," such as a picture of a car crash, makes it more powerful as a symbol of elite taste (2005 [1979]:35).

Bourdieu suggests that cultural capital in the embodied state is formed through *habitus*. Habitus "designates the system of durable and transposable dispositions through which we perceive, judge and act in the world" (Wacquant, 2006:6). According to Bourdieu, the system of dispositions or the "feel for the game" that an individual has is based on the internalization of objective structures learned as a child that continue to influence, and be influenced by, different contexts. Thus, as an internalization of objective structures, habitus is always mediated by fields. In *Distinction* Bourdieu (2005 [1979]) argues that it is always a combination of habitus (and its capitals) and fields that creates differentiated practices. He suggests that because members of particular classes have common features in their habitus they are likely to participate in similar cultural practices and possess similar lifestyles. From this perspective, taste, as a product of habitus, is one of the areas in which class relations are played out.

Bourdieu also suggests that cultural capital is institutionalized through educational qualifications. This, as Holt notes, "certifies the existence of the embodied form" (1998:3). Bourdieu claims that the education system sanctions the hereditary transmission of cultural capital as the "rules of the game" are already established to support those with greater access to resources. Once legitimated by qualifications, cultural capital can often be converted into economic capital in the labor market.

Legitimation is also the key to understanding the fourth type of capital that Bourdieu identifies: symbolic capital. Symbolic capital is the form that all types of capital (economic, social and cultural) take once they have been made legitimate within specific fields. Cultural capital, for example, has to be legitimate before it can have symbolic power and be used to maintain social dominance over those who do not possess similar tastes or competencies. As David Swartz suggests, symbolic capital is also often denied capital, or in Bourdieu's terms it is "misrecognized"; "it disguises underlying interested relations as disinterested pursuits" (Swartz 1997:90). For example, as Bourdieu documents in *Distinction* (2005 [1979]), the categorization of certain material objects as inherently beautiful works to secure the positions of those who have the symbolic power to make their judgments and definitions legitimate. This can result in the direct or indirect ridicule or abuse of those with the "wrong" type of taste, which Bourdieu calls "symbolic violence."

These concepts and arguments have been highly influential in recent discussions of class (see Crompton, 2008). Mike Savage (2000) is one of the academics who has discussed them at length. He argues that Bourdieu's idea of class as differentiation serves as a corrective to those, like Giddens and Beck, who think that class is no longer relevant. Savage (2000:xi) suggests that Giddens and Beck misinterpret the change to individualization as a decline of class cultures. Instead, he proposes that what has been interpreted as a decline in the relevance of class should be seen as a "shift from working-class to middle-class modes of individualization" (2000:xi). Savage writes that "by setting up the idea of individualization against the 'Aunt Sally' of traditional, collective class culture, some plausibility for [Giddens's and Beck's]...account can be mustered" (2000:105). He goes on to argue that individualization should be viewed as "resting on social, cultural and political struggles which permit some to claim the right to full individuality at the expense of others," and thus individualization is itself a product of class relations (2000:107). Therefore, Savage reclaims a culturalist approach to class analysis, while also highlighting how class is implicated in economic inequality.

Savage argues that this approach to class analysis is advantageous because it focuses on class as a relational process and as "modes of differentiation rather than types of collectivity" (2000:102). From this perspective, the emphasis shifts from the development (or not) of class consciousness to "the classed nature of particular social and cultural practices" (Bottero, 2004:989). Thus, taste and cultural practices place individuals in social space and construct "classed"[2] identifications. However, Savage is also critical of mechanically applying Bourdieu's theories, especially those in *Distinction,* to a British context. He suggests that they do not theoretically register the positive resources attached to the working-class culture and the power of populist motifs (2000:109). This point is particularly important when exploring the value of retro style and, as I suggested in Chapter 1, also applies to other international contexts. I come back to Bourdieu's understanding of working-class culture below.

Beverley Skeggs (2004a) also uses Bourdieu's concepts to critique the claims of Giddens and Beck. She suggests that their accounts assume that everyone has equal access to "resources by which the self can be known, accessed and narrated" and that there is no sense that "the possibility of having a self may itself be a classed, raced and gendered issue" (2004a:53). Skeggs argues that constructing a biography is not neutral and always "invokes a position in terms of social differentiation" (2004a:53). She, like Savage, argues that class inequalities have not disappeared (2004a:2). Indeed, Skeggs suggests that ideas surrounding the disintegration of class, and theories and processes of individualization and reflexivity, are "in effect, a re-legitimation and justification of the habitus of the middle-class that does not want to name itself, be recognized, or accept responsibility for its own power" (2004a:60).

Drawing on Bourdieu's concept of capital, Skeggs (2004a) demonstrates how class has not disappeared but is made and given value through culture, including through judgments of good or bad taste. She argues that this creates new forms of exploitation based on cultural appropriation and the ability to convert culture into symbolic capital, as well as traditional exploitation from production. Skeggs's approach includes the ways in which value is made and unmade through representation and consumption, breaking with more conventional Marxian perspectives on the construction of exchange value. As Skeggs notes, Bourdieu's theory of capital attempts to "dispute the centrality of the economy as a separate sphere, whilst also developing a model to illustrate how different resources and assets accumulate in bodies and are carried across social spaces" (Skeggs, 2004a:16). She argues that this type of analysis is particularly important given the "predominance of symbolic exchange in post-industrialization" (2004d:47). Thus, like Savage, Skeggs does not interpret the changes in the latter part of the twentieth century as the disintegration of class. On the contrary, both Savage and Skeggs argue that individualization and related theories of lifestyle illustrate the increased centrality of cultural categorization and distinction in the making of class.

While the theorizations of Savage and Skeggs arose partly in reaction to the individualization theses of Giddens and Beck, they question the validity of ideas regarding the change to more mobile identities in theories of postmodernism. They also cast doubt on the optimism that McRobbie and Samuel derive from the "fluidity across old class lines" supposedly represented by the production and consumption of retro style. This optimism is also challenged by studies of taste and domestic space that have found that consumption continues to be stratified along class lines and that lifestyle is central to the making of class rather than illustrative of its decline (Southerton, 2001a, 2001b; Taylor, 2008).

Interestingly, McRobbie's recent work takes a similar theoretical line. In *The Aftermath of Feminism,* McRobbie questions the individualization thesis of Giddens and Beck and suggests that they do not grasp that lifestyle is "productive of new realms of injury and injustice" (2009:19). McRobbie is critical of her earlier optimism regarding women's capacities to "turn around and subvert the world of consumer culture" (2009:2). She cites her work on women's magazines as an example of her misjudgment. However, she does not return to her work on retro style. While this may be because of the subcultural and countercultural origins of retro style and its anticonsumerist potential, I believe McRobbie's arguments about retro need to be reconsidered. Thus, in the empirical research in this book I ask whether the production and consumption of retro style are representative of the uncoupling of lifestyle and class or whether retro has an alternative history, one very much linked to cultural distinction and class position. To do this, I draw on some of Bourdieu's arguments and use some of his concepts.

EVERYDAY LIFE, GENDER AND SYMBOLIC EXCHANGE VALUE

There are some problems with Bourdieu's conceptual framework, particularly in relation to working-class culture and gender. These issues make a wholesale application of his approach inappropriate for an analysis of the production, consumption and representation of retro style.

The problems with Bourdieu's conceptual framework are evident in the mapping of different tastes in *Distinction*. Bourdieu observes that there is a correlation between taste for popular culture and those from working-class backgrounds. He suggests that working-class taste is shaped by both necessity and resignation and that this sensibility frequently results in pragmatic and functionalist aesthetics (2005 [1979]:376). Although Bourdieu describes working-class practices and dispositions as dignified (albeit in a rather nostalgic and romantic manner), his methodological and theoretical approach means that they are only represented as entering a zero-sum game. They feature at the bottom of Bourdieu's diagram of the "space of social positions," as lacking in cultural capital. While this is fine as a reflection of the dominant symbolic culture and an excellent model for understanding the way cultural distinctions are made, it consigns working-class culture to a position of inferiority. This is problematic because, as Claude Grignon and Jean-Claude Passeron (1985) argue, it ignores the "autonomous and creative styles of life, which are not negative or second-rate versions of the styles of dominant culture, and which are not reducible to function or utility" (quoted in Rigby, 2000:299). Grignon and Passeron suggest that working-class cultures "are neither fixed in a perpetual state of deferential awareness of legitimate culture, nor are they mobilized day and night in a permanent attitude of revolutionary confrontation" (summarized by Rigby, 2000:298). For example, as outlined in Chapter 1, the symbolic value of flying ducks in the media did not affect their value in my grandmother's eyes.

The diagram of the "space of social positions" in *Distinction* also highlights problems with Bourdieu's approach to gender. As Terry Lovell points out, if women were included, they would feature twice because women could be entered in terms of their own economic and cultural capital, as well as "in terms of the value of these holdings for their families" (2000:20). This problem, Lovell argues, is indicative of Bourdieu's view of women as capital-bearing objects who are markers of taste rather than capital-accumulating subjects who are makers of it. Bourdieu's model of capital, habitus and field also suggests that "masculinity exists in the public (via the economic) and femininity in the private (via forms of cultural reproduction)" (Skeggs, 2004b:22). This position is problematic because it reproduces the discourse of public and private spheres. It is also highly inappropriate when applied to a discussion of domestic retro style. As McRobbie (1994) suggests, women and girls have been central to the production and consumption of retro, and because the style has been widely adopted they have been involved in the making of "good" taste.

In my opinion it is feminist theory, particularly Skeggs's work, that has addressed these problems most successfully. As well as drawing on the concepts of Bourdieu, Skeggs is influenced by the Foucauldian tradition. She is concerned with how various models of the self are brought into being through discourse. This has led her to question the concept of habitus. She suggests that "the habitus is the embodiment of the accumulation (or not) of value given by the volume and composition of the different forms of capital (economic, social, cultural, symbolic), displayed as dispositions" (2004b:85). In this regard, fields, or the contexts that determine what capital is, are "a precondition of the habitus and the habitus will always submit to the field" (Skeggs, 2004c:29). Although Bourdieu was critical of the idea of the self and devised the concept of habitus in an attempt to move away from theories of conscious action, Skeggs (2004b:86) suggests that Bourdieu reproduces the idea of the individual as defined by the accrual of property and exchange value when using the concept of habitus. This, she proposes, is not dissimilar to the idea of the exchange-value self in discourses of possessive individualism.

As outlined above, the concept of the possessive individual was first consolidated in Enlightenment texts and represented a change in the way that certain European individuals thought about property and their own identities. In his discussion of fetish and its associations with European personhood, Peter Stallybrass (1998:186) observes that the "civilized" subject who could recognize the true (i.e., market) value of the object-as-commodity was historically constituted in opposition to those individuals who were seen as the objects of value and imbued their material goods with history and memory. Colonial subjects were demonized for their "irrational" relationship with material objects and denied the ability to accumulate value and build an exchangeable self (Kopytoff, 1986; Stallybrass,1998). So, too, were women and the working classes (Pateman, 1988; Skeggs, 2004a, 2004b; Strathern, 1992). As argued above, the discourses of possessive individualism influence the terms of selfhood prevalent in contemporary consumer culture. This means that certain groups continue to be structured out of the "social, cultural and epistemological status of the individual" (Cronin, 2000:285).

For this reason a perspective that considers the self to be defined by the accrual of property is problematic because it reproduces the "colonialist model of exchange-value" as "the defining factor in the construction of per-sonhood" (Skeggs, 2004a:11). It risks both representing those who are ex-cluded as lacking, and reproducing the rhetoric of the market that suggests that exchange value is the proper way to view the world. In addition, the model of the self as accumulating individual ignores "a significant part of social life" (Skeggs, 2004b:29). For example, Skeggs argues that due to the emphasis on the accumulation of capital, the values of "altruism, integrity, loyalty and investment in others" are often missing in Bourdieu's accounts (2004c:29). I would add that the intimate relations with material objects that are very much a part of everyday life are also neglected, a point I return to below.[3]

To address these issues, Skeggs recommends a model that recognizes that individuals have resources that are valuable in their own right but may not be exchangeable because they have not been made legitimate by fields. She suggests that "it is possible to re-work cultural capital not just as high culture if we think more generally about culture as a resource or a use-value which can be separated from the fields and the means by which it is *exchanged*" (2004c:24). Like Bourdieu, Skeggs uses exchange value in the broad sense to mean the exchange of symbolic value across a range of fields. However, draw-ing on Marilyn Strathern (1992), she adopts an approach that suggests that it is relationships and the processes of valuation, rather than equivalence, that create exchange value. Thus, it is when one party becomes interested in the cultural, economic, social, emotional or material resources of another that exchange may take place. Skeggs conceptualizes use value as value that goes beyond that which can be exchanged. Quoting Gayatri Spivak (1990), Skeggs suggests that use value has "no literal origin or referent, because . . . [it] will always exceed that which it claims to represent" (2004a:186).

By using both categories, use value and exchange value, Skeggs argues that it is possible to see how class distinctions are maintained while avoid-ing the reproduction of a ubiquitous model of the self based on the accumu-lation of capital. This allows the exploration of practices and value systems that exist outside the "dominant symbolic" (Skeggs, 2004b:88). She also suggests that this reworking of the relationship between practice, capital and field enables a better account of gender than the one that Bourdieu offers (2004c:24). By separating resources from fields it is possible to see how fem-ininity can be used as capital when it is symbolically legitimated, while also recognizing the complexities of gender relations. In this respect Skeggs is in-fluenced by feminist and queer theory, which has emphasized the contradic-tions of gender relations, unlike Bourdieu (2001), who suggested that women misrecognize masculine domination.

These differences come to the fore in Judith Butler's (1997) comparison of Bourdieu's conceptual framework and her own. Both Butler and Bourdieu use the notion of "performatives" to mean utterances that exemplify or bring about the conditions that they name and that are always authorized through social conventions and norms. For example, a marriage declaration secures a social contract and is authorized by various institutions, discourses and practices. It is the extent to which individuals are able to question, transgress or dislodge socially embedded performatives that differentiates Bourdieu's and Butler's opinions. For Bourdieu the authority of performatives derives from the power of social institutions and from habitus that "suggests no easy freedom to adapt or change the self" (Lovell, 2000:15). There is little space for resistance because individuals are always-already positioned and take on the "view of the dominant on the dominant on themselves" (Bourdieu, 2001:42). This means that, as Bourdieu argues in *Masculine Domination* (2001), traditional gender roles and family relations are reproduced through the habitus. He suggests that early experiences of parental bodies and the sexual division of labor naturalize gender inequality. However, there is scant acknowledgment of the different ways in which people live or of the contradictions and ambivalences of gender relations. For example, Bourdieu suggests that people in gay and lesbian relationships reproduce traditional gender roles.

For Butler, gender is *doing* rather than *being* and is a process open to reconstruction. She suggest that, rather than taking on the views of the dominant, individuals with no prior authorization can refuse domination and overthrow "established codes of legitimacy" (J. Butler, 1997:147). Using the example of drag acts, Butler illustrates how the performance of gender reveals the constructed nature of masculinity and femininity. She suggests that revealing the "regulatory fiction" of gender offers "performative possibilities for proliferating gender configurations outside the restricting frames of masculine domination and compulsory hetereosexuality" (1997:193). Thus, from Butler's perspective, there is a possibility that transgressive acts that seize their own authority by acting as if they owned authority can alter the meaning of performatives and change social norms and conventions.

The differences between Bourdieu's and Butler's frameworks are bound up with the social spaces they focus on. As Lovell (2000) suggests, both perspectives have advantages. On the one hand, Bourdieu's emphasis on the almost "permanent sediments and traces which constitute embodied culture" is useful for thinking through how inequalities are reproduced through custom and practice (Lovell, 2000:16). It is also useful for thinking though the difficulties in claiming authorization if your habitus is always represented in negative terms (Lawler, 2004). On the other hand, Butler's focus on the constructedness of gender and sexuality through play and masquerade is more able to deal with contradiction, and her emphasis on transgression offers space for a radical politics. If taken in their entirety these positions are irreconcilable. However, if one adopts an approach that separates use from exchange value, as Skeggs does, performances that are institutionally legitimate can be explored, and so, too, can authorizations that may disrupt symbolic legitimization.

This theoretical approach is the most relevant to the production and consumption of retro style and the most useful contribution to my analysis. It can account for the way that the appropriation of objects and styles by certain groups does not necessarily change or take away their value for their original owners. It enables me to consider the role of women in the production of tastes for retro and to acknowledge the complexities of gender relations as well as the possible challenge to traditional gender roles that the consumption of retro may represent. It also allows me to recognize the symbolic value of retro objects and styles while exploring the practices of retro enthusiasts that go beyond the accumulation of capital.

MATERIALITY, PRACTICAL COMPETENCIES AND AFFECT

As I have argued above, Bourdieu's theoretical framework is problematic not only because it reproduces a model of the self based on exchange but also because it misses a significant part of social and material life. A number of approaches have emerged within consumption studies that attempt to move away from symbolism and capital. I discuss two of these approaches here.

The first, relatively recent shift has been to explore ordinary consumption through materials, practices and routines (Shove, Watson *et al.,* 2007; Warde, 2005; Watson and Shove, 2008). For example, in *The Design of Everyday Life* Elisabeth Shove, Matt Watson and colleagues suggest that "the hardware of consumer culture and its role in the reproduction of social practice repeatedly fall between the cracks of disciplinary inquiry" (2007:2). In a discussion of kitchen renovation and DIY (do-it-yourself) they explore how everyday objects "configure the performances, routines and aspirations of domestic life" (2007:15). They focus on the distribution of competencies among various actors and argue that most consumption takes place "as part of the effective accomplishment of social practices," rather than for its own sake (2007:152). This perspective is influenced by actor-network theory (ANT).

Latourian ANT maps the ways in which human and nonhuman actors are configured and come together in networks. Each actor in a network plays a part in the unfolding of events, yet without each other they are lost. For example, John Law (1987), a key proponent of ANT, argues that the actors that contributed to Portuguese imperial expansion included kings, explorers and boat builders as well as reefs, building materials and tides. Without any one of these actors events would have been different. Therefore, ANT views the "stability and form of artifacts as the interaction of heterogeneous elements that are shaped and formed into a network" (Law, 1987:107). In actor-network analysis individuals are "engaged in activities that make and remake their competencies and capacities" (Silva, 2010:15–16). This is significantly different from the way individuals are conceptualized in the work of Bourdieu because power is thought of as deriving from combinations of actors and actions rather than the amount of power someone has. The description of actions is a common theme in pragmatic rather than critical sociology (Boltanski and Thevenot, 1999; Callon, 1991; Latour, 1987).

Perspectives on consumption and design that are influenced by ANT are useful because they take materials seriously and describe activities in detail. This means they "consider as many actors or persons as there are types of action and none of these figures . . . [are] ossified" (Benatouil, 1999:385). This is useful in relation to retro style because it highlights that the qualities of retro objects such as patina and age are material "realities." It flags some of the practical competencies needed to produce a retro home. It also emphasizes how material objects and subjectivity are always in process and created through practice. This resonates with the methodological approach to retro style outlined in Chapter 2.

However, pragmatic sociology and ANT have been criticized because power is represented "as capacity and effectiveness, while power as domination remains invisible" (Silva, 2010:16). I would suggest that this problem is apparent in the study of kitchens by Shove, Watson and colleagues (2007) referred to above. Their research is excellent at exploring how the design of kitchens and appliances encourages, restricts and discourages certain activities. However, while Shove, Watson and colleagues mention gendered divisions of labor and kitchen design in their review of the literature, the study does not develop an analysis in terms of gender relations. Instead, it suggests that specific products and designs are needed for the accomplishment of practices and does not explore the family politics or divisions of labor central to those practices. This is problematic because it neglects the way technology as a material object, knowledge and process enters into gender identity (Cockburn, 2004). The gender-neutral approach of ANT has been criticized more generally and has an uncomfortable relationship with the critical tradition informed by a feminist politics (Star, 1991). Indeed, while a pragmatic sociology is "genuinely attentive to the critical actions developed by actors," even Boltanski, whose sociology of critical capacities has been argued to be symmetrical to ANT (Guggenheim and Potthast, 2012), has suggested that "its own critical potentialities seem rather limited" (2011:43).

ANT-type approaches have also been accused of neglecting "human capacities for expression, powers of invention, of fabulation" (Thrift, 2008:111). For example, in Shove, Watson and colleagues' study (2007), the emphasis on activity and practical considerations avoids the exploration of aesthetic and emotional relations. Approaches to material objects informed by theories of affect have addressed these issues. Thus, this is the other approach that attempts to go beyond symbolism and capital that I briefly explore here.

Within cultural studies there has been a long history of studying material practices; however, in the last decade there has been a marked increase in work that explores the "immaterial material" using theories of affect. While the meaning of *affect* is contested, it is generally used to describe the capacity to act or be acted on (Seigworth and Gregg, 2010:3). A 1960s vinyl chair sticking to your bare legs on a hot day is an example of how material objects affect the body. This small instance is illustrative of the ways affect occurs "in the midst of things and relations...[as well as] in the complex assemblages that come to compose bodies and worlds simultaneously" (Seigworth and Gregg, 2010:3). Informed by the ideas of Gilles Deleuze, the theory of affect is different from emotion, which has been described as "cognified affect" (Massumi, 1987:xvi). A Deleuzian approach does not presuppose a subject as does the concept of emotion utilized by psychoanalysis. Instead, it focuses on libidinal energies that are not contained by the processes of inscription that classify and control the body (Deleuze and Guattari, 1987).

In the experience of the everyday, however, perception, affect, the senses and emotion bleed into one another (Highmore, 2011:182–183). The feeling of sitting on the sticky 1960s chair and of peeling your legs free may be pleasurable or painful and/or conjure up powerful memories. Ben Highmore's (2011) work on design and everyday life offers a way of thinking about how material objects work in relation to affect, the senses and emotion. He argues for a reclaiming of aesthetics, not in its dominant mode associated with end products and judgments of good and bad taste, but in the form of an everyday aesthetics concerned with sensate perception and the "ongoing-ness of process" (2011:44). Like ANT this means thinking about material objects not in terms of cultural symbolism or the meanings the owner invests in them but as actors in their own right. For example, Highmore describes the way a 1970s Habitat chair affects his movements, habits and memories. The choice of the Habitat chair is not insignificant. As I explore in Chapter 4, Habitat has been theorized as central to the change from "way of life" to "lifestyle." For Highmore, the role of the 1970s Habitat chair in his life exemplifies his argument that "life practices are not just 'consumer' choices but sensual and ethical responses to a world that makes its own demands on us" (2011:11). He suggests that style is "deeply social and significant," and while lifestyle "may be hedged in from all sides by commercial forces, it is not simply reducible to it" (2011:11). Highmore's theorization of everyday aesthetics is particularly useful for thinking through the affectual and sensual relationships that retro enthusiasts have with their objects. It also enables a discussion of the fantasy and nostalgia involved in the consumption and production of retro style without necessarily reading this as some form of childlike state or lack.

Nevertheless, I maintain that the concept of capital is useful to explore the way certain bodies are positioned, categorized and governed. It is precisely because Bourdieu's model reproduces social hierarchies that it describes the workings of power so well. Thus, I argue for an approach that explores the practices and sensual experiences of everyday life that can contribute to capital, as well as those that go beyond it. This means thinking about localized dynamics as well as wider social relations—about retro homes as a product of complex relationships between material objects, retro enthusiasts and their family and friends.

USING, EXPERIENCING AND TALKING ABOUT THINGS

The theoretical approaches to material culture and subjectivity discussed in this chapter have various methodological consequences in terms of ethnographic research. For example, studies concerned with the symbolic meaning of material objects tend toward narrative methods. This is because narrative approaches explore the ways in which objects structure the stories that humans tell about their lives, as well as focusing on how objects "acquire cultural meaning and power" (Woodward, 2009:60). As suggested above, studies of consumption focused on meaning and power have been criticized because they have tended to interpret material objects and their associated narratives as symbolic of social class and status (Bourdieu, 2005 [1979]; McCracken, 1988; Veblen, 1925). More recently however, narrative approaches have been used to explore the more complex symbolic, emotional and ethical relations that individuals have with material objects (e.g., Hurdley, 2006; Woodward, 2001). In a study of mantelpieces in homes, Rachel Hurdley (2006) suggests that objects in domestic settings inhabit the intersection between the social and the personal. For example, the same 1950s coffee table may create and reflect cultural capital but also be of psychological use and possess sentimental value if it has been the center of the living room for many years. The strength of narrative methods is that they can reveal both types of value. They can reflect the role of material objects as signaling status and good taste, but also as forming and managing "self-identity and family relations" (Woodward, 2001:120).

In the ethnographic research conducted to produce this book I have used narrative methods in a number of ways. By interviewing tastemakers and retro retailers I have been able to document the history of retro style as well as explore how value and meaning are created through buying and selling retro objects. By talking to retro enthusiasts I have been able to explore their accounts of their own subject positions as well as histories of their interest in retro. In addition, by using a narrative approach whereby interviewees were asked to give me a tour of their homes and select items to discuss, I have been able to analyze stories of acquisition and the memories evoked by retro objects. This approach is influenced by Ian Woodward's (2001) discussion of "epiphany objects." Woodward developed the concept, originally conceived by Norman Denzin (1989), to argue that objects can be used as anchors in interviews to stimulate narrative. He sees this method of interviewing as advantageous because epiphany objects "act as resources for thinking through broader social and cultural distinction" (2001:131). Using objects in this way also allows for taste to be described as a historical narrative, which is useful for contextualizing the production and consumption of retro style. This strategy also animated the interviews, with participants remembering more information and being more candid than in the first part of the interview, when they were asked to reflect on their background and their taste.

As acknowledged above, however, the tendency of studies of consumption to reduce material culture to symbolism has been much criticized. For example, Tim Dant has suggested that focusing on symbolic display leads to the overlooking of many of the ways in which people live with objects, such as how material forms lead "to certain types of actions and [curtail] others, or how the presence of objects within a life affects the bodily experience of those who use them" (2005:25). These types of observations have led a number of theorists, including Shove, Watson and colleagues and Dant, to argue for methods that explore human/object interactions. Thus, rather than asking people to talk about their things or to speak about their lives through material objects, the method of choice for studies of human/object interactions is often observation (Miller, 2012). In the ethnographic research completed for the book I have used video technology to record and observe retro enthusiasts, their domestic spaces and their interactions with their possessions. I have also observed working life in retro boutiques and at market stalls, taken photographs of these spaces and used a field diary to record my experiences.

However, even by using photography, video and a field diary it is difficult to record the "pluri-sensory" and affectual nature of our relationships with material objects (Pink, 2004). In order to explore the moods, rhythms and affects of everyday life Highmore argues for a "science of singularity" in which the "particular is studied as if it could contribute to a more general account of the world" (2011:2). Although these accounts will inevitably be provisional and contestable, Highmore argues that the everyday, including "the dynamic simultaneity of desire (and its sublimations), of confidence (and its undoing), of concentration (and its dispersal), require[s] a mode of description that is more tuned to orchestration than the ascription of meaning" (2011:2). I began the book by highlighting the narrative of flying ducks to explore the making and unmaking of the value of retro style. In doing so I referred to my own experience and relationship with these objects. In a similar vein, in the rest of the book I discuss enthusiasts' emotional and affective experiences.

As I am sure all the academics discussed above would recognize, the relations we have with objects are simultaneously symbolic, practical, emotional and affective. Through its material properties a retro chair determines how an individual should act and feel, and it is through narrative that the chair is rendered valuable in a culture. Thus, in my approach to retro style I attempt to bring together the theoretical and methodological perspectives outlined above. To do this I look at the practices with which objects and styles are embedded, used and valued in everyday life using a combination of methods. More detail regarding these methods, as well as the research design and analysis, can be found in the Appendix.

CONCLUSION

I began this chapter by outlining theorizations that suggest that cultural capital and the art-culture system have become central to consumer culture. I noted the relevance of ideas regarding the aestheticization of everyday life and lifestyle to the production and consumption of retro. I also suggested that the increase in value of authenticity within contemporary consumer culture might explain the popularity of the style. At the same time, however, I recognized the problems with assuming that aesthetic considerations (as defined by the art-culture system) are important to everyone. Thus, I proposed that the production and consumption of retro style might be limited to specific groups with high levels of cultural capital. By implication, this might mean that Bourdieu's ideas regarding the correlation between cultural capital and social class continue to be relevant.

Since Bourdieu's theorizations, however, the relationship between class, lifestyle and taste has been questioned. I gave an account of how in the early 1990s a number of social theorists argued that class had become less pertinent because individuals were free to make lifestyle choices. I identified similar ideas about the breakdown in the relationship between taste and class in McRobbie's and Samuel's discussions of retro style. In a review of more recent work on class and taste, particularly research by Savage and Skeggs, I questioned these conclusions. I documented how, rather than representing the disintegration of class, individualization and related theories of lifestyle demonstrate the increased centrality of cultural categorization and distinction in the making of class. These discussions led me to propose that retro style has an alternative history that is linked to cultural distinction and class position. Therefore, in the book I aim to explore the relationship between the production, consumption and representation of domestic retro style and class.

As well as documenting the discussions that led to this aim, in this chapter I also detailed my theoretical approach to the making of class and value. I suggested that an approach to class that utilized the concept of capital was advantageous in order to understand middle-class distinction making because the middle-class self has historically been bound with, and produced by, the accumulation of exchange value. I employ the concept of cultural capital to indicate the knowledge, values and practices that are valuable within a given field. Like Bourdieu, I consider cultural capital to be inherited through social position, objectified in material objects and legitimated by educational qualifications. Throughout the book I also explore the role of other institutions in the legitimation of cultural capital.

In the second part of the chapter I documented the limits of a Bourdieusian approach to gender and materiality. I suggested that Bourdieu's theories could not account for the ambivalences of gender relations or the ways in which women had been central in the making of domestic retro style. I outlined Butler's approach to gender as performance, as *doing* rather than *being*. The approach to gender that I take in this book is influenced by Butler's work because it allows for a politically empowering and potentially transgressive gender politics. I also suggested that the practical and sensual experiences of material objects were neglected in Bourdieusian accounts. This led me to explore studies of consumer culture that have drawn on ANT and theories of affect. I argued that these studies offered ways of thinking about the appeal of material objects beyond symbolism, which is particularly important in a discussion of retro homes, furniture and decorative objects.

To explore gender politics without considering class relations is short-sighted, and in a consumer culture in which certain affects are highly valuable it is important not to dismiss exchange. Thus, drawing on feminist discussions of Bourdieu's concepts, I proposed a model that focused on cultural resources, as well as cultural capital. The term *resource* is used to indicate the knowledge, values and practices that have use value but little or no exchange value as defined by the field. Using the concepts of resources and capital enables me to think about material objects and cultural practices as having many different use values, as well as having symbolic exchange value. As a reminder that an increase in the exchange value of an object may not affect its use value, I also use the concept of *regimes of value*, drawn from anthropology, to describe the "multiple, coexisting and variously related" contexts in which objects are valued (Myers, 2001:6).

I concluded the chapter by explaining the methods I used to document the symbolic, practical and emotional relations that retro retailers, tastemakers and enthusiasts have with their objects. Findings from this research are presented in Chapters 5 to 8 of the book.

4

A History of the Retro Aesthetic

I got interested in art deco and kitsch in the early 1960s. It was always around, but lots of people were getting into kitsch at art school in the 1960s.

Catherine, retro enthusiast (2006)

When I was sixteen I got into the mod revival scene, the '60s scene...even though it was 1980, everything based around it was '60s, from the scooters to the clothing.

Dave, retro enthusiast (2007)

I remember when I was little I liked to go to '50s parties, I used to do my hair in curlers and wear '50s dresses. I was in an acting class and I was obsessed with the movie *Grease,* and I loved the movie *Hairspray.*

Marianne, retro enthusiast (2007)

This chapter documents the history of the retro aesthetic in the cultural landscape of the everyday. The approach I take is inspired by retro enthusiasts' and tastemakers' accounts of the history of their interest in the style. As the quotes above demonstrate, enthusiasts mentioned their taste as being shaped by cultural products such as artworks, films and music; articles in magazines and newspapers; and the products and catalogs of high street retailers; as well as the availability of secondhand objects at jumble sales and car boot sales. Thus, in this chapter I explore a selection of these examples. While this is a rather eclectic mix of sources, a narrative of the development of the consumption and production of retro emerges. Three historical conjunctures appear significant: the 1960s counterculture, youth cultures in the 1970s and 1980s and mainstream media and retailing in the 1990s. This narrative highlights a potential popularization of the retro aesthetic, and thus I explore whether the production and consumption of retro style have grown. Throughout the chapter I engage with the argument that Angela McRobbie made in the 1980s that it was no "longer possible to pose the world of street style or second-hand style against that of either high fashion or high street fashion" (1989, reprinted in 1994:138).

I begin the chapter by briefly exploring the history of the consumption of secondhand goods, antiques and revival for the home in order to consider the difference between these forms of consumption and retro. I argue that the first retro-like objects can be found in the artworks of the European historical avant-garde. Drawing on the work of Mike Featherstone (1991), I suggest that the legacy of the avant-garde movements contributed to a change in attitude toward consumption and lifestyle among young people in the 1960s. I document the emergence of boutiques and furniture retailers that catered for these new consumers. I go on to outline the development of retro style in youth cultures, the media and retailing from the 1970s to the 1990s. I conclude the chapter by considering whether the popularization of retro style is illustrative of a wider sociocultural change in which mass culture has become bohemianized.

CONSUMING SECONDHAND, ANTIQUES AND REVIVAL

Throughout history, revivalism, appropriation and cultural borrowing have been common. This has partly been a result of a conscious desire to revive past styles. As John Pile notes, "From the earliest Renaissance beginnings there has been an interest in learning from the past and in borrowing elements to be used in a new context" (2005:231). This interest has resulted in both reproduction and antique furniture being included in the design of domestic interiors. In times when money and resources were scarce, the consumption of secondhand and inherited furniture also resulted from a lack of affordable alternatives. The histories of the consumption of antique, revival and secondhand are difficult to untangle and are all bound up with processes of industrialization. I explore these histories briefly here.

In the early industrial period technological advances increased the number of new goods that were manufactured and meant that "scarcity gave way to abundance" (Lemire, 2005:31). As Beverly Lemire suggests, in the early sixteenth century the significance of the secondhand trade grew because the increase in the consumption of new products meant that old items were surplus to requirements and could be resold and reused (2005:31). Lemire writes that consumption was two-tiered (1988). While the middle and upper classes had enough wealth to buy the new furniture and decorative objects they desired, much of the rest of the population were only able to afford secondhand goods purchased from junk shops, pawnbrokers and flea markets. Although the distinction between the two tiers may have been less marked than Lemire's account suggests (see Stobart, 2007), this separation seemed to continue long into the nineteenth century, with writers such as Charles Dickens, Thomas Carlyle and Henry Mayhew commenting on the secondhand trade in Monmouth Street and Petticoat Lane frequented by London's poor. However, by the late nineteenth century the size of this trade had decreased dramatically due to industrial production, which offered cheaper goods to larger proportions of the population.

Indeed, it was the development of industrial production throughout the eighteenth and nineteenth centuries that enabled the widespread manufacture of reproduction furniture and decorative objects. Aided by new technologies, larger-scale producers began manufacturing and marketing objects that copied the styles of ancient artifacts.[1] By producing new objects in the style of old ones manufacturers such as Wedgewood utilized and contributed to the taste for baroque and classical design. Wedgewood recognized that the value of ancient styles was partly due to their association with connoisseurship and the upper class. While retaining some of this exclusivity, Wedgewood capitalized on these connotations by making his ceramics more affordable to some of the aspiring middle class (McKendrick *et al.*, 1982). As mass industrialization intensified in the Victorian period, reproductions, produced as part of many historic revivals, became more available to wider sections of the British population. As Francis Collard notes, manufacturers and retailers interpreted the styles, designs and patterns available as part of revivals and offered "enormous choice for their customers by producing their own versions as well as supplying reproductions of actual historical models, some more accurate than others" (2003:48). From 1860 to 1890 department stores and furniture retailers such as Shoolbred & Co. of Tottenham Court Road and Heals in London filled their catalog pages and showrooms with interiors designed in the Gothic, Jacobean, Renaissance and Queen Anne styles (Collard, 2003).

Moreover, the late nineteenth century witnessed an increase in the buying and selling of antiques. As Deborah Cohen argues, prior to the 1880s "the suggestion that one should buy old furniture would have been greeted by most middle-class citizens with derision" (2006:148), yet after this time it became increasingly common to find antique furniture in middle-class homes. Old objects "served as a critique of a fast-paced age" and were desirable as a mark of distinction (2006:147). Consumption practices also changed in this period, with many consumers going to "salerooms, auction houses, bazaars, and curiosity shops to find objects that predated the machine" (2006:146). Late Victorian and early Edwardian consumers searched for unique and rare objects, and "proprietors spun fanciful tales around their objects, embellishing elderly specimens with noble pedigrees" (2006:152). Thus, antique dealers and their shops multiplied and flourished before World War I. The three histories introduced here—the consumption of secondhand goods due to a lack of affordable alternatives, the consumption of revival furniture and the consumption of antiques—continue into the present.

However, in the early twentieth century attitudes toward these practices changed. As Raphael Samuel acknowledges, "it [was]...modernism with its fetishisation of the new [and original], which [was]...the exception; revivalism, whether in the form of cultural borrowing or variations on a classical theme, has more often resembled the norm" (1994:110). The desire to sweep away the past was common in modernist literature, music, art, architecture and design (Attfield, 2000). As is explored in more detail in Chapter 8, in architecture and interior design this often resulted in an antipathy toward the bric-a-brac of domestic décor (Morley, 2000:61). The aversion toward the use of the past in furniture and interior design was part of the wider sentiment of modernism that was opposed to traditional bourgeois high culture and its tastes. At the same time, as Andreas Huyssen suggests, modernism "constituted itself through a constant strategy of exclusion" and an "obsessive hostility towards mass culture," which was frequently equated with domesticity and femininity (1986:vii).

However, the great divide between high art and mass culture was challenged as soon as it arose. Huyssen suggests that the philosophies and artworks of the European historical avant-garde attempted to establish "an alternative relationship between high art and mass culture" (1986:viii). Rather than sweeping away the past, many of the artworks produced by the European historical avant-garde, particularly artists associated with the Dada and surrealism movements, used everyday and outmoded objects. For example, pieces such as Marcel Duchamp's *Hat Rack* (1917) and Man Ray's *Emak Bakia* (1926) appropriated objects found on the street and at flea markets. By recontextualizing everyday objects in gallery space these artists hoped to challenge the boundaries of art as a concept and the status of the art institution (Goldsmith, 1983). This is where I would suggest the first retro-like objects are found. While the revival of styles was common in previous periods, the change in attitude toward the everyday and the outmoded is first evident in the artworks of the European historical avant-garde. These groups challenged the divide between high and mass culture, and the legacy of avant-garde movements contributed to the aestheticization of everyday life, which Featherstone (1991) suggests is characteristic of consumer culture. However, in their attempts to make everyday life into art the avant garde continued to "define their identity in relation to two cultural phenomena: traditional bourgeois high culture" and "vernacular popular culture as it was increasingly transformed into modern commercial mass culture" (Huyssen, 1986:viii–xi).

COUNTERCULTURE AND APPROPRIATING THE PAST IN THE 1960S

The valuing of the everyday and the outmoded famously reappeared in the work of neo-Dadaists and pop artists in the United States in the 1950s and 1960s and has been theorized as the inception of postmodernism (Huyssen, 1986). Like the European historical avant-garde, pop art challenged "modernism's relentless hostility to mass culture" and the bourgeois values with which it had become aligned (Huyssen, 1986:115). As Featherstone (1991:66) notes, in the art of the New York postmodern trans-avant-garde artists, such as Andy Warhol and Roy Lichtenstein, there was a double movement: to challenge the status of the work of art and the academy, and to assert that art could be anywhere and anything. In addition, more than the European historical avant-garde movements before them, pop artists embraced the "degraded landscape of mass culture," evident in works such as Lichtenstein's painting *Look Mickey,* which shows a scene adapted from a Disney children's book.

The pop movement was not only a U.S. phenomenon, and artists working in Britain also attempted to "efface the boundary between art and everyday life" (Featherstone, 1991:66). In the early 1950s, artists such as Edwardo Paolozzi and Richard Hamilton, "the fathers of London's Pop art movement," used images found in magazines, science fiction literature and advertising to create collage pieces (Osterwold, 2003:64). The reuse of everyday imagery and old and outmoded objects continued into the 1960s and is particularly evident in the work of Peter Blake. For example, in *The Toy Shop* (1962), Blake uses old toys and related ephemera to create a toyshop window. It has been suggested that this piece "developed as both a work of art and a store for his collection of objects" (Tate Website, 2009).

Two of the retro enthusiasts I interviewed, Catherine and Thomas, were involved in the British art scene in this period. Catherine identified her art school education and involvement in the arts in the 1960s as inspiring her interest in art deco and kitsch. The retro aesthetic prevalent in the pop art movement also influenced Thomas, who acquired many secondhand objects at the time, including a selection of glass pinball signs from a colleague he worked with at university and a 1950s jukebox. These personal narratives are illustrative of a wider turn toward quirky and eclectic interiors in the 1960s. They are also indicative of a change in the general attitude toward the distinction between high and popular culture as well as the outmoded and everyday among the young. As John Storey (2003:64) notes, high culture and its separation from the popular came to be regarded as the "unhip" assumption of an older generation with bourgeois values and tastes.

The mid-1960s witnessed the emergence of a different type of retailer to cater for young customers like Catherine and Thomas. In streets like Carnaby Street and Portobello Road in London, new shops and stalls started to appear, such as I Was Lord Kitchener's Valet[2] and Kleptomania.[3] Not unlike the antique shops in the same area, they sold odd pieces of secondhand furniture as well as clothing. Yet the objects that these shops sold were relatively new in "antique" terms; they were from a variety of periods and had often previously been viewed as junk. Victorian enamel signs, penny-farthing bicycles, old furniture painted with union jacks, stuffed bears, bowler hats, frock coats and military uniforms all mixed together in shops that played pop music and had a decidedly different and rebellious feel.[4] This contrasted with the more serious and overtly hierarchical business of buying and selling antiques. Rather than selling Chippendale sideboards that were recognized as valuable by association with high culture and good taste, these new secondhand retailers valued objects that were quirky, unique and not well established in design hierarchies. The shops were also different from junk shops because objects were carefully selected and the proprietors both followed and contributed to fashion trends. Although not defined as such at the time, these types of shops and stalls were the forerunners of retro shops today.

This change in attitude toward high culture and design meant that, as Dick Hebdige notes, the true legacy of pop was "not located in painting or purely academic analysis at all, but rather in graphics, fashion and popular music, in cultural and subcultural production" (1988:142). The cover of the Beatles' album *Sgt. Pepper's Lonely Hearts Club Band,* designed by Peter Blake and much cited as an example of retro style, exemplifies this point. The album, which is frequently associated with the Summer of Love, was released in 1967 and stayed at number one on the UK chart for twenty-seven weeks (*Rolling Stone,* 2003). This dual association with the mass market and the counterculture has led theorists such as Thomas Frank to suggest that "the counterculture, as a mass movement distinct from the bohemias that preceded it, was triggered at least as much by developments in mass culture as changes at the grass roots" (Frank, 1997:8). I return to this point below.

It was not only record covers designed by pop artists that took inspiration from the past. Many of the cultural products associated with the 1960s counterculture revived old styles. For example, art nouveau–inspired graphics were used to advertise clubs such as the UFO club on Tottenham Court Road in London. The record cover of the psychedelic rock album *Ogden's Nut Gone Flake* by the Small Faces, associated with the British summer of 1968 (Adams, 2008), took its inspiration from an old tobacco tin and clearly demonstrates the valuing of old Victorian objects that was common at the time.[5] The cover design is "representative of a traditional working-class symbol—the hand-rolled cigarette" and thus is also illustrative of a revaluing of objects traditionally associated with the working class (Thorgerson and Powell, 1999:113). This design is particularly important in the history of domestic retro style because it is often through association with past working-class culture that pieces of retro furniture and decorative objects become desirable.

In the mid- to late 1960s cultural products less obviously connected with music cultures also revived old styles. Restaurants, such as Wilton's in London, selected art nouveau furniture and pictures to attract customers

(Chapman, 1964:25). Clothes shops, such as Biba, also used Victorian, art deco and art nouveau objects in their shop interiors to mark their brands as distinct from "the plastic fantastic" ethos common in other retailers' strategies (Anderson, 2002).

The emergence of retro across different cultural locations was illustrative of a wider sentiment. As Jacqueline Botterill notes, while unease with mass production and its breaking down of social bonds was a feature of modernity, the period after World War II brought an even wider "fear that the processes of modern massification were obliterating individuality" (2007:108). For example, journalists (in magazines such as *Rave* and in newspaper columns in the *Sunday Times* and the *Guardian*) began to complain about the standardization of mass production and the role of the media in circulating tastes. Instead of relaying fashion trends, they began to describe ways to differentiate oneself through interior design. This included practices such as painting furniture yourself and incorporating secondhand or found objects into your interior (Chapman, 1964:30; "Brighter Than White," 1968:84).

Commercial culture, business and advertising influenced and reacted to this sensibility and became increasingly preoccupied with individuality, self-expression and the "conquest of cool" (Frank, 1997). One of the ways that producers and retailers could obtain the highly elusive badge of cool was by representing themselves and their products as authentic. To do this they partly relied on the established tradition of associating objects with the past. This had a new twist, however. Rather than emphasizing the grandeur of objects and their associations with the upper classes, manufacturers emphasized rustic charm and quirkiness.[6] As Irene Cieraad and Sjoerdtje Porte note,

> The students' social rebellion and Marxist admiration of the lifestyle of the old working class was mirrored in their nostalgic preferences. Soon very "incorrect" designs, like old sideboards, chairs with "misshapen," curved, and turned legs, and Simons' kitsch-defined pot-bellied stoves achieved an aura of respectability, especially when these items were handed down.... Popular must-haves were grandpa chairs, granny's tea tables, old household goods like sewing machines, enameled pots and pans, irons, and wooden coffee mills. These praised decorative objects crammed their student rooms, and functioned quite mistakenly as reminders of a pre-industrial past. (2006:281)

The valuing of these past objects and styles is different from previous revivals. Discourses of the fashionable interior had changed from promoting adherence to one particular style and decorating a room in this way, to an eclecticism that embraced many different styles in one room. For example, in an interview in the *Telegraph Colour Supplement* with Terence Conran, the founder of Habitat, Margaret Duckett writes about Conran's home. She states,

The furnishing format is deceptively simple. The rules are essentially common-place, and quite safe. First, degut your house regardless of its architectural style—although obviously good architecture counts when exposing the structural shell. Then mix old and new, junk shop finds with modern design (Conran's of course) and set it off against pure white paint, natural floors and existing propor-tions. (Duckett, 1968:26)

Retro style is part of this type of aesthetic, and although it was not defined as such at this time, interiors like this one are indicative of the beginning of retro in Britain. It did not matter whether consumers liked an Edwardian tea service or a Victorian hat stand; it was the way they put these objects together that became important. The style that the term *retro* was to define was wide-ranging and could categorize any group of objects and styles from the recent past. It was concerned with expressing individuality and difference from the mainstream. In this regard, the style "popularized the sentiments of mid-19th-century bohemian artists, throughout culture, by moving art outside official galleries, deeming everyday objects art, and everyone an artist" (Botterill, 2007:112). At the same time, retro was also in keeping with revivalist tradi-tions, which made it less radical and added to its popularity.

Retailers who produced and sold newly manufactured goods recognized and added to the trend for old objects and styles. They observed, and in some cases contributed to, the popularity of original retro objects. For example, in the same interview with Duckett, Conran and his wife, Caroline Herbert, were keen to emphasize that they shopped at antiques markets and junk shops as well as owning Habitat products (Duckett, 1968:26–30). Thus, in the 1960s, products, retail environments and marketing strategies that had been subtly decommodified became highly desirable to a specific group of producers and consumers. As the *Telegraph* article suggests, one of these producers was Terence Conran.

HABITAT AND THE POPULARIZATION OF ECLECTIC INTERIORS

Habitat opened its first shop on Fulham Road in 1964.[7] It sold furniture, soft furnishings and accessories. The influence of Habitat and Conran has been extensively theorized in the design and consumer culture literature (Chaney, 1996; Lury, 1996; Nixon, 1997; Whitely, 1994). It has been argued that Habi-tat was one of the first lifestyle brands and represented the beginnings of a new consumer sensibility. Habitat has been represented as innovative, in terms of both the products it offered consumers and its retailing strategy. For example, John Hewitt notes that Habitat was modern and that its "prod-ucts seemed to be part of the emergence of good modernist design as a popular concept" (1987:39). He also suggests that Habitat was innovative in its "pre-designed shopping programme" that encouraged consumption by inviting you to buy the whole look (1987:40). Other theorists, such as Nigel Whitely, have argued that "the Habitat style in the 1960s and 1970s appealed to the young and 'switched on' because it not only countered the prevailing British taste for 'repro', but because it expressed and confirmed a lifestyle" (1994:19).

Conran was innovative in his understanding of the market and the way in which he chose and displayed objects for the "pre-designed shopping programme" (so that any object would go with any other), and there is no doubt that this contributed to his success. He also made interior design more fashionable. For example, Elizabeth Good, a *Sunday Times* journalist, remarked on how Habitat had made consumers aware that interiors could be stylish (1964:43).

However, I would question the extent to which Habitat products countered the prevailing British taste for repro. As well as taking inspiration from ethnic designs, rural styles and continental Europe, Habitat objects and furniture were often influenced by the designs of previous periods. For example, they sold new versions of Victorian bentwood furniture and chesterfield sofas, army campaign chairs, French farmhouse kitsch utensils, old English butchers' aprons and Victorian apothecary jars (Figure 4.1). Fiona MacCarthy, columnist for the *Guardian,* wrote, "You can call Conran a plagiarist until the cows come home. The furniture he makes is not especially original" (1966:8). In addition, Elizabeth Benn (1964?) considered Habitat to be the "smart modern answer to the junk shop craze. Until recently young marrieds setting up home have gone to junk shops, but now there is Habitat," where one could buy new but old-looking furniture.

Indeed, in early Habitat promotional material this side of the business was emphasized. The catalog used stylish, but childlike and old-fashioned, illustrations of products. The captions describe the goods as simultaneously old and new. In a selection of objects from the catalog (Figure 4.1), the rocking chair is described as "Rock-a-bye Grand-Mama for Mods," the Victorian salt box as a "Pinewood salt box for old salts," the dish as "Stews like stews of yesteryear" and the oil lamp as "Shades of nights of old. Circa '64."

Given Habitat's success, these products and their humorous descriptions were obviously appealing to a certain type of young middle-class consumer. By 1970 Habitat had become a way of life "for a certain section of the middle class" (Carr, 1970:11). However, with this success also came the possibility of becoming too popular. MacCarthy commented, somewhat scathingly, on the success of Habitat:

> While he (ham fisted handyman) puts up his pinewood units with Melamine worktops and lots of drawers for clobber, she brings back a rough rush game bag full

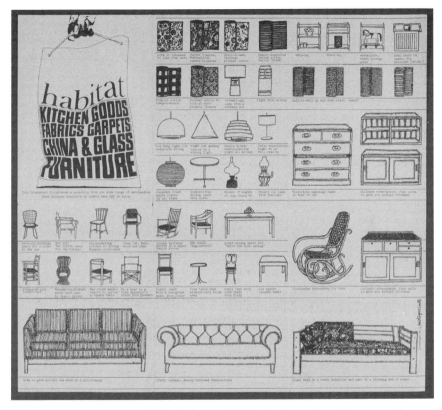

Figure 4.1 Habitat catalog (1964). © Groupe CAFOM. Courtesy of the National Art Library at the V&A.

of shopping and donning a butchers apron makes a rural weekend lunch: huge hearty stew with crusty rolls and creamy mounds of butter (made by wooden butter pat): then thinnest crispiest pancakes from a heavy cast iron crepe pan, and coffee drunk in red-enameled jolly workmen's mugs. These are Conran people. (MacCarthy, 1966:8)

However, criticisms of Habitat, such as this one, are uncommon both in writing at the time and in more recent theorizations. Habitat managed to supply products that drew on the past while avoiding being categorized as pretentious or inauthentic. One of the ways in which they did this was by embracing a retro aesthetic rather than a revivalist one. They appropriated products from more recent periods and valued objects associated with the working class or the rustic countryside instead of those linked with ancient civilizations and the aristocracy. The interior design of the shops and the ways the products were displayed also took inspiration from street markets and junk shops. Rather than being stacked on shelves, dishes, cups and cooking utensils were displayed individually and grouped with other complementary items. Baskets, pestles and mortars and urns were scattered around the shop floor. As Jean-Marie Floch notes, "It is via the layout of the shop that the various products are put forward as simple and beautiful things on the one hand and as encountered object on another" (2000:128).

In addition, Habitat avoided being viewed as a mass-market producer by emphasizing that their products could be mixed with existing styles. Pine chairs in the catalog of 1965 are described as "traditional Norwegian country-cottage pine chairs with seagrass seat, that blend perfectly with new furniture or family heirlooms." Furthermore, the identification of Conran himself as the artist and designer behind Habitat helped to associate the products and shops with an auteur rather than with industrial production.

In addition, I would suggest that it was Habitat's consumers, the young middle classes (this included many of the writers, critics and academics of the period), who defended the products and the brand against the critique of inauthenticity. While some reproductions consumed by the working classes were labeled kitsch, those consumed by the middle classes, such as Habitat products, were considered in good taste. Those who were in a position of relative power were able to authorize their own tastes while criticizing others. The reversal of the hierarchy of values attributed to objects that is evident in Habitat products (with greater value being given to products associated with the working classes rather than the upper classes) made this easier. Criticisms of snobbery could be avoided, and taste could be thought of as ascribed rather than achieved. Through misrecognition, as Pierre Bourdieu and Loïc Wacquant (1992) argue, the processes of classification and positioning involved in power relationships are hidden. It did not matter where the object came from, but it was the design of the object and the way styles were put together that became paramount. Thus, for the new middle classes in the 1960s, it was cultural capital rather than economic capital that demonstrated taste (although, of course, in reality economic and social capital were also necessary).

Habitat was one of the first organizations to recognize and contribute to the sensibilities of the new middle classes and their quest for life as art. Thus, it managed to carve out a space in the marketplace that was different from both newer mass-market retailers producing flat pack furniture (such as MFI) and more traditional furniture retailers selling modernist designs or reproductions of antiques (such as Heals). By the 1970s, the obvious references to the origins of its products had disappeared, and Habitat emphasized newness and innovation. Yet the company continued to produce objects that drew on historical designs and to highlight the versatility of their products in fitting in with other retro or antique shop finds.[8] The 1960s Habitat interior had also influenced the dominant aesthetic of the 1970s home. Farmhouse-style pine kitchens, natural flooring, bentwood furniture and chesterfield sofas became commonplace. However, in the late 1970s and early 1980s new and different appropriations of the past also began to emerge.

YOUTH CULTURE AND RETRO SCENES IN THE 1970S AND 1980S

After the 1960s the number of boutiques and market stalls selling retro furniture and decorative objects grew. By the late 1970s and early 1980s "retro-chic set a whole style for alternative culture" whereby retro retailers and market traders dealt in an eclectic mix of Victorian, art nouveau, art deco, 1940s, 1950s and 1960s styles (Samuel, 1994:86). This history is difficult to trace because retro shops and stalls are usually known through informal networks and local geographic knowledge and are temporally transient (Gregson and Crewe, 2003). Nevertheless, it seems that it was in the 1970s and 1980s that secondhand traders who described their goods as retro first emerged in Britain. As Samuel notes in his discussion of retro-chic, it was at this time that markets like Portobello Road and Camden in London became home to many part-time dealers who sold "off-beat" or "found-in-the-attic" goods (1994:96).

These traders were often part of the youth cultures and subcultures that emerged in the late 1970s and early 1980s in Britain who appropriated, revived and reworked historical styles. Indeed, it was the DIY (do-it-yourself) aesthetic of punk; the revival of the 1950s in rockabilly, psychobilly and new wave; and the reworking of 1960s styles in northern soul, mod revival and 2-tone that provided much of the source material for McRobbie's (1989) argument regarding retro style and postwar subcultures. She notes that female punk bands in the late 1970s, such as X-Ray Spex, wore 1960s ladies' two-piece suits as a war on conventional femininity; that Paula Yates, a 1980s television presenter, mixed 1950s glamour with punk (a style common among the music cultures of new wave, rockabilly and psychobilly at the time); and that 1960s movies such as *Blow Up* were raided in search of new ideas and provided part of the 1980s "soul-boy" wardrobe. McRobbie also notes that most of these subcultures relied on secondhand clothes found at jumble sales and flea markets (1989:24). The role of jumble sales in enabling teenage consumption was confirmed in interviews with retro enthusiasts. For example, Louise's love of 1950s music and the "rockin'" scene when she was a teenager meant that she often went to jumble sales to find cheap 1950s clothing and objects. She reflected on how those around her at jumble sales, including her mother, did not completely understand her love of the 1950s; this meant that she was able to acquire cheap retro clothing for herself and her friends.

The retro aesthetic was evident not only in the clothing choices of these youth cultures but also in the graphics on popular album covers, on flyers and in fanzines; the design of clubs and shops; and the choice of cars and scooters. For example, young people in the rockabilly scene in the late 1970s and early 1980s listened to records from the 1950s with graphic inserts from that period, and committed enthusiasts drove 1950s cars (Figure 4.2). Record covers and the publicity for psychobilly nights also revived 1950s styles, often with a more comic strip or horror film feel. In addition, mod revival and 2-tone enthusiasts reproduced 1960s-looking graphics in flyers and fanzines (Figure 4.3).

Many of the retro enthusiasts I interviewed had been involved in youth cultures in the 1970s and 1980s. For example, Andy and Louise located the emergence of their interest in retro in the "rockin'" scene in the 1980s when they listened to R & B, blues and rock and roll and dressed in original late 1950s and early 1960s clothing. As a teenager Louise also collected "odd '50s bits" for her bedroom. In addition, Dave's interest in retro style came

Figure 4.2   "The Rockin Crowd" (early 1980s). © Les Bailey.

Figure 4.3   Mod fanzine Go, Go (1985).

from his involvement in the mod revival and northern soul scenes in the early 1980s. He said that the lifestyle adopted by those involved in the scene was one that appropriated 1960s styles, including music, clothing and scooters. It was not until he moved into his own home that he started to become interested in retro interiors.

Enthusiasts who had participated in youth and music cultures in the 1970s and 1980s were keen to emphasize that their tastes were not typical of the time and were a select and minority interest. Thus, the revival of past styles by those involved in youth cultures in the 1970s and 1980s was part of antibourgeois and antimainstream sentiments, much like those of the 1960s counterculture.

However, the retro styles discussed above also influenced those who were not committed to one specific scene. Tim and Suzy suggested that although they were not involved in a specific subculture, the style, particularly the "new wave 1950s look," influenced their choice of clothing. It was in the early 1980s that they started going to charity shops and jumble sales more often. This is perhaps indicative of the "implosionary" effect of mass media and retailing in the 1980s, which meant that youth styles and fashions were "born into" the media (McRobbie, 1989:39). The revival of 1950s styles in the late 1970s and early 1980s, which Tim and Suzy refer to, was particularly visible. For example, articles in *19 Magazine,* a magazine aimed at young girls, gave advice about "getting the right 1950s fashion look" using the aesthetics from films, cars and interiors of the period (Rock, 1977). Around the same time, films, television programs and advertisements with retro aesthetics started to become more prominent.

Film was the inspiration for the first academic references to retro style (Baudrillard, 1994; Jameson, 1985). As I noted in Chapter 2, the term *retro* is said to have derived from French avant-garde cinema in the early 1970s. However, it was not until the late 1970s and 1980s that Hollywood blockbuster films really embraced the retro aesthetic. For example, in 1978 the release of the film *Grease* firmly positioned retro style in the mainstream.[9] Scenes showed a 1950s diner and bowling alley and lodged these interiors in the British cultural imagination (Marcus, 2004:34). The prevalence of 1950s style continued into the 1980s with films such as *Back to the Future* (1985) and the famous Nick Kamen Levi's advertisement (1985), set in a 1950s launderette. The advertisement associated Levi 501s with 1950s style, which was viewed as "cool, mythical and stylish" (Tomlinson, 1990:11). It linked the brand to both its authentic past and the fashionable status of the youth cultures explored above. This added to Levi's already growing sales, which increased from "80,000 in 1985 to 650,000 in 1986" (Tomlinson, 1990:11).

Films and advertisements were the inspiration for the younger interviewees' interest in retro style, myself included. For example, Marianne identified the film *Grease* as influencing her play as a child. One of her later inspirations was the cult film *Hairspray* (1988), directed by John Waters, which is set in the early 1960s and has a kitsch aesthetic. This inspired her to throw a 1950s party, and I remember copying dance moves from the film with friends myself.

Thus, by the mid- to late 1980s, retro, particularly 1950s and 1960s styles, was the domain not only of fashionable youth but of the wider population (both adults and children). As Guffey suggests, "a flood of kidney-shaped couches" and "tapas bars with pink and blue organic furnishings" had shifted the character of the 1950s "revival from teenage rebellion to middle-class aspiration" (2006:130). For some retro enthusiasts the popularity of 1950s retro started to lessen its appeal (see Chapter 7 for further discussion). Yet, for others, retro styles were not devalued enough by mainstream interpretations to change their taste. Thus, the consumption and production of retro in art and design, youth cultures and homes continued.

RETRO AND THE HOME IN THE 1990S AND 2000S

When those involved in the subcultures of the 1970s and 1980s grew up and moved away from home, the retro aesthetic went with them. The skills they had gained in finding clothes at jumble sales and car boot sales were put into practice to decorate their homes. Bargains could still be found. For example, Tim and Suzy found a 1950s three-piece suite at a car boot sale twenty years ago that they continue to display in their home.

However, as the popularity of retro style increased, some items of furniture and decorative objects became more difficult to find. To cater for the growing market, shops and boutiques focusing specifically on retro furniture emerged in the 1990s.[10] For example, Tom Tom, "London's oldest established twentieth century art and design emporium," opened in 1994 in central London (Dunkley, 2005). Owned by Tommy Roberts, the shop sold mid-century modern furniture and decorative objects with more of an emphasis on iconic pieces and designer names than had been the case in retro shops in the past. Items included early Habitat clocks, plastic desk tidies and furniture by designers such as Verner Panton, Pierre Paulin and Olivier Mourgue (Marsh, 1997).

The boom in popularity of retro style for the home, which was relatively tardy compared to that for retro clothing, seems to be part of, and influenced by, a wider interest in home decoration and the increase in turnover of fashion-led furniture in the late 1990s. The number of lifestyle magazines and television programs on the subject increased greatly. For example, Alison Clarke (2001) argues that the market for home-oriented lifestyle media expanded several times in the period from 1990 to 2000. Cheap furniture outlets such as Ikea also made fashionable furniture more affordable.

Ikea opened in Manchester in Britain in 1987, and most of the other British stores opened in the 1990s. The low-cost furniture and decorative objects produced by Ikea are well known, and their role in the making of ephemeral and temporary spaces has been well documented (Sparke *et al.,* 2009; Burikova, 2006). Ikea products have been described as having no provenance or charm and as reiterating modernist sensibilities of clean lines and functional aesthetics (Sparke *et al.,* 2009:229–269). Indeed, one could argue that when Ikea made fashionable furniture cheaper and more accessible to all, certain consumers and retailers became attracted to original retro objects as a means of distinction and individuality in a changing marketplace. This is an argument I explore in the next chapter.

While Ikea, like Habitat, has never marketed its products as retro, many of its products reproduce 1950s and 1960s Scandinavian designs, and this means they often feature in recent retro interiors. Ikea products are often so similar to retro originals that even retro retailers have found it difficult to distinguish between them. In Nicky Gregson, Louise Crewe and Kate Brooks' study of retro retailers, one of their interviewees said, "We bought an aluminium dish once, thought it was a 50s one, it turned out to be Ikea!" (2003:70). Thus, Ikea furniture not only changed home decoration in Britain but also contributed to the history of the retro interior.

While Habitat and Ikea have avoided naming their material objects as retro, other manufacturers and retailers have been keen to do so. The naming of reproduction products as retro peaked in the 1990s. Producers and retailers took inspiration from previous styles or relaunched old designs and marketed them as retro products. This has continued into the present. For example, the furniture producer Ercol recently relaunched some of its furniture designs from the 1950s to form an originals' range, and Typhoon, a kitchenware producer, has both a retro and a vintage collection. Retro styles have also become available from low-cost manufacturers and retailers in Britain. For example, both a steel standard lamp from the Argos catalog and a plastic kitchen scale from Matalan are defined as retro.

The spread of new products that are purposely decommodified, both by using past styles and by defining them as retro, represents a trend in business and the creative industries. As Botterill (2007:109) notes, the concept of authenticity has appeared in many recent popular business books on how to create value and attract contemporary consumers. Retro style is often flagged as one of the ways in which this can be achieved (e.g., S. Brown, 2001). In an interview I conducted with the research department of the advertising agency McCann Erickson, a desire for "basics," which included themes such as "retrofusion" and "authenticity seeking," was identified as one of the four consumer trends of the twenty-first century. The agency researchers suggested that the pace of scientific and technological development, work cultures and fear after 9/11 had created a consumer who craved stability, security and an authentic identity and was looking to the past to get it. Retro product designs, branding strategies or advertising styles would be employed particularly if the product was highly innovative, in an attempt to lessen the dehumanizing aspects of technology, or if the product was an established brand, in order to build on its authentic associations.

The number of examples of cultural products using retro aesthetics in the twenty-first century is substantial. These include products aimed at the mass market, such as the James Bond film *Casino Royal* (2007), which had a 1970s-style title sequence; the Hollywood remake of *Hairspray* (2007) with 1950s-style costumes and set; and an iconic Stella Artois advertising campaign (2009) using 1950s-style graphics. Retro aesthetics are also evident in cultural products aimed at more exclusive audiences. For example, the bar and restaurant interiors of Loungelover and Sketch in London combine 1950s-style teak chairs and tables, 1960s egg stools and more contemporary design pieces.

However, the wider use of a retro aesthetic does not necessarily mean that the style is devalued. As I demonstrate in the rest of the book, people continue to value retro objects and aesthetics even if they call them something different (vintage or mid-century modern), retro retailers find new ways to make the objects they sell desirable, and those working in the creative industries also continue to draw on the past for inspiration.

RETRO STYLE AND THE POLITICS OF POPULARIZATION

While the diverse range of sources documented in this chapter display a variety of retro aesthetics and revive styles from different eras, they all coalesce to give retro style value and meaning in the current cultural context. In some ways this is no different from the 1960s and 1970s, when art merged with popular and commercial culture, as was the case with the *Sgt. Pepper's Lonely Hearts Club Band* album cover designed by Blake.

However, there have been some significant changes since the art scene and the 1960s counterculture in Britain gradually disseminated retro-like aesthetics. As set out above, in the late 1970s and early 1980s retro styles became the mainstay of music and youth cultures and were increasingly "born into" the mass media and retailing (McRobbie, 1989:39). In the mid-1980s retro styles became common in Hollywood films, one of the most significant ways that young retro enthusiasts came into contact with the style. More recently, retro aesthetics can be found in cultural products aimed at mass markets and at more exclusive audiences. In terms of the domestic interior, high street retailers such as Habitat have disseminated the message that eclectic interiors that mix old and new styles are a sign of good taste, and low-cost retailers such as Ikea have made 1950s- and 1960s-inspired designs affordable to wider markets. Thus, although a variety of retro items can be found in all of the decades since the 1960s, there has been a popularization of the style and its associated values.

The popularization of retro style can be viewed as part of a wider bohemianization of mass culture (Binkley, 2007; Brooks, 2000; Frank, 1997; Wilson, 1999). As Samuel Binkley notes,

> Historically, bohemianism defines an aesthetic disposition which brings together a romantic investment in the authenticity and irreducible autonomy of aesthetic production as a practice of everyday life—one which operates against the perceived encroachments of a capitalist market in cultural goods patronized by bourgeois audiences. (2009:104)

In the 1990s Elizabeth Wilson argued that hedonistic attitudes, fashions originally associated with the avant-garde, and a bohemian aesthetic had gradually been disseminated to wider audiences (1999:26). She argued that we were "all bohemians now" (1999:24). As I outlined in Chapter 3, aesthetics and authenticity have become profitable in the contemporary economy. In addition, as documented here, the retro aesthetics that emerged from the practices of small groups of artists and members of subcultures have become commonplace. This is even more noticeable in the discussion of lifestyle media in Chapter 6. Based on this evidence, Wilson (1999) could be right.

However, rather than an indication of widespread bohemian values, the prevalence of retro may be linked to a particular trajectory of a section of the middle class and those who work in the cultural industries. For example, in his commentary on American society in the 1990s, David Brooks (2000) argued that the "new upper class" (Bobos) had values that derived from a fusion of the bourgeois world of capitalist enterprise and the "hippy" values of bohemian counterculture. Brooks (2000) suggested that educated "bourgeois bohemians" practiced "one downmanship" (a rejection of conspicuous consumption) in order to gain status. Retro objects and styles and the valuing of used, old and worn items fit with the values of this elite group. Thus, the prevalence of the retro aesthetic may be a consequence of many "bourgeois bohemians" owning, or working within, the cultural industries.

Critics such as Frank (1997) and Joseph Heath and Andrew Potter (2005) have suggested that the increased centrality of business in the cultural industries has meant that the distinction between a "bohemian space of expressive authenticity and a commodified space of mass consumption" has become even more implausible (Binkley, 2009:106). Because of this they have argued that the possibilities for cultural protest have been shut down.

Indeed, Frank proposes that it was the 1960s counterculture in the United States that changed the relationship between business and the cultural industries. He writes,

> What changed during the sixties, it now seems, were the strategies of consumerism, the ideology by which business explained its domination of national life. Now products existed to facilitate our rebellion against the soul-deadening world of products, to put us in touch with our authentic selves, to distinguish us from the mass-produced herd, to express our outrage at the stifling world of economic necessity. (Frank, 1997:229)

Frank even goes so far as to question the extent to which the 1960s counterculture was fundamentally opposed to the capitalist order. He suggests that the "counterculture may be more accurately understood as a stage in the development of values of the American middle class, a colourful instalment in the twentieth century drama of consumer subjectivity" (1997:29). He argues that one of the ways "hip consumerism" communicated with its middle-class consumers was by adopting retro styles. Indeed, Frank suggests that retro style is "hip consumerism's proudest achievement" (1997:227).

However, Binkley contests Frank's argument because it is simplistic and because it glosses over "the process of incorporation by which countercultural lifestyles were retailored for a new economic and cultural configuration" (2007:19). Binkley (2007:12) argues that the early lifestyle discourses of collective improvisation and caring in the countercultural movement of the late 1960s and early 1970s were overshadowed as lifestyles emerged as prepackaged commodities ready for individual consumption. Rather than a total emptying out of the radical values of the countercultural movement, he suggests that this process contributed to new, more complex versions of capitalism. Binkley suggests that in the late 1960s and 1970s businesses and the media began to speak in more authentic, intimate tones to more precise market niches, and the middle classes increasingly valued rebellion, defiance and individuality.

In Britain this is partly illustrated by the valuing of retro styles associated with art and youth subcultures and their dissemination by retailing and the media. In the 1970s and 1980s the middle classes seemed to become increasingly attracted to youth cultural styles. This is not to suggest that all of the middle class suddenly started to consume retro styles in the same way as those participating in youth cultures. Rather, it is to infer that the values of "hipness/coolness," "rebelliousness" and "authenticity," which Sarah Thornton (1997:115) associates with subcultural capital, became increasingly important to this group. This argument confirms Beverley Skeggs's suspicions regarding Thornton's concept of subcultural capital. Skeggs argues that "what

Thornton identifies as sub-cultural capital could be seen as a form of mis-recognition of a version of middle-class plundering, appropriation and dis-tinction-making" (2004a:150). The values associated with youth and music cultures are an attractive resource for the middle classes and those working in the creative industries. Thus, while retro emerged as a critique of traditional bourgeois high culture, the aesthetic is now part of that culture: it is found in the design of restaurants, shops, books and advertising aimed at elite groups. At the same time, due partly to its dissemination by the media, the retro aesthetic is also part of mass culture.

However, it is simplistic to view retro style solely as "hip consumerism's proudest achievement" (Frank, 1997:227). As Binkley suggests, it remains the case that the belief in the distinction between the mainstream and the alternative is "sustained in the minds, bodies and practices of bohemians (and those inflected with the logic of their practice), animating their conduct and opening them to perhaps more radical critical discourses on consumption as an ethically consequential mode of conduct" (Binkley, 2009:106). Thus, the critique of bourgeois culture and consumerism from which retro style emerged may well continue to influence the attitudes and practices of retro enthusi-asts. I return to explore this possibility in Chapters 7 and 8.

CONCLUSION

In this chapter I have proposed that the first retro-like objects were visible in the artworks of the European historical avant-garde and that this represented a change in attitude toward the everyday and the outmoded. I suggested that in the 1960s retro styles became more visible in art and in other cultural prod-ucts circulating at the time. Businesses such as Habitat began to use retro aesthetics to communicate to their audiences in more authentic tones. Retro style built on the traditions of revival and antique but also represented a new structure of feeling: one that was less concerned with maintaining cultural hi-erarchies and that placed more emphasis on eclecticism and individuality. Old and everyday objects could become desirable design pieces more readily than before, and more people could take part in this process. In the late 1970s and early 1980s the valuing of cool, rebellious and authentic styles intensified, and the speed with which retro styles were adopted and disseminated by the media and cultural industries quickened. This change in value could be one of the rea-sons why those who were involved in youth cultures in the 1970s and 1980s were able to capitalize on their cultural resources and make money selling retro styles. This argument is explored in much more detail in the next chapter.

In the 1990s and 2000s I argued that the number of retailers selling retro furniture and decorative objects grew and that domestic retro style was more widely circulated by the media. Although retro emerged in the 1960s as a critique of traditional bourgeois high culture, in this period it was increasingly found in the design of products and interiors aimed at elite groups. The aesthetic was also common in mass culture. This finding led me to question the politics of the popularization of retro style and to consider whether retro style is one of "hip consumerism's proudest achievements" (Frank, 1997:227). I suggested that retro does not challenge the values of art institutions or older generations as it once did and that the style may well have become part of middle-class distinction making. At the same time, however, I proposed that the legacy of the history of the retro aesthetic might mean that retro enthusiasts are open to critiques of inequality and consumerism.

5

Retailing Retro

The importance of retail spaces and those involved in the service industries in creating, establishing and communicating the value of goods has long been recognized by businesses and academic studies. As suggested in the previous chapter, retailing has been particularly important in the development of retro style for the home. Retro traders selling secondhand goods are even more central in the making of value because the production processes of the objects they sell are temporally and spatially distant. In this chapter I consider the cultural practices of retro retailers and traders, drawing on ethnographic research in three spaces: at boutiques, at markets and on the Internet. These sites are selected because they are where most retro enthusiasts buy their furniture and decorative objects.[1]

Retail spaces are interesting because they are contexts where production and consumption, and producers and consumers, come together. Historically, production and consumption have been "characterized as lying in cultural contradiction with one another—the rationalized, disciplined sphere of production and the free, hedonistic sphere of consumption" (Korczynski and Tyler, 2008:307). From this perspective, the structuring power of the producer meets the agency of the consumer in retail spaces. However, studies of cultural practice have complicated linear versions of the link between production and consumption and simplistic conceptualizations of the power relationships between producers and consumers (e.g., P. Jackson *et al.,* 2000). The relationship between the production and consumption of retro style is complex, and forms of exchange are multifarious. In the spaces I explore in this chapter, I find that retailers and their customers take on differing roles, and various power relationships are played out.

As well as exploring the diverse relationships between producers and consumers, in this chapter I consider the values attributed to various retail spaces. I suggest that the value of furniture and decorative objects differs according to where and how items were acquired. Modes of acquisition that are viewed as the least available and the least commercial seem the most desirable for retro retailers, tastemakers and enthusiasts. This has led me to draw up a suppositional scale of relative modes of acquisition (Table 5.1).

I begin the chapter by explaining the hierarchy in more detail and argue that it is indicative of the shifting terrain of distinctiveness central to the value of

Table 5.1 Scale of relative modes of acquisition.

Most valuable ("alternative")	Selective inheritance
	Found object
	Jumble sale/junk shop/charity shop purchase
	eBay/auction purchase
	Retro shop/boutique purchase
Least valuable ("mainstream")	High street retailer purchase

retro. I go on to explore how retro retailers and traders negotiate this terrain and how their success is made possible by the location of their shops and stalls, as well as their identities.

In the second half of the chapter I turn my attention to the buying and selling of retro items in informal retail networks, focusing specifically on jumble sales and eBay. Informal retailing networks are contexts in which individuals or small groups are able to sell retro objects without establishing themselves as permanent businesses.[2] Other key features include "sliding pricing systems, interpersonal relations of exchange, flexibility of social roles and affective as well as economic relations" (Gregson and Crewe, 1998:39). The production and consumption of retro have often taken place within informal retail networks, and it is partly for this reason that the style has been associated with the alternative, considered a democratic form of consumption providing consumers with greater degrees of agency and thought of as holding potential for consumer activism and empowerment. Thus, I conclude the chapter by reflecting on these ideas.

RETRO STYLE AND THE SHIFTING TERRAIN OF DISTINCTIVENESS

When the term *retro* first appeared on shop fronts and in retailers' advertisements in the 1970s, it was used to add value to goods and styles that were previously perceived as old-fashioned. As Raphael Samuel (1994:87) notes, when the shop American Retro opened in Soho in 1986 it was considered the height of style. To the owners of the shop and their consumers the term *retro* indicated that goods (both original and reproduction) were fashionable and authentic rather than poor quality and mass-produced.

Yet in more recent times the meaning of *retro* has become more nuanced, and in some cases the term has been discarded altogether, with consumers and retailers preferring to describe their material objects and tastes as *vintage* or *mid-century modern*. As suggested in Chapter 2, the value of retro partly rests on individuality, difference and distinction. It is mass production and high street retail that can destroy these qualities. Associations with popular low-cost brands such as Argos or Matalan can make certain retro objects and styles less desirable to retailers, tastemakers and consumers. For example, Edward, a writer and retro enthusiast, remarked,

> The public have become much more educated in the last ten years and seeing a growing market, more retailers want a slice of the pie.... And the kind of distinction that I was talking about is gradually collapsing, the distance between the old and new is closing down. It's actually very difficult sometimes to tell one from the other. (Edward, writer and retro enthusiast, 2006)

Because of this trend many consumers and retailers of retro style, including Edward, are turning to original objects and becoming more particular about them. Helen, a retro retailer, also reflected on this shift:

> It's more acceptable to have second hand or vintage now.... I think the interest has grown because it's more prevalent really, in that there is so much retro in the last four or five years. Retailers' lines are influenced by '70s things, right down to British Home Stores lighting.... It has become a lot more high street. A few years ago we were the only people selling lava lamps or '60s and '70s glass and now you can go into any cheap shop and buy a piece of glass that looks like it's '70s.... That's why other people really want the pure stuff. (Helen, retailer, 2006)

As is evident in these quotes, the increased reproduction of retro styles leads to an intensification of the distinction between reproduction and original in retro cultures. Although preferences for retro originals are complex (this is explored in Chapter 7), the majority of retro enthusiasts favor original objects. High street retailers are aware of this. As Angela McRobbie observed in 1989, secondhand clothes were sold alongside new ones in the shops of the fashion retailer Topshop. More recently, large upmarket department stores such as Liberty and Selfridges in Britain have begun selling original retro furniture and decorative objects (labeled as vintage) in their furniture departments. These pieces are often more expensive than new items.

The prevalence of original retro objects as well as reproductions in high street retailing environments may be one of the reasons why the hierarchy of value of retro objects is structured by their mode of acquisition. Buying an original retro object from Liberty seems to produce less cultural capital than purchasing the same object at a flea market. Although interviewees did not refer to these hierarchies overtly, they were often implied. The objects that interviewees chose to describe were much more likely to be ones they had found in junk shops or inherited from their grandparents than the retro items they had purchased in boutiques or from high street retailers (although many also had plenty of these objects in their homes):

> This clock is one of the things that I love and we had no intention of buying it. We found it in a junk shop in Wolverhampton. It's French marble and I would hate

to think how much it is actually worth because we didn't pay that much for it. It was in a shop of absolute tat, and there it was sitting in the corner. It's incredible to find things like that. It's special because of the way we found it. (Peter, retro enthusiast, 2006)

I have a whole collection of ashtrays that I found at different thrift stores. I really enjoyed finding them. You couldn't just go into a shop and purchase them. (Marianne, retro enthusiast, 2006)

That's my Granddad's old table from the 60s... when he died nobody wanted his furniture apart from me. (Louise, retro enthusiast, 2005)

It could be argued that these quotes simply illustrate the work of creative appropriation that all consumers engage in to combat the alienating affects of commodification (De Certeau, 1984; Miller, 1987). Of course, it is the case that all consumers are involved in these types of practices. However, my findings suggest that retro retailers and enthusiasts do not value all modes of acquisition equally. For example, although selective inheritance (keeping objects that you have inherited but have also chosen according to style) is valorized, unselective inheritance (simply keeping the same objects as your parents or grandparents) is not. Ownership of rare originals and acquisition of retro objects without purchasing them also generates value because these objects and occurrences are the least available. For example, a 1960s interior bought entirely from eBay would indicate much less cultural capital than one consisting of various jumble sale buys and found objects. These items have been made singular by being more difficult to acquire, and their value derives from this fact. Thus, to attract certain customers, it seems important for high street retailers selling retro goods to mimic modes of acquisition in more alternative spaces. For example, when Topshop holds a jumble sale, or Habitat displays its objects as "encountered," they attempt to add value to their goods.

Yet the extent to which the wider population attaches value to original objects and more alternative modes of acquisition is debatable. Certainly there is some evidence that those who work in advertising agencies and for large manufacturers or retailers such as Selfridges, Argos and Topshop think that their customers are attracted to the retro aesthetic.

However, buying retro goods, particularly items that are mass-produced or sold on the high street, is not a guarantee of cultural capital and an individual and authentic identity. As Anne Cronin notes in her discussion of gender and consumption, "certain overlapping groups have suffered compulsory exclusion from terms of individuality" (2000:277). Cronin describes how popular discourses of individuality and identity in contemporary consumer society take as their center ideals of an authentic inner self that should be expressed through an "innate" capacity for "free choice" (2000:275). Thus, those who are excluded face an impossible imperative of "doing oneself," a project or goal to be aimed at, and "being oneself," a projecting forward of an already established identity. The goalposts of good taste are continually moving, and discourses of authenticity are remade to ensure certain individuals are excluded. The moment that "doing oneself' becomes more accessible, in this case through the mainstreaming of retro style and the democratization of retro knowledge that that entails, the ways of "authentically being oneself" change. For example, greater importance is placed on eclecticism, consumption of original objects and less commercial modes of acquisition. These ways of "authentically being oneself" require higher levels of cultural capital and a preestablished identity that has the ability to authorize its own tastes. Thus, excluded individuals are continually reembedded in retraditionalized roles and norms (Adkins, 2000).

With this in mind, I would question whether hierarchies of material objects, consumption practices and individuals have been flattened. As retro styles have increasingly featured in the product designs and marketing of high street producers, distinctions between original and reproduction, alternative and mainstream, and ultimately those who can distinguish between them and those who cannot, are continually remade. This process is even more apparent in retro boutiques and market stalls.

LOCATING RETRO MARKET STALLS AND BOUTIQUES

An association with the alternative is essential for retro traders to retain their distinctiveness in the marketplace. In their study of retro retailers, Nicky Gregson and Louise Crewe (2003:33) found that the location of traders in towns and cities was particularly important in this regard. Although the choice of geographic location is often dictated by life circumstances rather than a conscious market decision, and the importance of location may have diminished somewhat due to the popularity of eBay, the position of shops or stalls continues to be paramount to survival. To distinguish themselves from high street retailing and junk shops, boutiques and market stalls need to be located in the appropriate area. These tend to be areas that are associated with small-scale creative industries, where artists, designers and musicians can be found. As Sharon Zukin (1988) argues, these industries are often catalysts for the revaluation or gentrification of districts in cities and towns. Gentrification, where older, cheaper and unkempt housing is revived or refurbished, has been the focus of a great deal of research (see T. Butler, 2003:9). Central to most of these theories is a critique of the transformation of working-class areas into middle-class ones.

Districts of cities and towns that are undergoing gentrification are attractive for stallholders and retro retailers because they provide potential

Figure 5.1   Broadway Market in Hackney, East London (2007). © Author.

consumers with high levels of cultural capital, revived market cultures and cheap rents. The revival and restoration of old buildings, commonly Victorian or Georgian, has been a large part of the process of gentrification in London, and the aesthetics of these areas make an ideal setting for retro boutiques and market stalls. Retro furniture and objects suit these environments because they complement the minimal and shabby-chic style in which most buildings have been renovated. For example, the retro retailers I interviewed felt that they "fitted in" in areas with old buildings and were keen to emphasize the "character" of the locality of their market stall or shop. They defined their locations as noncorporate and free from "bland high-rise buildings."

The gentrification of Broadway Market in Hackney, East London, illustrates this point. Set up by the Tenants and Residence Association and Hackney council in 2000, it is now a flourishing market with traders selling organic food, arts and crafts and retro items (Figures 5.1 and 5.2). At the time I conducted the ethnographic research, the street was also home to a number of shops, including four retro retailers selling furniture and decorative objects: one relatively new and temporary and three more permanent shops, the oldest of which had been open since 2004 (Figure 5.3).

Figure 5.2 Stall selling retro objects and vintage ceramics, Broadway Market, Hackney, East London (2007). © Author.

For the traders and retailers I spoke to, the history of the market and of the buildings in the area contributes to the atmosphere that consumers enjoy. The restored Georgian and Victorian shops make perfect settings for today's boutiques due to their size and character, and most businesses are thriving. However, retro retailers were ambivalent about this process:

Figure 5.3   Broadway Retro on Broadway Market, Hackney, East London (2007). © Author.

I've lived in East London for a while and it is changing. In some ways it's good for business, as long it doesn't become too corporate. . . . I kind of liked it when it was a bit more downtrodden. It had a bit more character. (Keith, trader, 2006)

As well as demonstrating Keith's thoughts about living in East London, his ambivalence toward the process of gentrification also reflects the position of retro retailing in the marketplace. Keith's business, like other retro retailers and traders, depends on a location that is not "so run down" that there are no potential customers nor so mainstream as to destroy its "character" and demand high rents. The need to demonstrate character was also evident when discussing interiors and displays. For example, Cathy, another retailer in East London, told me it was important to maintain the "East End hovel look" to make consumers feel that they were getting a bargain. Steve, a retailer in Islington, also mentioned that the shop must not look "overly displayed"; otherwise, consumers might think that the objects were new or feel unable to sit on furniture or pick up objects. Thus, for retailers it is important that they occupy a space somewhere between jumble sale and art gallery. Most of all, their location should maintain its association with the alternative.

Yet, as Gregson and Crewe suggest, "inscriptions of the 'alternative' in the retail landscape—particularly when constituted in opposition to the 'mainstream'—are inherently unstable geographically" (2003:33). Areas gradually change though reinvestment and revaluation, and their associations with the alternative and their attractiveness to those in the creative industries decreases. Thus "more marginal spaces are sought out by those looking to escape the incursions of the mainstream" (Gregson and Crewe, 2003:33). This is evident on a larger scale in the histories of markets and shops selling retro goods and their locations. From Portobello Road and Carnaby Street in the 1960s, to Camden in the 1970s and 1980s, and then Brick Lane and Spitalfields in the 1990s, the opening and closing of retro stalls and shops can be tracked across London. These changes coincide with larger trends in the gentrification of London, moving from Inner North London (Camden and Islington) and West London (Notting Hill and Portobello Road) east to Hackney, Tower Hamlets and Walthamstow, and more recently to South East London (T. Butler, 2003:9). Within these areas the process is a gradual one, with market stalls often being the first to appear. As market stalls become successful they often change into more permanent shops. As shops become more established and areas become even more popular, they are likely to attract investment from bigger, more mainstream businesses and different types of visitors. Spitalfields Market in East London is one of the most obvious examples of this: over ten years it has changed from a weekend flea market to a space akin to an upmarket shopping center (Figure 5.4). In the period between the ethnographic research and the writing of this book, Broadway Market has also changed considerably, with many retailers and traders experiencing increases in rent.

When these changes occur, stallholders and retailers have a number of choices. They can move to find cheaper, more alternative areas; become more commercial; or get out of the business altogether. Moving to a different area

Figure 5.4   Spitalfields Market (2011). © Author.

is, of course, much easier for those with temporary stalls or shops. For those with more established businesses, it is much more difficult. Gregson and Crewe found that gentrification created two distinct product strategies for those who could not change location: "a retreat historically into vintage" or critical comment on the mainstream "through juxtaposition, parody and hybridity" (2003:38). I also found these strategies in my research with retro retailers.

The retailers I spoke to who had been established for ten years or more had inevitably witnessed changes in the areas in which they were located. Some of them had gradually become more exclusive and specialized by focusing on what they defined as mid-century modern furniture or twentieth-century design. When I visited the shops the items on sale were recognizable as design classics and were often quite expensive. The cutting-edge, antihierarchical and alternative feel of other retro shops was also less evident in these spaces. Customers tended to be collectors with relatively high disposable incomes who would travel large distances to find the "perfect" piece. It is in this niche market that the distinction between retro and antique is at its most fluid. For example, the majority of stands in Alfie's Antique Market sell retro goods. The displays of goods in the market are similar to those in other high-end[3] retro boutiques. Stands are understated in order to draw attention to "key pieces." This results in interiors that are white, minimal and similar to art galleries (Figure 5.5).

Other retro shops have seen their locations become increasingly commercial. Catering for the gift or tourist markets, they have mixed originals with reproductions and have increasingly stocked cheaper novelty items, such as

Figure 5.5 Alfie's Antique Market (2006). © Author.

shot glasses and ashtrays (Figure 5.6). Yet, to remain distinct from the high street shops in their vicinity, they often cultivate kitsch, over-the-top or crowded shop fronts and interiors. In some cases the shop, rather than the products, becomes a destination in itself. For example, the frontage and interior of Flying Duck Enterprises in Greenwich often attracts visitors who reminisce about childhood games and toys rather than buying large or expensive pieces.

Although retro shops and stalls have different locations, interiors and types of display, they all aim to distinguish themselves from the mainstream. One of the other ways that retailers do this is through personalization. As both buyers and sellers, retro retailers have close connections with the objects they sell and are able to communicate this to consumers. Like Victorian antiques traders, retro retailers often narrate their objects to make them more attractive to consumers. They pass on information about the designers of objects, the periods in which they would have been made and, in some cases, their past lives. This is significantly different from the information consumers receive from high street retailers.[4] Not only does the product's back story fabricate an aura of authenticity (Zukin, 2004:184–185), but it also provides consumers with information about the objects and styles in which they are interested.

Figure 5.6 Flying Duck Enterprises (2006). © Author.

In addition, retro retailers' businesses often emanate from their own interest and passion for retro, and their stock can often be conceptualized as "part personalised collection" (Gregson and Crewe, 2003:67). The most extreme example of this is Showhome, "a house, a home, and the most personal shopping experience you could hope for" (Showhome, 2007). Showhome was set up by two enthusiasts for Scandinavian and British design who opened their 1970s house as a retail space in June 2003. Customers can visit the house and buy the furniture, which is a mixture of retro and more recently produced items. Showhome's marketing material suggests that this "takes away the risk" from buying retro pieces of furniture because all those on display are guaranteed as design classics. Retro retailers such as this one also help reduce the time involved in sourcing retro furniture and objects because many items can be found and bought in the same place.

However, as Gregson and Crewe note, "the attempts of retro retailers to constitute spaces where the premises of exchange run counter to the commercial mainstream are themselves both read and condemned by others as indicative of the very same tendency" (2003:74). For some, usually more committed consumers of retro style, the lowering of time and risk that is involved in consuming retro objects and styles from retro boutiques detracts from its pleasure (a point explored further in Chapter 8). As suggested by the scale of hierarchies of acquisition, purchases from retro boutiques are considered less valuable than retro objects acquired in other ways, such as jumble sale finds, because the retailer has selected and defined the objects. Although I do not in any way wish to echo the view that some retail spaces and objects are more authentic than others, the critique of retro retail as too mainstream is instructive. Not only are retro retailers and traders influenced by the processes of gentrification but they are part of the process themselves, a point that Gregson and Crewe (2003) do not acknowledge. Retro retailers and stallholders do this through their choice of neighborhoods and investment in locations, their role in attracting different types of consumers to areas and their contribution to the popularization of retro style as well as by revaluing objects and styles.

REVALUING OBJECTS AND STYLES

Retro retailers and traders change the context of objects and styles and play a part in increasing their value with the knowledge that they generate about them. For example, a 1950s Formica table may look cheap and old-fashioned in a dilapidated council flat, but in a retro boutique with a retailer mentioning its iconic status and authentic origin, its value is transformed.

   This process of value enhancement makes the role of retro retailers particularly interesting because they come into contact with both the previous owners of objects and their potential consumers. Retailers' reflections on these two groups are very distinct, as this excerpt from an interview with Cathy demonstrates. When asked about her customers she said,

> It is middle class...yes, it's middle class, because of the position on the market. Although you can't tell from looking at them I would say quite a lot of them are sort of dress-down city people. Dress-down Saturday it is on the market. There is a lot of money walking about. (Cathy, retailer, 2006)

When asked where and who she sourced her stock from, she said,

> I source a lot of things from house clearances in Epping, Chigwell, Loughton and Chingford, so it is your posher East End people who have moved out, um...and are robbers! (Cathy, retailer, 2006)

In these quotes from Cathy, we see the potential owners of retro objects (middle-class "dress-down bankers") juxtaposed with the previous owners of objects ("robbers" who live in Essex). Location is used to signify the class and style of both previous owners and potential ones. Essex signifies the "posher" working class who moved out of London in the 1960s and 1970s and could afford to buy mass-produced furniture. This is contrasted with the gentrifiers who live in London and enjoy its cultural ambience; for them, living in the "home counties" or "the provinces" is unthinkable (T. Butler, 2003:7). Locations such as Essex become ideal sources for retro retailers. Due to differences in regimes of value, decorative objects and furniture can be acquired cheaply at house clearances, auctions and junkyards and sold at a profit in London. Objects, such as Ercol sideboards, cocktail bars, glass fish and G-Plan dressing tables, are bought at bargain prices and are desirable to retailers and consumers partly because of their associations with bad taste, something that has long been associated with Essex.[5]

Cathy's comments also contrast middle-class buyers with working-class sellers in terms of occupation. Although the reference to those from whom she sources objects in Essex as "robbers" was meant as a joke, it links the working class with criminality. An age-old stereotype, this is nothing unusual, yet at the same time it glamorizes the objects that Cathy sells. Compared to a boring job in banking or insurance in the city, saying that the previous owners were robbers gives objects a history that is exciting and subversive. This is representative of a larger trend of celebrating East End gangsters and criminality in the media (Skeggs, 2004d:59).

Those retailers who have been established for longer and supply a high-end market are more likely to source their stock in continental Europe, because it has become more difficult to find high-quality retro and modernist furniture in Britain. The greater prevalence of modernism, discrepancies between fashions for retro and the strength of the pound at the time I conducted these interviews enabled retailers to source original objects relatively cheaply abroad.

> 99% of the stuff is from Europe. I have contacts there.... Most of the furniture comes from Germany, Denmark, Scandinavia, Sweden. Finland you get a bit. Italy and France...Europe was full of new designers with new ideas in the 1950s. It must have been wonderful. (Eloisa, retailer, 2006)

As this quote from Eloisa demonstrates, for high-end retailers "Europe" also symbolizes a certain sophistication and association with modernist design, which most British products do not.[6] Yet the cost of shipping furniture makes the process more expensive, and many retailers said they would prefer to be able to look at items in person before they purchase them. Thus, if they can find British furniture and objects to sell that meet their customers' standards, they would prefer to do so. For example, retailers spoke about an emerging trend for 1980s black ash and high-tech furniture, which could be potentially profitable because these items continue to be relatively easy to find in Britain.

The revaluation of retro objects and styles explored here can be compared to the process of urban gentrification. In a study titled "Muscles, Motorcycles and Tattoos," Karen Halnon and Saundra Cohen argue that theories of gentrification usually applied to housing are also applicable to "symbolic neighbourhoods" in popular culture, a process they term "aesthetic gentrification" (2006:34). They document how middle-class men have appropriated symbols of working-class masculinity (muscles, motorbikes and tattoos) and argue that these types of appropriation reinforce class distinctions rather than exemplifying postmodern "egalitarian sharing and status fluidity" (2006:52). Halnon and Cohen suggest that the appropriation of objects and symbols by a section of the middle class diminishes their value for the working class.

In regard to this latter point, the theory of aesthetic gentrification is rather simplistic. For example, the sale of a 1950s Formica table in a London boutique and the declaration of its fashionability in lifestyle magazines does not necessarily mean that its value will change for someone who has owned the table for fifty years. Even in the process of urban, rather than aesthetic, gentrification, the working classes are not always geographically displaced; instead, they become less obvious in environments increasingly tailored toward the middle classes (T. Butler, 2003:15). Thus, rather than arguing that aesthetic or urban gentrification always leads to displacement, it is more useful to think in terms of "regimes of value." Regimes of value, as Arjun Appadurai (1986) notes, account for differences in the distribution of social, cultural, technical and aesthetic knowledge. When objects, styles or districts are appropriated by fractions of the middle class, there may not necessarily be any change in the way those objects or styles are valued by other groups.

With the addition of these revisions, however, the theory of aesthetic gentrification does conceptualize the process of revaluation that retro objects and styles go through and the spaces in which it takes place. To make a profit, retro furniture dealers capitalize on differences between regimes of value. It has been suggested, by Skeggs (2004a) in particular, that the process of aesthetic gentrification, or "boundary plundering," is one of the ways that the new middle classes generate status in contemporary culture. Thus, rather than acting as arbiters of highbrow taste, the role of cultural intermediaries becomes the "translation and evaluation of other cultures" (Skeggs, 2004a:148).

IDENTIFYING RETRO RETAILERS

Cultural intermediaries, as outlined by Pierre Bourdieu in *Distinction,* are those individuals who have occupations involving "presentation and representation (sales, marketing, advertising, public relations, fashion, decoration and so forth) and in all the institutions providing symbolic goods and services" (2005 [1979]:359).[7] Bourdieu also identifies artistic craftsmen and art dealers as having relatively high cultural capital and, although they are close in some respects to other entrepreneurs, locates them in a similar position to cultural intermediaries. As mediators between producers (both original manufacturers of objects and their past owners) and consumers, and as possessors of high cultural capital, retro retailers fit into this group. In *Consumer Culture and Postmodernism* (1991), Mike Featherstone develops Bourdieu's theorizations further. He suggests that cultural intermediaries do not promote a single lifestyle but seek new markets to appropriate from and to cater for. The process of buying goods in one regime of value and selling them in another— undertaken by retro retailers—fits well with this definition. For retro retailers, past popular culture becomes an ideal source for products that are both new and recognizable to consumers.

To find potentially valuable items retro retailers need knowledge of design history, awareness of contemporary fashions and creative flair. Yet, as Gregson and Crewe note, it is "retro sellers' knowledges and tastes which provide the basis for their competitive edge, rather than their artistic or creative talent per se" (2003:63). Instead of seeing "market failure as a sign of success, or at least artistic integrity," as McRobbie (1998:6) found in a study of fashion designers, retro retailers valued the more commercial skills that helped them make a profit. For example, Cathy was keen to emphasize that she had always been a good salesperson. In this regard, retro retailers seem more similar to entrepreneurs or art dealers than artists.

The importance of making a profit was also highlighted when retailers spoke about finding items for their shops and stalls. As retro style has increased in popularity, sourcing items has become increasingly difficult. Influenced by the media, the general public are more likely to know the value of retro style. This makes cheap pieces hard to find, and a healthy profit margin more difficult to achieve, as the following quotation demonstrates:

> The buying is hard compared to the selling. The items sell themselves, rather than, you know, the other way around. (Steve, retailer, 2006)

The work of retro retailers is framed by both the cultural and the economic. Retailers' understandings of their products, the market and their competitors are social and cultural as well as being produced within an economic framework. Likewise, the skills of sales and sourcing are both economically necessary but depend on appropriate social and cultural capital. The interdependency of the cultural and the economic in the work of retro retailers is not unusual. As Paul du Gay and Sean Nixon argue, focusing on cultural intermediaries "can bring to light...the interdependence and relations of reciprocal effect between cultural and economic practices" (2002:498). Retro retailers seem no different in this regard.

Retro retailers are unique in other ways, however. The existence and growth of those defined as cultural intermediaries have been theorized as a reflection of the expansion of higher education and "the formation of a highly sophisticated and educated audience for cultural goods" (Wright, 2005:119). This is a convincing argument with regard to most intermediaries where qualifications are needed to get a job, in publishing, for example. However, in a field such as retro retailing where barriers to entry are not institutionalized and knowledge of retro style is not established in the education system (perhaps apart from art and design education), this history is more complex.

In her discussion of the unofficial job market offered by retro style, McRobbie (1994) argues that retail spaces enable entrepreneurial members of subcultures, particularly women, to start businesses. She suggests that retro retailers are often lower-middle-class art school graduates unable or unwilling to get jobs in the more mainstream creative industries and that it is cultural capital gained through involvement with subcultures and art schools that enables retailers to revalue old objects. A decade later, in ethnographic research conducted with retro retailers, Nicky Gregson and Louise Crewe found that half of their twenty-one interviewees had attended a university or college to study arts-based subjects, while the other half had become involved in retro style "through long-standing familial or personal histories of buying second-hand commodities" (2003:89).

The findings of my research with retro retailers were not radically different from McRobbie's and Gregson and Crewe's studies. Two out of six retailers interviewed had university degrees, one in an arts-based subject and one as a teacher, while the others had learned about retro retail through involvement with the antiques trade, as collectors, from their parents' love of jumble sales or as members of youth cultures. Many retailers had attended adult education courses to learn craft skills to aid their businesses. The number with university degrees is slightly lower than McRobbie and Gregson and Crewe would suggest. This may be a product of a small sample and the difference between a study of the retailing of retro furniture and one of clothing. However, it also seems to be related to the backgrounds of the retailers. Five out of six retro retailers and traders came from lower-middle-class or working-class backgrounds. This was made obvious from discussion of their life histories and from their parents' occupations, outlined in more detail in Appendix 2. Interestingly, three of the interviewees had family connections in retail, specifically in, or near, the areas where their shops were located, which may have given them valuable local knowledge.

The backgrounds of retro retailers are different from those of the enthusiasts for retro style that I have interviewed. This difference is not apparent in either McRobbie's (1994) or Gregson and Crewe's (2003) studies; neither distinguishes between retro retailers and retro enthusiasts. In some ways this is instructive. Like consumers of retro style, retailers demonstrate a keen interest in art and design and have knowledge of retro style that they have developed over many years. As part personalized collections, stalls and shops work to attract customers with similar style. Thus, retailers and consumers have much in common and share a mutual appreciation of each other's tastes and cultural capital.

However, retailers' educational qualifications were lower than those of the enthusiasts interviewed (nine out of twelve retro enthusiasts had the equivalent of a BA [Hons] qualification or higher), and enthusiasts were more likely to come from middle-class backgrounds. These differences are partly due to the skills that retailers need to make a living from selling retro objects and styles. Retro retailers have to demonstrate their cultural capital when talking to customers and have to be capable of legitimating their own tastes. They also require the appropriate knowledge to be able to buy objects at house clearances in more working-class areas. As Skeggs notes, "It is not just high cultural capital that relies on the right knowledge; there are also aspects of working-class culture that also need the 'right' accumulated knowledge" (2004d:60). For example, bargaining and acquiring items cheaply would be more difficult if the individual selling the item thought that the purchaser was a pretentious snob. Therefore, it seems that the combination of these two types of resources is most likely to be found among those from working- or lower-middle-class backgrounds who have acquired knowledge about retro though education, family circumstances and life experience.

The backgrounds of retro retailers also connote working-class authenticity while remaining tailored to middle-class values and tastes. For example, when reflecting on retro retailing in the 1960s, Tommy mentioned that his customers were more middle class and aristocratic than himself, yet his identity as working class and as a retailer defined him as "cool."[8] This cool status has enabled many retailers to make a living from a relatively creative occupation. As four out of six of the retailers I interviewed were female, it may also confirm McRobbie's suggestion that retro style enabled women to influence design trends and gain cultural capital in the process. I return to consider this point in more detail below.

Easy entry into retro retailing does not necessarily mean, however, that the practice is always democratizing or a sign of social mobility. Retro retail is a precarious business. Retailers earn a relatively low wage, and shops frequently close. While I was conducting the ethnography one retro shop in the study changed hands, and two shops shut down. Therefore, although retro retailers' cultural capital is recognized as legitimate in the symbolic economy, their ability to convert this into economic capital without academic qualifications is less successful than for their more middle-class customers. In this sense, retro retailers are different from other intermediaries whose cultural capital can earn them high salaries and whose jobs are viewed as highly desirable.

These findings suggest that although cultural consumption has become increasingly important in the making of class, economic and social capital continue to be influential. The sourcing of retro objects and styles to make a profit is a different prospect and demands a different class identity from personal consumption. Although retro retailers are very literally "translating and evaluating other cultures" (the role attributed to cultural intermediaries), their social class seems no different from that of small retailers from previous periods.[9] The skill necessary for the job, particularly the accumulated knowledge that retailers need to source cheap objects, distinguishes them both from other cultural intermediaries and from retro enthusiasts. Thus, I think a more nuanced account of cultural intermediaries' role and of their relationships to both the producers and the consumers for whom they mediate would help to draw out some of the differences in intermediary occupations as well as the "family resemblances" (du Gay and Nixon, 2002:498). Of course, this argument is made more complex by the production and consumption of retro style in more informal retail networks, where in theory everyone can become a retro retailer.

INFORMAL RETAIL NETWORKS AND ENTREPRENEURIALISM

The concept of the cultural intermediary has been questioned in recent years. Nowhere is this more apparent than in the work of Maureen Molloy and Wendy Larner (2010). In their study of the New Zealand fashion industry they argue that it is almost impossible to determine exactly where culture is mediated because the boundary between cultural production and consumption has become blurred. Therefore, they suggest that the status of the cultural intermediary can no longer be associated with particular professions. To exemplify their point, Molloy and Larner demonstrate how all those in the fashion field take part in producing, mediating and consuming fashion and fashionability. They suggest that the notion of the cultural intermediary is particularly inadequate in relation to new forms of entrepreneurial work in which women are more likely to be involved. The fashion industry, they write, has contributed to the "the emergence of new occupations, and the associated proliferation of small businesses has allowed women to develop new economic opportunities through the mobilization of both 'entrepreneurial' and 'aesthetic' labour" (Molloy and Larner, 2010:373). Molloy and Larner suggest that their argument has much in common with McRobbie's (2009) analysis of women and consumer culture in *The Aftermath of Feminism.* They write that McRobbie suggests that "success in spheres associated with female consumer culture—fashion, beauty, cosmetics, media—has become a new pathway for women's economic independence as fashion and beauty have become major industries and a key part of global capitalism" (Molloy and Larner, 2010:373). One could perhaps add retro retailing to this list.

While McRobbie's recent work is highly critical of what consumer culture offers women and feminism (more so than Molloy and Larner seem to acknowledge), her earlier work on magazines and retro was more positive. In relation to retro, McRobbie argued that the style offered young working-class women the chance to take part in, and influence, fashion trends. This argument was particularly strong in relation to retro because of the informal retail networks such as jumble sales, car boot sales and flea markets that were central to the style in the 1980s and 1990s. In differing ways these spaces meant that women and girls could buy secondhand goods relatively cheaply. Jumble sales are the most obvious example of this point.

Jumble sales have not been the focus of much academic research. This is probably due to their local, temporary and relatively unimposing status because they are often held in church halls and community centers. The sales are generally organized to raise money for charities, schools or local communities; people are asked to donate unwanted objects, which are then sold. Consumers are usually charged a small entrance fee (from 20p to £1). Objects and clothing, piled up on trestle tables, are sold cheaply, and retro bargains are, or used to be, easy to find. At their inception, jumble sales attempted to perform two charitable works simultaneously: they raised money for good causes and provided outlets of cheap secondhand goods for those who could not afford new items. Thus, while the primary aim of holding a jumble sale is to raise money, and payment is taken for goods, quite often this is a token payment. Gretchen Herrmann (1997), in a study of U.S. garage sales, found that because price was negotiable those who appeared to have less money (children, teenagers, old people and those in need) often paid less for the goods they desired. From my own experience and discussions with jumble sale organizers this is also the case in Britain. Because goods given to jumble sales are surplus to requirements, stallholders and organizers are keen to extend the life of objects. They prefer for objects and clothing to be used by someone rather than be sold by weight to the ragman or destroyed at the end of the sale.

As highlighted in the previous chapter, in the 1980s and 1990s many retro enthusiasts capitalized on the potential retro items to be found at jumble sales. For example, Suzy spoke of finding Homemaker china for 20p a plate, which now sells for £30 each on eBay. Retro objects were so commonplace that many small boutiques used jumble sales as their primary mode of sourcing objects. As Tim (Suzy's husband) told me, Suzy was skilled at finding retro bargains:

> We started going to jumble sales for our own look and then Suzy thought "I can make a living out of this." (Tim, retro enthusiast, 2006)

In the 1980s Suzy opened a shop in South London selling vintage clothing and decorative objects. She would go to jumble sales around the southeast of England to source items for the shop. Although Suzy had attended a university she was unlike some of the other enthusiasts interviewed because she came from a working-class background (see Appendix 2). She had seven brothers and sisters, and as a consequence "hand-me-down" clothing was common. Suzy suggested that it was this, her interest in fashion and the influence of punk and new wave that gave her an insight into the value of objects found at jumble sales and car boot fairs. Tim was also involved in the decision to start retailing retro. Thus, it was also Suzy's relationship with Tim, who had a more middle-class upbringing, which heightened her awareness of the profit to be made from selling retro.

Suzy's narrative seems to echo many of the arguments about the unofficial job market that McRobbie (1994) makes in "Second-Hand Dresses and the Role of the Rag Market." McRobbie argues that changes in fashion and consumer culture "come from below, from those who keep an eye open for redeemable pieces which are then re-inscribed into the fashion industry" (1994:153). This is certainly the case in this instance because Suzy's selection of pieces for the shop undoubtedly contributed to fashion at the time.

However, this unofficial job market was fragile and short-lived in Suzy's case. As vintage clothing and objects became more difficult to source and rents more expensive, she had to close the shop. Nevertheless, the experience and cultural resources she had gained in retro retailing enabled her to get a job managing secondhand retailing for charity shops (a job in which she continues to be employed). Suzy now lives a middle-class lifestyle as displayed by her income, house, taste and partner's occupation (see Appendixes 1 and 2). Perhaps, then, her involvement in retro style, combined with other factors, such as a university education and her marriage to Tim, contributed to her social mobility: from working class to middle class. Social mobility is often meaningful only in relation to intergenerational dynamics, and Suzy seemed to feel different from her parents and the rest of her family. The influence of youth subcultures, her partner and her experiences at university enabled Suzy to legitimate her own tastes and name them as "retro." As retro style became more popular, the capital to be gained from her interest became more exchangeable. This confirms McRobbie's and Molloy and Larner's suggestion that involvement in consumer culture has opened up new pathways for women. At the same time, however, Suzy's narrative also exemplifies the precarious nature of "creative" labor.

As time went by savvier jumble sale organizers or stallholders would recognize more collectable objects and increase the price accordingly. They would also do this if they identified the buyer as an antique or retro dealer. In the 1990s, the spread of knowledge to organizers and stallholders, but more importantly to those who donated objects to jumble sales, meant that retro objects could seldom be found, and this is still the case today. Many consumers of retro style talk nostalgically about buying objects for very little, which would be difficult in today's market. These reflections could simply be interpreted as evidence that the retro styles they are interested in, once cutting-edge, have become established and popular (appearing on *Antiques Roadshow,* the popular UK television show, for example). To some extent this is convincing because newer retro objects from the 1980s are easier to find. However, jumble sales have decreased in number, and the quality of goods has diminished.[10] Although there has been a small resurgence of jumble sales or swap meets organized by artists or those who work in the fashion industry in London, these bear little resemblance to their predecessors.[11] In the current period most retro objects that may once have been donated to jumble sales are increasingly being sold in different environments. For example, asked where she bought her 1930s and 1940s objects and clothing, Mary found charity shops, car boot sales and jumble sales less fruitful than a new source of retro goods:

> eBay has been quite a revelation to me and American eBay is fantastic. So that's made a real difference because about, sort of, 10 years ago the vintage stuff, clothing especially, was drying up and it was getting hard to get hold of stuff. We were paying silly prices for things and eBay has just been brilliant.... I don't think charity shops or car boot sales are as good as they used to be.... These days you hardly see a jumble sale. (Mary, retro enthusiast, 2006)

THE RETRO "PROSUMER" ON EBAY

All the retro enthusiasts and retailers I interviewed had used eBay and suggested that the site had fundamentally changed the consumption and production of retro. The website's popularity not only changed the location of the retailing of the style but also influenced the categorization and knowledge involved in its production and consumption.

Before discussing the consumption and production of retro style on eBay in more detail, I want to outline the meaning of the term *prosumer* referred to in the heading above. The concept has two definitions that are relevant to this part of the chapter, both of which are concerned with the merging of the roles of producers and consumers. Alvin Toffler (1980) coined the term to predict that consumers would increasingly be doing the work of producers. This was based on a prognosis that businesses would need to employ strategies of mass customization to make their goods stand out in the marketplace and that advances in technology would lead to greater consumer choice. In a later book, *Revolutionary Wealth,* Alvin and Heidi Toffler (2006) adapt the definition of the prosumer and use it to define the work of the "non-monetary economy," which includes everyday tasks such as cooking and decorating. The Tofflers argue that "marketing executives and managers, advertising agencies and investors, CEOS and venture capitalists, bankers, lobbyists and strategic planners" should all recognize the value of "prosumption" because it has the power to democratize economic relations without impoverishing the wealthy (2006:154). Thus, they call for the economic recognition of all unpaid labor.

The term *prosumer* has also been used by consumer groups and activists to mean a noncorporate or DIY (do-it-yourself) approach to consumption that does not rely so heavily on the structures of capitalism. For example, the RGT (Red Global de Trueque), a global bartering network that began in the economic crisis in Argentina, uses the term *prosumer* to describe its members. The RGT is comprised of a number of groups who hold weekly flea markets to exchange their wares. In a similar vein the term has also been adopted by voluntary simplicity movements to mean making goods or growing and producing food. Although these two uses of the concept of the prosumer are ideologically distinct, both are valuable to understanding production and consumption on eBay.

eBay, or AuctionWeb as it was formerly known, was launched in the United States in 1995 as a free auction site. In 1996 it became a profitable venture when payment for listings was introduced. Much has been written about the history of eBay and the trust involved in buyer/seller relationships on the site, which I do not have room to consider here (e.g., Resnick and Zeckhauser, 2002; Van Swol, 2006). Instead, in this part of the chapter I am interested in the way that the relative simplicity[12] of the buying and selling process on eBay allows individuals to become producers and consumers with little investment or resources. In the official history of eBay, Adam Cohen claims that this was one of the reasons why Pierre Omidyar designed the site. He wanted to create the perfect market in which the playing field would be level. "Buyers would all have the same information about the products and prices, and sellers would all have the same opportunity to market their wares" (Omidyar, quoted in Cohen, 2002:6).

However, as Nathan Scott Epley suggests, marketing director Mary Song realized that the media and potential users of eBay were not interested in hearing "about a 30 year old genius who wanted to create the perfect market," so she created a more "human" story (2006:151). "This invoked both romance and collecting culture: Omidyar began eBay, she announced, to help his fiancée find and trade PEZ dispensers" (Epley, 2006:151). The emphasis on collecting has continued in the marketing and press coverage of eBay, and more recent British eBay advertisements have featured retro goods. This is an attempt to lessen the alienating effects of new technology and to humanize the image of the brand (Desjardin, 2006:31).

The deliberate emphasis on collectables and retro objects in the marketing of eBay also reflects a substantial amount of the buying and selling that takes place on the website. eBay is a rich emporium for retro objects and styles, and its development has opened up the marketplace for their production and consumption. Networks that were once local—for example, the sourcing of retro objects at jumble sales, car boot sales and charity, junk and retro shops—have become increasingly global through eBay. Many enthusiasts of retro style welcomed this. For example, three of the enthusiasts interviewed were excited to explore and use the U.S. site before the British one was developed in 1999. The almost instant popularity of eBay with enthusiasts of retro style was probably due to the fact that the site functioned in a similar way to auctions and other informal networks that they were used to. For example, the bidding system on eBay makes it easier to "get a bargain." It also delays gratification, resembling the physical search for retro objects in other sites such as jumble sales. By appropriating some of the features associated with more alternative retailing spaces, eBay also distinguishes itself from the high street.

However, while eBay mimics some of the characteristics of informal retail networks, it also organizes trade on a global scale and allows larger numbers of people to access and participate in these relationships at any one time with relative anonymity. Transferring labor from one large organization to many small producers also means that the site manages to maintain both scale and specialization. The sheer number and variety of objects for sale on the site make eBay ideal for consumers with niche interests. For retro enthusiasts this means that the inconsistencies in the value of retro objects in different areas or countries can be capitalized on. For example, original 1950s Formica dining suites that are rare and relatively expensive in Britain are commonplace in the American market.[13] Utility furniture from the 1930s, which is difficult to find in London, seems plentiful when the search includes the rest of Britain. By implication, this has reduced the extent to which retro retailers can charge high prices for certain pieces. For example, many owners of retro boutiques spoke of the impact of eBay on their businesses; it has caused some retailers to close down or start selling on the Internet themselves.

The buying and selling of retro objects on eBay also influence the practices of retro enthusiasts.[14] Search features on the site mean that the time spent scouring jumble sales, car boots or junk shops can be saved. Purchasing objects on eBay does need commitment, however. For example, two enthusiasts, Peter and Mary, hired a van and dedicated a weekend to driving from the southeast to the northeast of England to collect the rare 1950s bathroom suite they had bought on eBay. However, such narratives seem to be limited to highly committed enthusiasts. Due to the off-putting transportation costs of large items of furniture and the culturally specific nature of objects and their photographs and descriptions, trade is most frequently conducted within local and national contexts. As Jon Lillie notes, although eBay is virtual, it "revolves around the trade of material goods that are contextualized and given meaning within actual geographical places and communities" (2006:95). This is evident in the arrangement of online groups and communities on the site, which are divided by location, such as "South East England," as well as by interest, such as "Collectables."

By creating forums and groups on the site, eBay encourages discussion and sharing of knowledge related to products or styles. At the time of writing, groups on the community section of the site that could be categorized as retro included "Art Deco Lovers," "Retro Computer Gamers" and "Mid-Century Collectors." Mostly centered on objects or styles, these communities discuss product features, prices and rarities and are similar to the discussions that can be heard at collectors' fairs. The community aspect of eBay is an attempt to insert taste, discernment and the performance of knowledge (intrinsic to the act of collecting) into the site. However, somewhat central to this performance, as Rebecca M. Ellis and Anna Haywood note, is the notion that objects

> should be geographically scattered and retrieved from spaces of "unknowingness" such as boot sales, swapmeets and junk shops....Collecting on eBay, however, challenges this ritual by making formerly "private" or "hidden" objects public and readily accessible to anyone with an internet connection and the ability to conduct online research. (2006:46)

Therefore as Ellis and Haywood point out, the geographic impact that eBay has had on the trade of retro goods has been accompanied by the spread of knowledge about retro style.

As discussed in Chapter 2, the definition of *retro* is contested. eBay is interesting with respect to this changing definition because it is individuals rather than established retailers who use the term. However, the more widespread the usage of the term *retro* on eBay has become, the more others have shied away from it. As suggested earlier in this chapter, the impulse for the redefinition of retro objects as vintage or mid-century modern by retailers has partly been driven by the increase in reproduction items described as retro. eBay seems to blur the distinction between original and reproduction goods even further. For example, a search for an "original 1960s lava lamp" will reveal a number of reproduction objects.[15] Thus, the way sellers describe objects on eBay and the search terms they choose change how retro objects and styles are categorized both on eBay and in a wider context.

One of the most notable changes is how brand names have increasingly been used to describe retro objects. For example, a stool is described as a "Rare Early Verner Panton CONE STOOL Retro Modernist." The reference to the designer of the object, Verner Panton, would once have been irrelevant, but as knowledge of retro design has increased, names such as Panton have become valuable marketing tools and are included in descriptions. On eBay the recognition of manufacturers' or designers' names seems to go even further. Not only do objects designed by Panton appear when searched, but "Panton" (like "Ercol," "G-Plan" and "Eames") has also been adopted as way of describing the periodization of retro objects. A lampshade is described as "Stylish POP ART Wall Lamp 1970s * PANTON Era." This trend seemed to irritate some retro enthusiasts:

> There are so many names on eBay now. If you put Verner Panton or someone into a search you get loads of crap that wasn't designed by him. (Andy, retro enthusiast, 2006)

To Andy, the use of brand names (particularly those used incorrectly) represents the commercialization of the style. Specialist knowledge, once confined to groups of collectors or enthusiasts, has become public and is placed in the hands of those who cannot use it "properly." Although other media such as lifestyle magazines and television programs contribute to this, eBay is especially influential because object descriptions and histories are communicated in great depth. For example, in the following description of a sofa bed (Table 5.2), the reader is told not only about its materials, its size and its original designer but also of an award that it received and a book in which it has been documented.

Sharon Zukin suggests that by consuming histories on eBay, which does not necessarily involve consuming products, "we develop a vast amount of archaic production knowledge. Like a collector, then, we become, in a sense, the producer of these objects" (2004:246). Thus, reading detailed descriptions distributes knowledge of retro objects and styles more widely. This knowledge is tailored to the conditions of the market. For example, it is clear in Table 5.2 that the writer is knowledgeable about the values of retro enthusiasts and the conventions of writing for eBay and of marketing copy more generally. Therefore, on eBay buyers become experts in retro objects, as Zukin suggests, but sellers also become experts at marketing them.

Table 5.2   Description of 1957 sofa bed (2007).

1957 SOFABED DESIGNED BY ROBIN DAY FOR HILLE

Very rare "Convertible Bed-Settee" designed in 1957 by Robin Day for Hille, UK. Won a Design Centre Award in 1957 and documented in "Robin and Lucienne Day" by Lesley Jackson.

Mahogany end panels, upholstered foam mattress, rubber webbing and black stove enamelled flat steel legs. The backrest folds over and down to turn the sofa into a bed. 194cm long by 85cm deep by 64cm high.

The sofa is in overall good condition, the heavy frame is in excellent condition, the end panels have been repolished and have a good deep colour, the legs have no rust or paint chips. The fabric is brown with a dark green weave and is in very good condition. Although I have always used the sofa as is, it does ideally need the webbing tightening [sic] or redone. The foam on the backrest has also slipped down at some point. It would be a very simple job to have the sofa refoamed and reupholstered and would look stunning. I can provide contact details for the weavers who made the original fabric for these sofabeds and are still producing it today.

As mentioned above, eBay allows individuals to become retailers of retro style with relatively little effort. The following quote is indicative of the ease with which retro objects can be bought and sold:

—I'd always wanted a sideboard. We got this from eBay. (Louise)
—For £60 or something. (Andy)
—My Granddad's one was better, but we'd already got this one, so we sold Granddad's one. (Louise)

(Andy and Louise, retro enthusiasts, 2006)

The ease of becoming a producer or consumer on eBay has led writers, such as Adam Cohen, to suggest that "all sellers are created equal, all buyers have equal chances to bid, and, most importantly, old offline hierarchies no longer apply" (2002:68). To some extent this is the case. The anonymity afforded by email communication and eBay user IDs lessens the distinctions and differences that can be capitalized on in other environments. For example, purchasing an object on eBay can be a less daunting process than going into a rather exclusive-looking retro shop, and prices are not heightened for those who appear wealthy. As Lisa Bloom notes, "On eBay, clients as well as businesses are not so easily coded through appearance, age, education, class or gender as they are in traditional auction settings" (2006:232).

However, it would be wrong to argue that eBay is an undifferentiated space. In the first instance, to trade on eBay one must have access to an Internet connection and "seem to possess a stable identity, verified through a user ID and password, a permanent address, and a credit card" (Hillis *et al.,* 2006:5). In addition, in place of physical presence, descriptions and images become the objects of scrutiny. As Ellis and Haywood suggest, collectors "project back onto eBay analogies between finding virtual spaces of unknowingness and finding them physically in the geographical hunt" (2006:59).

Misspellings, miscategorizations and inaccurate descriptions are all signs of a potential bargain for collectors and retro enthusiasts. For example, typing "Deckchair" into a search rather than "Deck Chair" may unearth postings that others have not found and thus have not bid on. Poor photography or display of objects may also signal a potential bargain. For example, sideboards that are of similar size, design and period sell for different amounts of money on the site because of the context in which they are displayed. A sideboard displayed in a gallery-like space accessorized with retro items will frequently sell for more than a sideboard outside a garage or in a front room accessorized with nineteenth-century-style china ornaments.

Over time the number of postings on eBay with badly taken images and personalized stories is decreasing. As Mary Desjardin (2006:31) finds, 10 percent of eBay sellers are responsible for 80 percent of its sales and thus form the core of eBay's profitability. These are often small retailers rather than individuals, and this is partly a consequence of high rents and the processes of gentrification that I outlined earlier in the chapter. Thus, to sell objects effectively, individual sellers develop more professional-looking postings. It is likely that this is the cause and the effect of the increase in books dedicated to "making a profit on eBay" (Gookin and Birnback, 2005; Sinclair and Livingston, 2005).

Yet it is personalized stories and photographs of previous contexts that make goods attractive for more committed consumers of retro style. In contrast to catalogs or advertising for Habitat or Ikea, images are not retouched, and descriptions are more focused on object specifications. In addition, naïve and misspelled descriptions and photographs taken in owners' homes singularize objects and make them unique. As James Leo Cahill suggests, eBay flatters "anti-consumption fantasies with the promise of a decommodified ex perience, exemplified by the amateur aesthetic of the images and the often 'folksy' narratives that accompany objects and help personalize the anonymous transactions" (2006:192).

Aware of this attraction, some sellers add personal touches to their postings, which are very professional looking in other ways. For example, one sideboard is described as "very good condition, despite have spent 40+ years in a busy family home." Other postings have even more elaborate narratives describing why the item is for sale. For example, a wedding dress sold for a large amount of money on eBay because of the detailed and humorous accompanying narrative (Hillis, 2006:173).[16] Internet forums, help pages and the numerous guides about selling successfully on eBay recommend that sellers highlight their carefully tailored personal stories (Prince, 2007:145). For this reason, eBay represents a wider commodification of personal experiences and identities as well as objects. As Roberta Sassatelli notes, "Modern consumers are asked to actively participate in the process of de-commodification, producing themselves as the source of value" (2007:148).

Not only does eBay represent and promote commodification of the self, but it also increases awareness of the commodity potential of all objects. Although there have always been sites that have done this, eBay, as Zukin argues, "stimulates us to experience life as if everything is for sale.... It naturalizes market ideology" (2004:249–250). She suggests that rather than a "world of collectors" (as eBay, or Hillis and colleagues [2006] argue), we have become a "world of sellers." However, unlike both Hillis and colleagues (2006) and Zukin (2004), I would suggest that the world of collectors or sellers is also stratified by social characteristics including class. This is not to suggest that there are no members of the working classes who buy and sell on eBay. Rather, it is to argue that the double-pronged commodification of objects and selves represented by eBay fits well with the theories of possessive individualism discussed in Chapter 3. Selling the self and those material objects attached to the self is made possible by the "ability to authorize and institutionalize one's own perspective" (Skeggs, 2004a:153). The economic market, in which the selling of the self takes place, which comes to be represented as neutral, is predicated on "individualized interest, rational calculation and productive value" (Skeggs, 2004a:31). Thus, although eBay may appear to offer any entrepreneurial individual the chance to make a fortune, those who cannot sell the self and authorize their perspective are less able to participate.

At the same time, however, because the buyers and sellers on eBay are less coded by their bodily dispositions, they may be able to seize their own authority by acting as if they have it. For example, with the right marketing know-how an elderly working-class woman could sell off her possessions as "granny-chic." This is partly because it is the aesthetics and narratives of those who are unable to participate that are most attractive. Resources that elude commodification and evoke authentic characteristics are desirable. Thus, an ideal selling strategy on eBay would be to photograph a piece of furniture in an environment that defines it as retro while also describing its authentic origins. This approach is similar to the one used by the owners of retro boutiques, and as more established retailers trade on the site it has become more common. This is one of the reasons why retro enthusiasts found it harder to capitalize on unknowingness on eBay than they did at jumble sales and car boot fairs.

eBay also differs from other informal retail networks such as jumble sales and car boot fairs because it is a large organization that profits from the unpaid labor of its buyers and sellers. Sellers do the unpaid work of marketing and distributing goods that a more conventional organization would need to undertake, and buyers are also asked to work for their goods in the form of bidding, emailing, collecting and giving feedback (Hillis *et al.*, 2006). Therefore, eBay is a good example of the type of prosumption that the Tofflers (2006) are recommending: the economic recognition and capitalization of unpaid labor by corporations. This discussion of eBay highlights the difference between the Tofflers' definition of prosumption and the one used by activist groups.

Instead of bringing production and consumption closer to each other, as occurs in other informal retail networks like jumble sales, on eBay buyers have limited contact with sellers. For the consumer, this means that it is difficult to appreciate the labor used to make artifacts and it becomes harder to experience the past lives of goods. Although descriptions and images on eBay attempt to do this work, they are much more likely to be influenced by the conventions of marketing and advertising and mediated by the market than are face-to-face encounters in other spaces. Thus, in comparison to other informal retail spaces, prosumption on eBay furthers the commodification of experience that many consumer groups and activists criticize.

These criticisms of eBay do not apply to all informal retail networks that take place on the Internet. Freecycle (an email list where people give away things they no longer need for free) is based on local networks, makes use of surplus goods and does not make a profit. Those offering items are much less likely to write sophisticated marketing copy, and gestures of goodwill, such as the offer of a coffee in exchange for items, can mean that individuals living in the same area meet each other.

Although retro enthusiasts were the early adopters of eBay, they did not mention Freecycle (even though some Freecycle groups began in 2004). More recently, in the areas where I have lived (East London and Brighton in Britain) I have noticed that retro items are seldom given away. This is telling of the demographic of Freecycle in these areas, where there are numerous retro shops and people who value retro furniture and decorative objects. It may also be evidence of burgeoning knowledge about retro items and their potential exchange value more generally.

Therefore, underlying the second half of this chapter is a narrative of the increased commercialization of retro style and its related informal retail networks. Although eBay is unlikely to replace physical venues altogether because multisensory shopping experiences are important to consumers of retro style, it has influenced the existence and popularity of other retail spaces. What were once more local forms of production and consumption in informal retail spaces (which offered some possibility for working-class youth to consume retro goods) have been replaced with more commercial spaces that are contingent on external regimes of value.

This process means that the economic capital (although minimal and often short-lived) and cultural capital that Suzy gained from involvement in producing and consuming retro would be more difficult for working-class youth to accumulate today. Suzy benefited from the popularity of retro style, and her practices and values became widely valued as capital. This contributed to her social mobility. At the same time, the popularity of retro has made it harder for people like Suzy to do the same today. eBay is just one part of the rapid communication and dissemination of retro knowledge that makes finding a bargain or starting a trend without sufficient economic capital a much more difficult prospect.

CONCLUSION

In this chapter I have explored how retro retailers and traders are involved in making and unmaking the value of retro style. In the introduction to the chapter I set out a scale of relative modes of acquisition in which I suggested that the rarest, least commodified and most alternative forms of acquisition held the most value for retro enthusiasts. I argued that the hierarchy of acquisition is indicative of the shifting terrain of distinctiveness that the production and consumption of retro style represent. The modes of acquisition that are most valuable depend on a preestablished identity that can authorize her/his own taste. Therefore, although I am in total agreement with McRobbie when she argues that the retro aesthetic has spread throughout mainstream design and retailing, new means of distinction are found and excluded individuals are continually reembedded in retraditionalized roles and norms.

The shifting terrain of distinctiveness has a significant impact on the practices of retro retailers. Retro retailers have to work to maintain their association with the alternative, and they do this through the location of their shops and stalls, as well as the display of their products. In these activities retailers are involved in the processes of urban and aesthetic gentrification. By appropriating and revaluing objects and styles, retro retailers capitalize on different regimes of value and are symbolically and materially translating and evaluating other cultures. These activities have been associated with cultural intermediaries, and thus I explored the identities of retailers in relation to these theorizations. I found that in terms of class position the retro retailers in this study were different from the majority of consumers of retro style and other cultural intermediaries. Those who made a living from selling retro furniture and decorative objects tended to be from working- or lower-middle-class backgrounds. This was partly because retro retailers needed appropriate knowledge to source items in more working-class areas, as well as an ability to demonstrate their cultural capital when selling goods. While retailers have high levels of cultural capital legitimated by the media and the market, their knowledge is not institutionalized by educational qualifications, and this restricts their social mobility: many retailers have similar class backgrounds to their parents.

The theorization of retro retailers as cultural intermediaries is further complicated by informal retail networks where barriers to enter the marketplace are less defined. In agreement with McRobbie's work I found that informal retail networks have allowed women to participate in the fashion industry. For example, when retro goods were cheap and easy to find in the early 1980s, those from working- or lower-middle-class backgrounds, like Suzy, capitalized on spaces of unknowingness, and this contributed to their social mobility. Nevertheless, retro retailing is a precarious business, and as the style became more popular, objects became harder to source. This made it harder to capitalize on cultural knowledge without significant economic investment.

These findings regarding the popularization of retro lead to the final point arising from this discussion of retro retailing: the implications of the commodification of the relations of exchange in informal retail networks. In interviews with retro retailers and enthusiasts I have found that the consumption of retro style has moved from spaces like jumble sales to ones like eBay. I suggested that the processes that underpin exchange on eBay create and reinforce middle-class modes of distinction, including the selling of the self. In addition, as retro objects are sold on eBay, their past lives are mediated: they are influenced by global market values and by the conventions of marketing and advertising. Thus, chains of production and consumption become more obscure, and the interpersonal and affective relations of exchange found at other informal retailing sites are less common.

However, as retro styles become more available from high street retailers and eBay, modes of acquisition such as jumble sales and swap meets become more valuable for retro enthusiasts in search of difference and individuality. The recent (re)emergence of jumble sales and Freecycle is partly a product of this trend. Retro objects acquired in alternative spaces create and represent high levels of cultural capital based on the exploitation of unknowingness and differences between regimes of value. At the same time, however, these alternative sites may also offer greater opportunity for understanding chains of production and consumption and recognizing the large amounts of waste that we produce.

6

Retro Interiors and Lifestyle Media

I began this book by referring to the recent proliferation of the term *retro* to describe particular objects and styles and used the *Guardian Weekend* magazine to illustrate this point. This example is just one of many representations of retro style in lifestyle media during the past twenty years. In this chapter I explore some of these representations in more detail.

Media texts such as lifestyle magazines and television programs have symbolic power that goes beyond the media field. As Nick Couldry suggests, when the media "intensively cover an area of life for the first time (as in the past decade in the fields of gardening or cooking) they alter the internal workings of that sub-field" while also increasing the wider influence of the media across the social terrain (2003:12). For example, representations of retro influence the production and consumption of the style; change the practices of collecting, interior decoration and home improvement; and also reinforce the centrality of the media to these activities.

This is nothing new. The media have always played a part in the formation of taste cultures and everyday practices, and there is a long history of magazines and television programs that focus on interior decoration and DIY (do-it-yourself; Bell and Hollows, 2005, 2006). However, as the quote by Couldry suggests, the number of lifestyle magazines and programs increased dramatically in Britain in the 1990s (Bell and Hollows, 2005; Brunsdon, 2003). This provoked many detailed academic studies of lifestyle media. Many of these contest the idea that lifestyle is illustrative of a detraditionalization of social roles in postmodernity or late modernity (Bell and Hollows, 2005; Bonner, 2003; Heller, 2007; G. Palmer, 2004; Taylor 2002). Instead, they argue that it is in makeover programs, reality shows and magazines that struggles over taste, gender and class are played out.

As David Bell and Joanne Hollows have suggested, "At the core of understanding lifestyle media is the issue of class" (2005:11). This is illustrated by the on-screen relationships between experts and participants in lifestyle programming, which are fraught with class tensions (Heller, 2007; McRobbie, 2004). It is also evident in the middle-class tastes and aesthetics produced, circulated and promoted by lifestyle magazines and television programs (Holliday, 2005; Taylor 2005). The circulation of middle-class tastes and aesthetics, Bell and Hollows observe, raises an interesting contradiction regarding the role of lifestyle media. They argue that lifestyle media produce distinction but also demystify and democratize (Bell and Hollows, 2005:11). For example, Ruth Holliday (2005) has proposed that the circulation of the modernist aesthetic by lifestyle media democratizes the style in terms of gender and class. While interior design magazines, makeover programs and valuation shows are arbiters of good taste, the popularization of these tastes often leads to devaluation. As Bell and Hollows put it, "If everyone knows how to 'pass', having learnt the rules of dress, cuisine, home décor and so on, then how is distinction to be maintained?" (2005:11).

In this chapter I consider this question. In doing so, I explore how retro style communicates distinction and how it makes interior design accessible. The extent to which lifestyle media are involved in either of these activities varies according to the medium, genre and imagined audience. Thus, I analyze a range of lifestyle media and related representations of retro style, which include makeover programs, interior magazines and valuation shows. From this analysis, a range of different retro tastes and aesthetics start to appear. In the last part of the chapter I consider the similarities and differences between lifestyle media and niche/micro media with smaller audiences.

CHANGING ROOMS AND RETRO STYLE AS THEMED INTERIOR

Changing Rooms (BBC, 1990–2004) was one of the first and most popular home makeover programs produced in Britain[1] and was one of the earliest lifestyle television programs to use the term *retro* to describe interior styles. In the program two couples make over each other's houses under the influence of the *Changing Rooms* team, which consists of a designer (the most famous being Laurence Llewelyn-Bowen, Linda Barker and Anna Ryder Richardson) and a builder ("Handy Andy"). At the beginning of each episode the designer and a neighbor discuss what is wrong with the existing interior. This process usually gives the designer an opportunity to critique the taste of the homeowner. For example, in one episode Linda Barker remarks, "The room looks much better now all their furniture is out," implying that the old furniture and knick-knacks are in bad taste. Although this shaming is not perhaps as strong as it is in more recent lifestyle programming, such as in fashion makeovers or parenting programs (Biressi and Nunn, 2007; McRobbie, 2004), it both undermines the taste of the participants and maintains the authority of the designer.

It is the power relations and differing tastes of those involved in the makeover (neighbors, homeowners, builders, presenters and designers) that form the narrative of *Changing Rooms*. The highest points of drama are created by incongruities between the wishes of the neighbors and those of the designers. Apart from one episode in which two middle-class women from Camberwell manage successfully to undermine the authority of the designer,[2] the wishes of the neighbors are often ignored because they are viewed as knowing little about design. Handy Andy, the cockney builder, is also framed as lacking understanding of the design concepts used on the show. He is presented as good at manual labor but not quite so good at intellectual and creative tasks, such as measuring for shelves or designing interiors.[3]

The explanation of retro style is one of the devices used by the producers to frame the designers as knowledgeable and the interiors as distinctive. For example, Handy Andy is frequently filmed saying that he does not understand the styles in question. This gives the designers a chance to explain past styles and demonstrate their own cultural capital. It also teaches audiences that retro styles are desirable and easy to achieve, and they are shown how to "do it themselves" using affordable and modern materials, such as medium-density fibreboard (MDF). In comparison to other lifestyle media explored below, the history and periodization of the styles used are not discussed in detail, and although categorized as retro, designs are firmly rooted in the present to prevent them from being misinterpreted as old-fashioned. The outcomes are retro interiors that are brightly colored, boldly patterned and coded as feminine. This is perhaps a result of the mostly female design team, as well as the foppish Laurence Llewelyn-Bowen. For example, in a bedroom called "Romantic Retro Retreat," lozenge shapes inspired by 1970s wallpaper have been painted on the walls in shades of pink. In another room entitled "Retro 1950s Soho Bar" yellow walls are painted with 1950s-style graphics, and a brown sofa is covered in scatter cushions. In contrast to retro interiors inspired by modernist aesthetics, these rooms are not ones that those in the design elite would consider to be in good taste.

Indeed, the owners of the houses themselves do not always consider the style to be good taste. As episodes of *Changing Rooms* develop, interiors that were once full of a mismatch of objects and styles are removed in favor of a themed room or retro interior. This, as Lisa Taylor notes, can involve the removal of working-class aesthetics to make way for "the imposition of a middle-class coherent design concept" (2005:115). The homeowners are often unhappy at the transformation of their interior, in which objects invested with meaning and value have been lost. Taylor suggests that this is an example of "symbolic violence *par excellence*" (2005:115). By asserting their higher cultural capital, designers establish and impose their good taste on participants whether they want it or not.

The often negative reactions of participants to the transformation of their interiors are, of course, part of the appeal of the "big reveal" at the end of the program. The shock of the homeowners at the removal or destruction of their possessions is the focus of extreme close-ups to "capture" the "knee-jerk reaction of the ordinary person...[as] primary public spectacle"

(Moseley, 2000:312). To some extent, these expressions of dismay and disgust can question the taste of the designers and destabilize their positions as tastemakers. As Holliday notes, "The authority of the designer is sometimes undermined by the failure to orient their design to customer specifications" (2005:77).

The designers on *Changing Rooms* have also been the focus of wider critique. For example, Mark Kennan, a *Sunday Times* journalist, is critical of *Changing Rooms'* designers imposing their "tacky" tastes on the public:

> Since this hybrid format invaded our screens in the mid-1990s, hundreds of seemingly sane people have volunteered their homes to the whims of a pack of roaming vandals wielding swathes of fake fur, truck loads of spray paint and that miracle whip of their trade, MDF (that's medium density fibreboard to you). (Kennan, 2003)

On the surface this critique seems similar to academic analyses of makeover television. However, while Kennan critiques the designers on *Changing Rooms* as "vandals" he simultaneously condemns the participants as "Mr and Mrs Mustn't Complain" from "Cosy Old Terrace, Somewhere Street, East Boredom." This characterization of participants as the duped masses with no individual or unique taste is in fact similar to the critique of participants' tastes and interiors at the beginning of the program. In *Changing Rooms* the participants are pathologized for having bad taste and disordered modes of living, and in discussions of the program in the press, they are chastised for going on the program in the first place.

Kennan's critique of *Changing Rooms* is made possible because of the program's position as mass entertainment and as a producer of low-budget interiors. As Penny Sparke (1995) has argued, taste for decoration, chintz and craft has frequently been associated with femininity and thought of as uncivilized. One could argue that the binary oppositions set up in modernist discourse between masculinity and femininity continue in Kennan's critique of *Changing Rooms.* This is point I return to below.

In addition, although retro styles are used on *Changing Rooms* to categorize interiors as distinctive and designers as knowledgeable, the emphasis on retro as easy to understand and achieve is frequently more prominent. Activities that have historically generated high levels of cultural capital and have been associated with the middle classes, such as connoisseurship and the valuing of authentic originals, seldom appear on the program. Thus, the presence of retro interiors on *Changing Rooms* contributes to the mainstreaming of retro and devalues a style that is partly prized because of the cultural capital involved in its definition. However, since the last episode of *Changing Rooms* in 2004, the discourses on what constitutes valuable retro style and entertaining lifestyle media have both changed significantly.

DICTATED BY DECADE: RETRO IN NEWSPAPER STYLE SUPPLEMENTS

In comparison to the interiors displayed on *Changing Rooms,* the retro interiors found in newspaper style supplements have tended to make more obvious historical references. This has been most apparent in the *Guardian Weekend* magazine (May 26, 2007) and the *Independent Magazine* (March 1, 2008), which have published entirely retro issues and included features and editorials on retro food, cars, fashion, gardening and homes. It can be assumed that the production of these retro supplements meant that a large percentage of the readership of the *Guardian* and the *Independent* was identified as interested in the style. The *Guardian* characterizes its readership as "affluent, young urban consumers" (Guardian website, 2008). This was presumably one of the reasons for the choice of the Rubik's Cube on the front of the magazine, a toy that was particularly popular in the early 1980s and that is a nostalgic symbol for many of the readers who would have been children at the time. The *Independent Magazine* has a photograph of another childhood toy, the space hopper, which was popular in the 1970s. This was probably used to attract their slightly older demographic (National Readership Survey, 2008). Therefore, these retro-themed issues both reflect and produce the contemporary tastes of a section of the young urban middle class.

This demographic was particularly evident in the style section of the *Guardian Weekend* magazine. The section featured consumers in their living rooms surrounded by their retro objects from various decades (1950s, 1960s, 1970s and 1980s), dressed in period clothing and with an accompanying commentary about their interests (Figure 6.1). These images were not dissimilar in style to those taken by the photographer Martin Parr, particularly those in his book *Sign of the Times: A Portrait of the Nation's Tastes* (1992). Thus, rather than a practical guide to creating a retro interior, the photographs in the *Guardian Weekend* magazine represent knowledge and taste for contemporary art: a largely middle-class interest (Silva, 2006a).

The retro enthusiasts depicted in the images also give clues to the identities of retro enthusiasts more generally and the producers and consumers of the *Guardian.* All of the five homeowners in the article are in their thirties. This not only reflects the age of the *Guardian Weekend* reader but is also a desirable age in terms of retro style: not too old, such that retro objects could be misconstrued as old-fashioned, nor too young and therefore lacking in the economic and cultural capital needed to buy a house or to be knowledgeable about retro objects to fill it with.

It is also apparent from the images and commentary that all the homeowners are high in economic capital. Although their occupations are not mentioned, most are clearly well-off with privileged backgrounds. For example,

Figure 6.1 Gillian Milner and partner, 1970s style (2007). © Richard Waite.

Greg Stevenson has a 1960s prefab in Wales as a second home, Sarah-Jane Magee says that it was her father's love of vintage cars and racing of Aston Martins that got her interested in the style, and Gillian Milner talks of the 1970s orange blow-up chair that she bought for her swimming pool.

In addition, the images of their interiors and the accompanying commentary show that retro enthusiasts are high in cultural capital and have considerable knowledge of the styles and periods in which they are interested. For example, Sarah-Jane talks of the long history of her interest in the 1950s and the American collectors' fair (the Hershey Autojumble) that she goes to. Most readers would not have heard of this fair, and Sarah-Jane's knowledge of where to buy good authentic original objects positions her as an expert. Her shopping practices command high value according to the hierarchy of modes of acquisition outlined in Chapter 5. The photographs of the interiors also communicate the authenticity of the enthusiasts' tastes. For example, there are no objects or architectural features that do not fit the style of their chosen period. Thus, the representations of retro enthusiasts as high in both cultural and economic capital in the text help to position retro interiors as distinctive and desirable.

There is one homeowner, however, Kannan Chandran, who appears to have less cultural capital. Kannan is the owner of the 1980s interior (Figure 6.2). The image was smaller than the other images featured in the magazine and was placed at the end of the article. This is because the revival of 1980s style is one of the most difficult to represent as favorable, both because of the proximity of the period to the present and because of its associations with

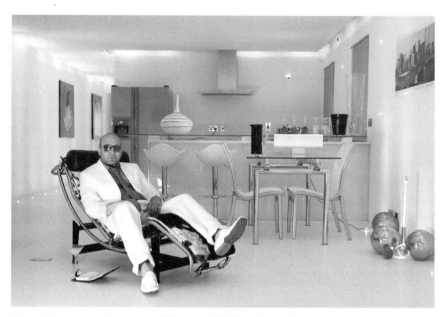

Figure 6.2   Kannan Chandran, 1980s style (2007). © Richard Waite.

yuppie culture and conspicuous consumption. Thus, to create distinction with 1980s style, the owner would have to have extremely high cultural capital and possess an identity that was undoubtedly avant-garde.

Kannan is not represented in these terms. He is quoted as unknowingly creating a 1980s-style interior. When describing his flat he says,

> It's a two-bedroom flat adjacent to Chelsea Harbour, in London. I bought it in 2004. It didn't look as it looks now—it was very '70s, very old-fashioned. I gutted it. I suppose the look is kind of '80s Miami Vice. I didn't intend it to look '80s—I meant it to look 21st century. (Booth and Steiner, 2007:91)

Kannan is marked as different from the other homeowners. He did not adapt his style to the period in which his flat was built. He did not appreciate authentic 1970s style, and, worst of all, he did not intend to create a 1980s interior. Kannan is the only nonwhite homeowner in the article. Although it could be argued that this is coincidental, I believe it is telling of the complex relationship between taste, cultural capital and race. Because Kannan is Asian, he is already associated with certain dispositions and tastes, which means that it is more difficult for him to "play" with retro styles without being represented as old-fashioned. The limits of appropriation are explored further in the next chapter.

In the *Guardian Weekend* magazine, retro style is not used only to convey distinction. Although aesthetically very different from *Changing Rooms,* the tastes and styles of retro enthusiasts are also made achievable. The title of the piece is "Step Back in Time: Meet the People Who Revel in the Home Styles of the Past...and Get the Look, Too." The ability of the reader to "get the look too" is reinforced by adjacent photographs of reproduction retro objects that readers can buy. In addition, decades are used almost like brands to make objects and styles recognizable. For the untrained eye it is easier to recognize 1970s style when all the iconic objects of the 1970s are put together and labeled as such, rather than included in an eclectic mix of retro objects. Due to this, certain objects become shorthand for certain periods. For example, orange patterned wallpaper, pin art pictures and avocado bathroom suites become synonymous with the 1970s. Thus, like on *Changing Rooms,* the dominant aesthetic in these retro supplements is one of design coherence. Yet the interiors in the *Guardian Weekend* and the *Independent Magazine* are also framed by decade. This makes the styles depicted appear authentic and relatively recognizable.

MAKING YOUR OWN MODERNIST MARK: HIGH DESIGN AND RETRO STYLE

In high-end[4] lifestyle media, such as *Elle Decoration* (1989–), an interior decoration magazine, and *Grand Designs* (Channel 4, 1999–), a self-build and architecture television program produced by TalkBack Thames, it is periods and design movements, rather than decades, that are used to contextualize and clarify retro styles. Unlike both representations of retro style discussed above, the term *retro* is avoided in these formats. Although it was frequently used in *Elle Decoration* in the 1990s, as retro became more popular the magazine started to use the term *mid-century modern* to describe retro objects and styles. By doing this *Elle Decoration* associates the items within its pages with modernism, as well as famous artists and designers like Frank Lloyd Wright and Charles and Ray Eames. The magazine also stakes out its distinctive position in relation to other lifestyle media: mid-century modern style in *Elle Decoration* is represented as completely different from the retro styles shown on *Changing Rooms.* Likewise, the renovations or architectural projects on *Grand Designs* are usually categorized by design movement, and many of the projects are influenced by modernist designs. The production, circulation and promotion of modernist style by high-end lifestyle media is not unusual. Since the beginning of the twentieth century, modernist architecture and design have been depicted as the epitome of good taste (Attfield, 2000).

However, magazines and television programs such as *Elle Decoration* and *Grand Designs* have bigger readerships and higher audience figures than the architecture and interior design magazines from earlier decades.[5] Therefore, it has been argued that lifestyle television programs have disseminated and popularized the styles of modernism (Holliday, 2005). Holliday suggests that modernism has come to signify gender neutrality. She writes that there is a sense that television "home shows are democratic in a way that first wave modernism never was" (2005:77). She argues that because modernism is a highly recognizable style, it "makes obtaining the cultural capital necessary to appreciate it a relatively straight forward exercise" (2005:80). Holliday concludes by proposing that "perhaps this time around modernism can offer the democracy it promised but never delivered at the beginning of the twentieth century" (2005:80).

Both *Grand Designs* and *Elle Decoration* are keen to appear accessible to all. *Grand Designs* and its presenter, Kevin McCloud, a Cambridge-educated architect, emphasize the democratic role of the program. In an article in the *Observer,* McCloud said, "I've always enjoyed taking complex ideas and making them accessible. . . . We talk about engineering and architecture, and people get it" (Blanchard, 2003). By accentuating his role as educator rather than expert, and because he is not involved in the design or building of the project himself, McCloud avoids the criticisms of earlier television experts as "vandals" imposing their tastes on unwitting participants. Discourses of accessibility are also present in *Elle Decoration.* For example, the editor of *Elle Decoration* has suggested that there are "beautiful buys for every budget" in the magazine and that good taste is not a question of money or class position (Ogundehin, 2005, quoted in Potts, 2006:156).

The modernist aesthetics circulated by architecture and interior design programs and magazines undoubtedly mean that the style is better known and appreciated. It is also true that these media sometimes include relatively cheap pieces of furniture and decorative objects. However, high-end lifestyle media perform subtle acts "of distance and distinction" (Bell and Hollows, 2005:12). Thus, by proposing that modernism is more democratic the second time around, Holliday (2005) replicates the rhetoric of lifestyle media rather than analyzing the subtle acts of distinction that are produced. I have observed three related discourses that allow *Elle Decoration* and *Grand Designs* to appear democratic while also upholding distinctions that are particularly relevant to the value of retro style. These are commitment to the consumption of originals and quality craftsmanship, individual style and eclectic taste.

The first, commitment to the consumption of originals and quality craftsmanship, is most evident in the narratives of *Grand Designs*.[6] In an attempt to distinguish itself from other lifestyle media, and in a reflection of the values of its participants and consumers, *Grand Designs* emphasizes the knowledge, time, skill and labor that go into building and designing an interior. On the program practical skills are valued. This is illustrated by McCloud's pieces to camera, in which he explains how a new building material works or discusses the craftsmanship that has produced a bathroom, kitchen or staircase. This is very different from the quick and easy interior decoration depicted on *Changing Rooms.* In addition, unlike *Changing Rooms,* where makeovers were completed in a short time frame, projects may take place over a number of years on *Grand Designs.*

This return to more realistic timescales for DIY projects and the valuing of craftsmanship could be understood as a revival of the egalitarian design education that Charlotte Brunsdon (2004) identified as characteristic of lifestyle media in postwar Britain. However, unlike earlier lifestyle television programs where the same renovation projects continued throughout the series (e.g., *Furnishing on a Shoestring,* 1975), the viewer of *Grand Designs* is shown the completion of a building and interior in one episode. In addition, due to their large budgets, the majority of projects on the program are far from achievable for all. Thus, I would suggest that the emphasis on producing and consuming handcrafted quality originals on *Grand Designs* is less about egalitarian DIY education and more about the demonstration of high cultural capital.

It is commitment to handcrafted quality originals that allows McCloud to maintain his status as expert in the majority of episodes.[7] This was particularly evident in an episode in which a couple, two pilots from Surrey, built a modern yet art deco–inspired house (Series 5, Episode 18). At the beginning of the episode the participants are portrayed as knowing little about art deco. For example, they do not own any art deco furniture or wear any 1920s or 1930s clothes. This establishes McCloud as a knowledgeable expert who has a higher level of cultural capital than the couple and who is more able to distinguish between good and bad reproductions of art deco styles. Partly under McCloud's influence, the couple go on a research trip to Miami to find authentic inspiration for their house. After this research they make some key decisions regarding the design of their interior. They change the modern bathroom to something more art deco, and they decide to buy an original 1930s dining suite; McCloud views both these steps as praiseworthy. The cultural capital that the couple have accumulated in research and the extra effort involved in finding and buying an authentic piece are highly valued.

Yet the tensions between the design statements that McCloud considers to be kitsch and the ones that he suggests are authentic continue to be emphasized. This is illustrated by McCloud's rather sarcastic tone of voice when discussing the kitchen design, and his smirk at the reproduction art deco extractor fan that the couple have designed. Although the kitchen is bespoke and crafted in maple, which McCloud seems to value, its lack of authentic or original design leaves it open for criticism.

Although emphasis is placed on handcrafted quality originals on *Grand Designs,* no lifestyle television program can be fully committed to the consumption of original retro objects in the way that retro niche media often are. The commercial media industries have a vested interest in maintaining high levels of consumption of new goods (Taylor, 2002:479). In addition, the knowledge and time involved in sourcing original objects are problematic for lifestyle television. Showing a master craftsperson making a bespoke kitchen guarantees a shot of the finished article; however, in the quest to find a particular type of art deco bed there are no guarantees of success.

At any rate, an extreme commitment to replicating an art deco home would conflict with the two further discourses found in high-end lifestyle media: commitment to individual style and eclectic taste. Both in *Elle Decoration* and on *Grand Designs* this is expressed in a critique of people who slavishly replicate period styles. For example, in an article about the renovation of a mid-century modern home in *Elle Decoration,* Fiona MacCarthy asks,

> How do you bring a mid-twentieth-century home back to its best without living in a time warp? That's the challenge one couple faced when they found this Modernist gem in their hometown of Odense, Denmark. Here, they share their solutions. (2006:97)

The reader is then advised on how to rip out the previous owners' efforts to turn modernist homes into country cottages, such as fussy patterned carpets; how to restore valuable but shabby pieces, such as a kitchen designed by the world-renowned German kitchen makers Poggenpohl; and how to make their own design statements because "no-one wants to live in a museum." While in isolation these markers of good taste might be easy to achieve (it is relatively easy to recognize fussy patterned carpet and rip it out), together they become more complex. For example, adding your own touches in the eyes of *Elle Decoration* would probably not mean including your collection of Beatrix Potter figurines in your mid-century modern interior.

However, appropriate eclectic taste is valued. This is evident in an *Elle Decoration* article about the 1960s and 1970s interior owned by Marc Anthony Rees (Figure 6.3). Rees is quoted as saying,

> I used to live in Berlin and I fell in love with the fusing of the simple socialist housing of the East with the elaborate art nouveau apartment blocks of the West. I was also really inspired by a bar there called Wohnzimmer, which mixed vintage wallpaper and Louis XIV chairs with pieces from the sixties and seventies. I like the idea of mixing styles and also wanted to incorporate my Welsh heritage and childhood memories to create a place that said something about me. Using old family pieces as a starting point made the whole thing much more personal. The kitchen, for example, is built around my parents' old table and chairs, while hanging above my bed is a blown-up photograph of the house I grew up in. (Wilkes, 2006)

Figure 6.3   Marc Anthony Rees's bedroom (2007). © Hugh Burden Photographer.

Like the stories of retro enthusiasts in the *Guardian,* Rees's experiences of living in Wales and Berlin combine to make his interior seem more authentic. The way he has tastefully selected inherited pieces also gives him more status in the hierarchy of modes of acquisition. Thus, in *Elle Decoration* both individual and eclectic tastes are valued, and interiors that demonstrate these characteristics fill the pages of the magazine.

The discourses of individual and eclectic good taste also contribute to the narrative and drama in the art deco house episode of *Grand Designs.* From the outset McCloud says, "Building a house is difficult, building something period, something inspired by a bygone era, now that is really tricky" (*Grand Designs,* Series 5, Episode 18). Throughout the episode McCloud continues to highlight the difficulties in producing an interior that is new and original as well as period and authentic. He suggests that the art deco house can end up looking like "a dry academic exercise, or worse, a weak insipid attempt." As in *Elle Decoration,* good taste is viewed as somewhere between these two extremes.

Therefore, although some of the means of distinction are clear to the avid consumer of *Grand Designs* and *Elle Decoration* (a commitment to buying original authentic modernist pieces), others (eclectic and individual good taste) are harder to achieve. For example, it is difficult to identify what makes Rees's parents' chairs and table seen as good taste and another person's inherited objects not so. This, I would suggest, goes back to the identity of the owners and their ability to legitimate their own taste, as we saw with the example of Kannan in the *Guardian Weekend* magazine. By making taste personal and individual, high-end lifestyle media manage to avoid being perceived as hierarchical design dictators while simultaneously judging appropriate taste and maintaining authority. Methods of distinction continue but are reworked to appear democratic. Programs and magazines, such as *Grand Designs* and *Elle Decoration,* maintain this subtle illusion. However, other lifestyle media seem to manage it less successfully.

PROBLEMATIC PARTICIPANTS AND VIEWERS: RETRO COLLECTORS AND VALUATION

So far in this chapter I have considered how retro style, in its various guises, has reinforced the distinctiveness of lifestyle media and the cultural capital of its experts. However, these power relations are not inevitable, particularly when retro enthusiasts and collectors are involved. This is evident in two lifestyle television programs, both involving the valuation of retro goods.

The first example is an episode from a series called *To Buy or Not to Buy* (BBC, 2003–), in which a couple of retro enthusiasts, Joanne and Kevin, looked for a retro home. The usual premise of the series is that two experts compete to see who can find the best properties for the participants. While the house hunters are looking around the property, the presenters-cum-estate agents, Kristian Digby and Ed Hall, listen to their comments and talk, often mockingly, about their tastes. However, in the episode in question, it is clear from the outset that both experts find it difficult to understand retro style and therefore to discuss Joanne and Kevin's taste. For example, Kristian says, "It's still a heady mix for me to get my head round, the fact that she loves all the things that everyone else would hate." The presenters also find it difficult to predict the properties and style of interiors that Joanne and Kevin will like. For example, before entering a house designed in the early 1960s, Kristian shows Joanne and Kevin some 1960s wallpaper and material samples that he thinks will encourage the couple to buy the property. However, Joanne and Kevin disregard them as "too flower power" while also trying to make Kristian feel better by saying that "the house looks pretty cool though."

Joanne and Kevin's specific tastes and their specialized knowledge of mid-century architecture, styles and building techniques continue to undermine the position of the experts throughout the program. This makes for enjoyable watching as the participants get their own back. Yet while this is a subversion of the normative narratives of lifestyle television, it does not disrupt hierarchies of taste altogether. Joanne and Kevin are able to question the authority of the experts because they are connoisseurs and their knowledge of original and authentic items demonstrates higher levels of cultural capital. In addition, Kevin is highly skilled in refurbishing and renovating retro homes.

At the same time, however, their passion for retro makes their practices and tastes marginal and thus not wholly compatible with the values of the property market. This comes to the fore when Joanne comments on an en-suite bathroom. She says, "We could always take it out and put in a walk-in wardrobe." This is the undoing of the experts-cum-estate agents, and Kristian says, "I can't, I can't, oh, I can't listen." Ed explains, "Five years in the mines [being an estate agent] and he's never heard this. Someone wanting to rip out an en-suite and turn it into a cupboard!" Thus, it is at the moment of market valuation that Kristian and Ed attempt to regain their position as experts.

The difference in values between lifestyle television experts on the one hand and retro collectors and enthusiasts on the other is also evident in the series *20th Century Roadshow* (BBC, 2005). A spin-off from *Antiques Roadshow, 20th Century Roadshow* toured the country asking the general public to bring in their twentieth-century objects. Alan Titchmarsh, of the garden makeover program *Ground Force* (BBC, 1998–2005) and the Christian show *Songs of Praise* (BBC), presents the program together with a number of other experts. In each episode twentieth-century objects are discussed and valued. The mini-narratives of these valuations are similar to those on *Antiques Roadshow* (BBC, 1979–) and on many of the other lifestyle programs based on the valuation of goods.[8] Members of the public are encouraged to tell the expert and viewer how they acquired their objects, the expert talks about the background history of the objects, and then they are valued. As Francis Bonner suggests, valuations "pose as detective stories by opening with the enigma posed as 'What is this object?' but reveal, by their culmination in a valuation, that the enigma instead is what is this object worth?" (2003:191). Therefore, the drama in valuation programs rests on the unknowing owners' surprise at their objects' monetary value. As Bonner notes, sentimental value is recognized "primarily as a compensation for negligible economic worth" (2003:154).

Valuation is even more prominent on *20th Century Roadshow* than on *Antiques Roadshow*. From the outset the title sequence presents the program as concerned with monetary value. It shows a domestic interior with three white lines in the center of the screen. As the camera moves to different rooms in the home, the white lines (presumably meant to represent experts) stop on retro objects and the date and price of the object appear on the screen. Retro enthusiasts interviewed in this research were critical of the emphasis on price and valuation on *20th Century Roadshow*. For example, when asked about the program, Edward, a writer and retro enthusiast, said, "You know a lot of telly encourages or almost tells people to look at everything around them and just see a bank statement and I don't like that" (2006).

Of course, this criticism could also be leveled at *Antiques Roadshow,* but *20th Century Roadshow* failed to deliver on another count: the drama of the moment of valuation. On *Antiques Roadshow* the drama is created by the difference in knowledge between the expert and the member of the public. As Bonner notes, "The story of origin is the only major discursive form available to the owners, the non experts" (2003:197). The less the owner of the object knows about the antiques market, the more shocked he or she is at a high valuation. Simon Shaw, the series editor of the *Antiques Roadshow,* has related this knowledge and recognition of market values to class. He claims that "the more middle-class the venue, the less interesting the finds" (quoted in L. Cohen, 2008). He suggests that programs made in northern industrial towns have been much more successful due to their demographic profile. Thus, like the retro retailers explored in Chapter 5, television producers capitalize, albeit less directly, on the differences in regimes of values specific to certain locations and classes.

However, on *20th Century Roadshow* the members of the public were usually collectors of the objects they brought in. This meant that they were not surprised at the valuation because they frequently knew more about the objects than the experts did. Thus, the authority of the expert was questioned. In *20th Century Roadshow,* this was so commonplace that in most episodes the collectors spoke more about the objects than the experts did. As in *To Buy or Not to Buy,* the experts frequently tried to regain control by considering whether the collectors would get their money back if the objects were sold. These attempts to demonstrate superior knowledge of the market were usually unsuccessful because collectors either knew the market value of the item or did not care about it. This made the program rather dull, as Edward commented:

> It was totally lacking that human element, totally lacking. It was completely sterile and they had too few people that we could identify with, that happened to have, you know, a Pierre Paulin chair or some piece by Hans Wegner, that's what I was hoping for. Someone saying "My Mum was a funny old Mum in the fifties, our friends all had G-Plan furniture and she bought this funny stuff from Scandinavia, but we hated it." (Edward, writer and retro enthusiast, 2006)

The "human element" that Edward was looking for on *20th Century Roadshow* was a member of the public who was not an enthusiast or collector. This was unlikely because the press release for the program invited people "with contemporary collectables from film, fashion and furniture to toys, travel and TV to come and have their items valued by experts" (BBC Press Release, 2004). It was even less probable because someone who did not know that 1960s Scandinavian furniture was valuable would not take it to *20th*

Century Roadshow in the first place. Unlike antiques, where age is an obvious marker of value, the knowledge required to define valuable retro or twentieth-century style is more specialist. Although *20th Century Roadshow* contributed to popular knowledge of retro collectables because it got 5.6 million viewers each episode, it did not meet the requirements of collectors or the wider public. This was indicated by bad reviews in the press and only one series (see Gill, 2005). It was too specific and educational for the average viewer, and not specific enough for the retro enthusiast or collector.

However, as the retro enthusiasts' website *Retroselect* commented,

> The fact that the experts and production staff of BBC Antiques are so square, so dated, so lacking in style or cutting edge, and so totally out of touch with modern British tastes, is, ironically, good news for retro lovers. It means that prices are not yet inflated through TV exposure. (*Retroselect,* 2008)

So, as this quote demonstrates, the failure of *20th Century Roadshow* was positive for retro enthusiasts because it limited the circulation of knowledge about retro style. Although retro items have been the objects of valuation in other programs such as *Antiques Roadshow, Flog It!* (BBC, 2002–) and *Cash in the Attic* (BBC, 2002–), they feature only occasionally. Committed retro enthusiasts and collectors have other niche and micro media that cater to their needs.

ENTHUSIASTS AND COLLECTORS ONLY: NICHE AND MICRO MEDIA

Niche and micro media have low circulations and are narrowly targeted. Micro media are distinct from niche media because they are often nonprofessionally produced. As Sarah Thornton notes in her study of club cultures, micro media "are essential mediators amongst the participants in subcultures. They rely on their readers/listeners/consumers to be 'in the know' or in the 'right place at the right time'" (1997:151). While retro collectors or enthusiasts do not form a subculture, retro books, guides, websites and blogs circulate information just as the micro media that Thornton identifies do. Thus, these texts play an important role in the production, circulation and promotion of specialist knowledge about retro style; I outline some of this knowledge here.

Media that are self-published often arise from and bind those with similar interests (Leonard, 1997; Triggs, 2006:81). As mentioned in Chapter 4, fanzines were frequently produced by those involved in youth and music cultures and often promoted retro aesthetics. Indeed, the look, editorial style and content of zines was often "backward looking" (Thornton, 1997:140). Fanzines have been theorized as democratic forms of communication and have often been linked to resistant communities partly because of their position outside the institutionalized media field (for example, see Duncombe, 1997). As fanzines have disappeared in favor of websites, blogs and chat rooms (Hodkinson, 2005:596), arguments about the democratic potential of grassroots media have continued. It has been suggested that the World Wide Web is a democratic tool that flattens media hierarchies, enables wide participation and facilitates postmodern "flexible identities" (Leonard, 1997:111; Rheingold, 2005 [1994]; Turkle, 1995).

In the research conducted for this book, I did not find any fanzines focused exclusively on retro interiors. I did, however, find many websites and blogs dedicated to the style.[9] One of the most comprehensive websites is www. retrotogo.com. Launched in 1995, the site is a spin-off from www.modculture. co.uk, a listings site for those interested in going to mod events. It defines itself as offering "around 10 items or news stories per day, covering everything from architecture and art to fashion and design, not to mention gadgets and technology, books, film, cars, cosmetics, food, sport, travel—in fact anything interesting with a retro edge" (Retrotogo, 2012). While some of its audience may be collectors of specific eras, brands or objects, the website addresses a general reader who is enthusiastic about retro objects and embraces a retro lifestyle.

On www.retrotogo.com it is the acquisition of retro objects that receives the most attention. The site, especially the home page, is structured around specific retro products. Each day it features new items that can be bought online by clicking a hyperlink. The short features usually include a photograph of the object, a short description, the price and the details of the retailer. In this respect, www.retrotogo.com is not unlike a retailer's catalog and is written in a style similar to advertising and promotional copy.

The way that the style is framed on websites and blogs echoes its portrayal by mainstream retailers and lifestyle television. These similarities emphasize the "dense intertextuality and extra-textuality" between promotional, lifestyle and micro media (Bell and Hollows, 2005:9). Thus, as Thornton argues, media that are self-published, such as micro media, are not necessarily pure, autonomous or emergent (1997:138–139). To varying extents they are also a product of, and contribute to, wider disputes over taste, class hierarchies and consumerist ideologies. In this case, retro taste is portrayed as good taste, and readers are addressed as avid shoppers. Ironically, the interlinkages between the values of subcultural groups evident in micro media and those present in mass media, which Thornton astutely recognizes, were not reproduced in her concept of subcultural capital. As argued in Chapter 4, to view subcultural capital as different from cultural capital is problematic. While certain minority groups do have some distinct values and practices (as is explored below) these are not wholly different from those of the rest of society.

The "catalog-like" style of www.retrotogo.com also represents and encourages openness toward reproduction retro objects. For example, when discussing a retro table, the editor suggests that "there's not a lot of difference" between the original and the reproduction, "except one is a lot cheaper." The website is also more inclusive in terms of interiors, and this continues in parts of the website that are not focused on acquisition. In a section called "Retro Homes" readers are encouraged to send in their photographs and a few words about their retro houses, rooms or furnishings. Rather than being judged and critiqued as tastes frequently are on lifestyle television, contributors are thanked for their contributions. This encourages other readers to send in their photographs and promotes the consumption and display of retro interiors more generally.

Although one should be wary of conceptualizing www.retrotogo.com as wholly inclusive because it is likely that contributors already have an interest in retro before they engage with the site, the environment created by www.retrotogo.com is less critical and judgmental than most lifestyle media. The editor of the site and other contributors seem genuinely pleased to find other enthusiasts. This inclusivily occurs even if contributors' interiors do not seem to fit with the aesthetic promoted elsewhere on the website, which tends to be minimal and modernist styles inspired by the 1950s and 1960s. For example, comments on retro rooms include "This is hyper-cool. Could you please show us pictures of the kitchen?" "I love the 70's kitchenalia you have, it's a shame it's often difficult to find or impossibly expensive," and "beautiful. I adore it. Now can I move in with this man?" The satisfactions and pleasures involved in discussing specialist interests with others are more apparent, and are partly made possible, through micro media on the Internet. As Chris Atton (2002:76) suggests, websites and forums, or e-zines, offer new opportunities for sociality. The differences between the discourses of lifestyle media and those found in niche and micro media are even more distinct on the websites and blogs created by retro collectors.

While the distinction between enthusiasts and collectors is blurred, self-defined collectors tend to be individuals interested in specific brands, pieces of furniture and decorative objects, rather than those with a general enthusiasm for retro lifestyles. Websites and blogs written and read by retro collectors are usually highly specific and as a consequence do not often use the term *retro* to define their objects. An example of one of these sites is www.midwinterdirectory.co.uk, a resource for collectors of Midwinter pottery. Midwinter ceramics and tableware, particularly items produced in the 1950s and 1960s, have often been associated with retro style both in the press and in academic texts (e.g., Franklin, 2002). The site www.midwinterdirectory.co.uk includes images and prices of almost all of the ceramics produced by the company. Collectors send in the photographs used on the site, and prices are determined by the most recent sale price on eBay.

The centrality of monetary value in cultures of collecting, exemplified by the niche and micro media discussed here, is one of the reasons for theorizations of collecting as imitating the structures and relations of capitalism. As Russell Belk notes,

> In the process of collecting collectors rehearse and imitate the market-based economy in which we are increasingly embedded. . . . Among these structures and relations are competition, commodity trading, and buying, accumulating, and later selling at an anticipated profit. (1995:55)

The competitive nature of collecting is also evident on www.midwinterdirectory. co.uk. Many of the photographs used on the site are of items that are difficult to acquire. For example, a coffeepot is used to illustrate a pattern rather than a plate or a cup. This hints at the one-upmanship involved in the pursuit of rare original objects by avid collectors.

However, it is problematic to view collecting as simply rehearsing the market-based economy (as Belk [1995:56] recognizes). The Midwinter directory not only represents competitiveness and buying as an investment but is also a friendly and inclusive virtual environment. The information on the home page begins with a disclaimer:

> First let me explain that we are *not* Midwinter experts, just amateur collectors. The idea of the site is to offer a useful guide to design names and approx value where possible. (Colin and Angela, 2008)

This statement protects against any criticisms that the avid collector might have. It also adds to the modest and personal tone of the site. On the home page the editors also introduce themselves as Colin and Angela and welcome readers. In addition, like on www.retrotogo.com, Colin and Angela seem grateful for the contributions of other collectors. On the home page they write, "A BIG THANKYOU TO EVERYONE WHO HAS CONTRIBUTED and particular thanks to Joan & Bob who have supplied 'pagefulls' of photographs" (Colin and Angela, 2008). Interestingly, both the editors and main contributors are couples, which may contradict claims regarding collecting as an individual pursuit (Belk, 1995:68).

Of all the examples in this chapter the Midwinter directory seems to be the site that is most similar to theorizations of a virtual community in which discussions create a web of personal relationships (Rheingold, 2005 [1994]). Midwinter collectors post images and discuss their collections, and the

website has a question-and-answer page where editors and contributors identify Midwinter pottery. The community is relatively accessible in comparison to
collectors' groups prior to the web. Colin and Angela do not seem worried that
their knowledge will be devalued or that prices of Midwinter pottery will go up
if they include others. Instead, they encourage contributions and call for help
to find images of "missing designs."

While this may be a sign of Colin and Angela's egalitarian spirit, it is also
due to the nature of collecting as a practice. Collecting Midwinter pottery is
specialist and requires high levels of commitment and dedication, so it is
unlikely to become a popular activity. In addition, because Midwinter collectors concentrate on originals, this imposes a relative scarcity that means it
would be difficult for a significant amount of the population to be involved in
such an activity. Even when objects become fashionable, as is the case with
Midwinter, collectors benefit from the rising prices of their existing collections. Although this can make acquiring new objects more difficult and some
collectors worry about increases in prices (Ellis and Haywood, 2006:58),
the discussion on www.midwinterdirectory.co.uk does not communicate this
anxiety.

The Midwinter directory is also less concerned with style, aesthetics and
individuality than those micro and niche media written and read by enthusiasts. This is because the type of collecting encouraged and represented
on the site revolves around the acquisition of sets. Collectors are keen to
know and acquire all the possible permutations of Midwinter pottery, and
the directory is a list that helps them do this. Thus, rather than being based
around cultural knowledge, this type of collecting is based on commitment to
acquisition.

The seeming irrelevance of style and design to these types of collectors is
also communicated by the design of the site itself: www.midwinterdirectory.
co.uk is designed with function rather than fashion trends in mind. It uses
unfashionable fonts and has clashing colors, and the images on the site
are often of poor quality. This disregard for fashion corresponds with the
practice of collecting itself, which, as Belk notes, "differs from most other
forms of consumption in being relatively immune from fashion obsolescence"
(1995:66). The site focuses on lists, pottery marks and identifiable characteristics rather than eloquent descriptions, beautiful pictures and fashionable
designs. Therefore, the website is at odds with the aesthetics and practices
defined as desirable in other lifestyle media. As explored earlier in the chapter, magazines aimed at more affluent and exclusive markets, such as *Elle
Decoration,* promote eclectic and individual retro aesthetics. Consuming every
piece of china produced by one factory irrespective of its design contradicts
this idea of good taste and therefore is unlikely to represent and generate
cultural capital.

This discussion of niche and micro media demonstrates a difference between the values and practices of retro enthusiasts and those of retro collectors. For enthusiasts, the value of retro objects is based on the acquisition of distinctive, unique and individual styles. Therefore, increases in the popularity of retro can signal a decrease in value. While origin and price are important to collectors, they are motivated by more specific rewards related to the practice of collecting itself: for example, finding and displaying a rare tea service, irrespective of whether it is fashionable or deemed to be in good taste.

CONCLUSION

In this chapter I have argued that retro style is used as a mode of distinction in magazines and on television. Retro is a way of maintaining and furthering the cultural capital and symbolic power of experts and the media. Yet the style also makes period styles accessible. In lifestyle television and magazines, audiences are addressed as consumers and are shown how to recognize retro styles and "get the look" too. Thus, lifestyle media are also involved in the popularization of retro style. This confirms Bell and Hollows's (2005:11) theorization that lifestyle media play a key role in producing distinction but also demystify and democratize. In this regard, lifestyle media can be seen as key in the production, circulation and promotion of styles, therefore contributing to fashion obsolescence and high levels of consumption.

However, the ways in which distinction and accessibility are communicated vary across media formats, and this is where a hierarchy of types of retro styles seems to appear. Lifestyle television programs aimed at wide audiences, such as *Changing Rooms,* show retro style as a desirable and coherent themed interior and attempt to make it easy to understand and achieve. While communicating period authenticity and advocating practices high in the hierarchy of modes of acquisition, newspaper supplements such as the *Guardian Weekend* magazine show readers how to get the look by decade. High-end lifestyle media such as *Grand Designs* and *Elle Decoration* claim accessibility while promoting a subtler mode of distinction through effort, individuality and eclectic taste. On *Changing Rooms,* retro interiors are themed and produced using reproduction pieces. In the *Guardian Weekend,* interiors are carefully reproduced and characterized by decade using original objects, and on *Grand Designs* and in *Elle Decoration* they are eclectic and individual, mixing original and reproduction. Of course, this is not static, and like the mass production of retro objects, once styles are disseminated and associated with the mainstream, their authenticity and distinctiveness deteriorate. Thus, the media and cultural industries become involved in a constant search for new and more authentic practices and styles, of which retro style is one manifestation.

Yet what is interesting about high-end lifestyle media and the valuing of effort, eclecticism and individuality is that methods of distinction are hidden, which makes them more difficult to appropriate. Legitimate effort, eclecticism and individuality are contingent on the appropriate context and identity of the owners and their related capital. While *Elle Decoration* would not recognize most people who put their collection of Beatrix Potter figurines in their mid-century modern home as having good taste, those with extremely high levels of cultural capital made legitimate by the arts market, such as artists and designers, may be able to do so and be judged as avant-garde. The continual appropriation and legitimation of styles in the media reflect a change in middle-class values. Rather than cultural capital related to the possession and knowledge of specific cultural forms, it is the display of a wide range of styles and knowledge of other cultures that is valuable. In this process the media become central because they circulate and institutionalize cultural capital. While this mode of creating distinction may appear less hierarchical, not everyone can create individual and eclectic retro interiors that are considered authentic and/or in good taste. This finding reinforces the arguments I made in Chapter 4, which suggested that certain groups are excluded from the terms of individuality.

In my analysis, I have found that the term *retro* is more likely to be used in a commercial context, and because the appropriation of styles has become part of middle-class distinction making, retro does not challenge the values of art institutions or older generations as it once did. However, the emphasis placed on effort, the acquisition of handcrafted quality originals and practical skill discussed in this chapter is particularly intriguing and seems to transcend commerciality. On *Grand Designs* this is used as a means of distinction. In *To Buy or Not to Buy* and *20th Century Roadshow,* it is the device that enables highly committed retro enthusiasts and collectors to disrupt the normative balance of power between experts and participants.

In addition, some of the practices of those interested in retro objects continue to be marginal and new media technologies aid enthusiasts to share knowledge and create relatively inclusive communities. This was especially evident in micro media created by collectors, and this leads to the last point emerging from this chapter: the difference between "collecting" and "consuming" retro style. Throughout my analysis of media texts I have found that the values of retro enthusiasts revolve around style, uniqueness and difference. Although retro collectors value origin, I observed that they are less concerned with style and fashion. This may make collectors' practices less representative of the aestheticization of everyday life and less compatible with lifestyle discourses than those of retro enthusiasts. I consider this point in more detail in the next chapter.

7

Retro Homes, Taste and Cultural Distinction

This chapter of the book takes up the themes of individuality, appropriation and popularization that have been central to my argument so far and explores them in the context of the home. In this chapter and the next, I concentrate on people who describe themselves as interested in domestic retro style and explore the interiors and lifestyles that result from this interest. These individuals could be defined in many ways: as householders, as consumers, as producers or as enthusiasts. I argue that they are simultaneously all of these things. They are householders because they rent or, more commonly, own their homes. They are consumers because they consume retro objects to go in these homes. Although they are not paid, they are producers because they appropriate objects and produce retro interiors. They are enthusiasts because they have a strong commitment to one particular style. I have chosen to frame the interviewees as the latter, as enthusiasts of retro style. This is not because enthusiasts are not householders, consumers or producers but rather because this enables me to explore the wide range of activities (consuming, producing and homemaking) that are involved in the creation of a retro interior.

Representing interviewees as enthusiasts also draws attention to the way in which they were selected—not by age, class or gender,[1] but by their interest in retro style. As mentioned in Chapter 2, I took this approach in order to assess the validity of the claim that the relationship between lifestyle and social position had disintegrated. To do this, in this chapter I consider the aesthetics of retro interiors and the ways in which enthusiasts seek to construct and display distinctive lifestyles. I also explore how enthusiasts talk about their ideal homes and their own identities. I focus on whether those who make similar aesthetic choices and have similar lifestyles are linked in terms of their social position. However, as Joanne Hollows suggests, "the meaning of home-making strategies cannot simply be reduced to the meaning of class differences" because this often misses "the complexity of household consumption practices" (2008:82). Thus, I also explore the emotional and practical relationships that retro enthusiasts have with their objects and interiors.

DESCRIBING AND USING RETRO FURNITURE

In tours of their homes, retro enthusiasts told me how decorative objects and pieces of furniture were acquired and why they were important. As many theorists have argued, material objects are intrinsic to the construction and maintenance of identity and are central to people's relationships and to the process of homemaking (Busch, 2005; Clarke, 2001; Hurdley, 2006; Makovicky, 2007; Miller, 2001, 2008). As such, retro items materialize individual and collective histories and are loaded with value and meaning. This was obvious in the stories retro enthusiasts told me. For example, the first and most important item that Mary and Peter showed me was a marble clock they had found in a junk shop and purchased as a present to commemorate their wedding anniversary. The clock took pride of place on the mantelpiece in their lounge. Tim and Suzy also described the story behind a piece of 1960s Czech glass they had bought on a special weekend in Prague. The piece of glass sat on a shelf in their dining room and was obvious to guests when they entered their home. As joint purchases acquired on important occasions, these pieces had become significant in enthusiasts' relationships as well as in their domestic interiors. Both couples, like the majority in this study, conveyed a strong sense of their joint involvement in the decoration of the home and described how their tastes and interiors had mutually evolved.[2] Appreciating, discussing and buying retro furniture were fun activities that couples could participate in together and were an enjoyable part of their lives. I return to consider the co-construction of retro interiors in more detail in the next chapter.

Inherited retro objects were also important because they reminded enthusiasts of family members. For example, Louise spoke with fondness of the pieces of furniture she had inherited from her grandfather. Catherine also told me that she had inherited furniture from family members. Now that she and Thomas were going to move back to the area where her family had lived, she was happy that she could "take the furniture home." Thus, like pieces of furniture and decorative objects in other people's homes, objects belonging to retro enthusiasts embody social relationships in a personal and familial sense.

Enthusiasts' homes also reflect wider tastes and ideals. Consequently, there were many commonalities in the types and styles of furniture that were displayed in retro enthusiasts' interiors. Cocktail bars and cabinets, sideboards, coffee tables, radiograms and jukeboxes have become synonymous with retro style and symbolic of particular periods. For example, the cocktail cabinet is associated with the glamour of the art deco period, and the cocktail bar with the hedonism of the 1950s, 1960s and 1970s. These pieces of furniture were central in many retro enthusiasts' interiors and frequently took pride of place in lounges and dining rooms. While it is partly the size of these items that makes them obvious to guests (myself included), it is also the absence of these objects in modern interiors that adds to their conspicuousness.

The design of these objects also facilitates certain practices that are more time consuming than their modern equivalents. For example, preparing a drink using a cocktail cabinet takes more time than grabbing a can from the fridge, and putting a vinyl record on a radiogram with a temperamental stylus is more time consuming than pushing a button on an iPod. These activities are enjoyable partly because they are different from, or punch through, everyday experiences of time as hurried and immediate. It is also the materials of cocktail bars and cabinets, sideboards, coffee tables, radiograms and jukeboxes that make them popular and pleasurable. A radiogram is a substantial piece of furniture frequently made of relatively high-quality teak, the workings of the record player and radio are usually easy to repair, and the knobs and dials are attractive. These material differences alone make using a radiogram appealing for retro enthusiasts.

The materials of retro "statement pieces" also make them glamorous. Jukeboxes usually have bright lights, sparkling metal back plates and colorful graphics. As Nigel Thrift (2008) suggests, color can be one of the ways glamour is experienced. Other means include sound, "the play of brilliant or subdued light [. . . ,] powerful smells [. . . ,] haptic association [. . . ,] and pace" (Thrift, 2008:16). Many retro objects are rich in these qualities, and so are the practices they facilitate. For example, the sound quality from a jukebox, as well as its look and feel, transports people in their daydreams and fantasies to different worlds, ones that often cannot be fully realized in the everyday. As Thrift writes, material and sensual experiences make "cherished imaginary abstractions seem attainable," and while they occupy an imaginary space they are "no less real for that . . . [because] imagination is itself lived experience" (2008:14). I return to consider the role of fantasy in relation to retro enthusiasts' domestic practices in more detail in the next chapter.

The experiences and narratives that interviewees told me about their objects appeared mentally rehearsed, if not previously verbalized. This is unlike previous studies of domestic space, in which it has been suggested that supplying detailed accounts about choices of furnishings, decorative objects and family heirlooms is a relatively strange and unnatural process (Makovicky, 2007:230). Narratives were particularly rehearsed when talking about statement pieces that were likely to provoke questions from friends and family (and the interested academic). Indeed, the value of these objects also partly derives from the space they create for retro enthusiasts to tell stories about their acquisition. As suggested in Chapter 2, buying a retro item cheaply and going to great lengths to get it home reflects high levels of cultural capital. This is not to argue that the practices that these material objects encourage are not enjoyable in their own right, especially in a society that is "time poor." Nor is it to deny the material differences between old and new items or to dismiss the personal and social attachments that enthusiasts have with their possessions. However, statement pieces also provide opportunities for their owners to discuss their unique tastes, to highlight their highly committed shopping practices and to demonstrate their cultural knowledge. As Beverley Skeggs argues, it is through reflexivity and the "telling of the self that social processes of positioning, of value, of moral attribution, are put into effect as a manifestation and maintenance of difference and distinction" (2004a:120). As discussed in Chapter 3, self-reflexivity and the ability to relate to oneself as property are intimately linked with middle-class regimes of value. Thus, the ease with which retro enthusiasts were able to describe and discuss their interiors is a result of their high levels of cultural capital and their social position.

Statement pieces were not the only items valued by retro enthusiasts. Less conspicuous objects like mantelpieces, shelves and cabinets were also important because they enabled retro enthusiasts to exhibit precious decorative items. While other homemakers value mantelpieces, shelves and cabinets as well (Makovicky, 2007), storage and display are even more significant to retro enthusiasts. For example, some interviewees went to great lengths to find the appropriate cabinets and shelving. Andy and Louise had a large 1960s hearth built to display their objects and design books. Tim and Suzy had 1950s-style shelves made to display their objects and collections of old Penguin paperbacks (Figure 7.1).

As both these examples indicate, books were highly significant to retro enthusiasts, and many were keen to talk to me about them. Books were viewed

Figure 7.1   Tim and Suzy's 1950s-style bookshelves (2006). © Author.

as sources of invaluable information and as aesthetic objects in their own right. They were also thought of as reflecting and constituting enthusiasts' own identities, as this quote from Louise illustrates:

> I always think it would be really funny if someone did a Lloyd Grossman thing and they looked at our bookshelves. They would say "they are definitely interested in design." (Louise, retro enthusiast, 2006)

Although the emphasis placed on the display of design books may have been a consequence of the interviewees reacting to my own status as an academic, it was also a display of their extensive design knowledge. All of the enthusiasts had learned a great deal about the styles they were interested in and in this regard were connoisseurs. Most enthusiasts also had a relatively good understanding of the social history of the periods they were passionate about. As Heike Jenß (2005:191) found in her study of 1960s fashion enthusiasts, this contradicts theorizations of the production and consumption of retro style as a random plundering of the past whereby history is a lost referential.

As well as demonstrating cultural knowledge, design books contextualize and legitimate the items that retro enthusiasts select. Enthusiasts often used reference books to design authentic-looking interiors, and it was not uncommon to see books about specific retro objects next to the pieces themselves. Thus, as well as being connoisseurs, retro enthusiasts are similar to curators of museums and art galleries, arranging their objects and surrounding them with appropriate information. The similarities between retro interiors and gallery spaces can also be seen in the overall design of retro enthusiasts' homes.

THE DESIGN OF RETRO INTERIORS

As discussed above, retro enthusiasts owned similar items of furniture. They were also interested in styles from similar periods. Broadly their periods of interest fell between 1930 and 1970, and the most popular styles were art deco and those from the 1960s. While many of the enthusiasts had originally been interested in the 1950s, their tastes had gradually changed. They continued to like certain designer items from the 1950s such as fabrics designed by Lucienne Day or ceramics by Terence Conran, but in general many objects from this decade were viewed as too "mass market," a point explored below in more detail.

The shared interest in retro also manifests itself in a valuing of largely modernist-style interiors, and the majority of retro enthusiasts valued "clean lines" over excessive decoration. Although some of the retro enthusiasts represented in the media enjoy kitsch, crowded and bright interiors, I did not find any. Most interior walls had been painted in muted colors like white, cream, green and beige. There was also an absence of wallpaper, carpets and curtains in favor of blinds, painted floorboards and vinyl (Figures 7.2 and 7.3). The gender politics of this taste are explored in more detail in the next chapter.

Figure 7.2 Tim and Suzy's dining room (2006). © Author.

Figure 7.3 Peter and Mary's lounge (2006). © Author.

The valuing of clean lines was highlighted by enthusiasts' descriptions of their taste; most enthusiasts were keen to emphasize that retro style was certainly not about "clutter." This emphasis was an attempt to preempt what they thought were many people's perceptions of the style.

> We have never been into clutter. Sometimes you assume that people who are into retro like a room full of just everything. (Suzy, retro enthusiast, 2006)

> I like clean lines...although you may not realize it. At Christmas the clutter is terrible. There is lots of applied decoration everywhere, which is completely against what ordinarily my taste would be. (Peter, retro enthusiast, 2006)

As the quote from Peter demonstrates, the attainment of an ideal retro interior is often disrupted by the practices and practicalities of everyday life. This was especially true if circumstances meant that retro enthusiasts' homes were relatively small. For example, Catherine and Thomas had been forced to move into a smaller house, and much of their art deco furniture was held in storage. Dave also had little spare room in his flat. While he considered his flat to be in the ideal location and loved the architecture, sometimes he thought he had purchased too many pieces of furniture for such a small space. Due to these constraints, the interior decoration of Catherine and Thomas's and Dave's homes was more crowded. In addition, both Catherine and Dave, like Chris, were more prone to collecting than other enthusiasts.

Despite these practicalities, most retro enthusiasts valued minimal interiors in which retro furniture and objects were positioned in enough space to be displayed and viewed. For example, when guests walk into Tim and Suzy's house they find themselves in a white room. There are shelves on the left-hand side on which 1960s pieces of glass are displayed, a dining table and chairs at one side of the room and two other retro chairs by a window. Compared to the majority of homeowners' front rooms, this space feels very sparse, and the similarities to an art gallery are hard to miss.

As outlined in Chapter 3, in his discussion of postmodernism and consumer culture, Mike Featherstone (1991:26) suggested that sections of the middle class had become increasingly engaged in the practice of making life like art. Although Featherstone was referring to a general turn to lifestyle, the interiors of retro enthusiasts seem to be art-like in a very material sense. Thus, retro enthusiasts are an exception to Alan Warde's theorization that "most people would prefer a comfortable to a beautiful life" (2002:194). In fact, Suzy told me that she "doesn't do comfy."

By making their homes into gallery-like spaces, retro enthusiasts also distinguish their interiors from other types of revival. For many, bad taste was synonymous with the country cottage look with its chintz, antiques and trinkets and the English pub with its dark walls, horse brasses and patterned carpet. The majority of enthusiasts conceptualize their tastes as urban and thoroughly modern. Thus, the styles of the country cottage and the pub are avoided partly because of their associations with older generations and provincial petit bourgeois taste.

Retro enthusiasts' rejection of clutter has its origins in the discourses of modernism, where adornment, ornamentation and display were attacked in favor of functional interiors (Attfield, 2000:12). As Ruth Holliday notes, "Decoration was firmly equated with the uncivilized—the savage, the childish and the feminine," and the aesthetics of the pub and country cottage were established as inferior in design terms (2005:72). As documented in Chapter 4, it was this hostility to mass culture that the European historical avant-garde and the pop movement reacted against and that led to the beginnings of retro sensibilities, including the appropriation of old and outmoded objects previously associated with the working class. Thus, what is interesting in retro enthusiasts' interiors and their descriptions of bad types of revival is the combination of aesthetic values that have their origins in both modernism and postmodernism. The legacy of these two movements is also obvious in enthusiasts' attitudes toward original furniture, decorative objects and architectural features.

VALUING AND LIVING WITH ORIGINALITY

As discussed previously, the original is privileged in retro cultures. This was reinforced by discussions with retro enthusiasts and was obvious in the furniture and decorative objects they displayed in their homes. Retro enthusiasts, like retro retailers, usually convey originality by discussing age, origin and quality. For example, Tim, who had an eclectic retro interior, was proud to announce that he didn't think they had a "single piece of new furniture in the house" and went on to suggest that this was because secondhand retro objects are unique and different. For many the possession of original items was related to the construction and maintenance of a unique identity. When discussing his enthusiasm for retro style, Dave, who was keen to show me that he even had original kitchen utensils, said,

> We, me and my friends around me, we set out to be individuals, in what we collect, how we think, what we wear and in every aspect of our lives. (Dave, retro enthusiast, 2007)

The valuing of authentic origins was also obvious in the architectural styles that retro enthusiasts preferred. Unsurprisingly, many enthusiasts' visions of ideal homes were buildings that were designed in the periods they were interested in. While the majority of enthusiasts had not realized these dreams,

Peter and Mary had found their perfect art deco building and were in the process of restoring it to its former glory using as many original materials as possible. Enthusiasts who did not live in houses designed in their ideal period all lived in houses or flats that were constructed before 1970. While only a minority of the British population lives in new houses because of the age of housing stock, enthusiasts also said they preferred old buildings. For example, Sylvia considered old buildings to have their own intricacies and character that made them much more interesting. She, like Catherine, expressed her dislike of fake or modern-looking additions to old houses.

What architectural features do you dislike?

White plastic double glazed windows, I hate most of all, especially doors that match, and little plastic stained glass motifs in the top windows, and artex and textured walls ... beams, especially mock beams. (Catherine, retro enthusiast, 2006)

Even those with houses that did not match their passion for certain periods were critical about the removal of original architectural features. Thus, to some extent, enthusiasts felt controlled or "haunted" by the styles of their houses (Miller, 2001). For example, Suzy said that they had retained and restored the dado rails and ceiling roses in their home but that these didn't "really go with their minimalist style." Tim and Louise also identified the problems of living in a Victorian house. They said they had chosen their house because it was old on the outside but also because the previous owner had removed the internal Victorian features that would have clashed with their modernist style. This was important because they would have felt guilty removing them themselves. The obligation to retain old architectural features is partly due to an awareness of the value that original fireplaces, dado rails and skirting boards add to a house when it is resold.

These findings regarding originality are similar to those of previous studies of consumers of retro clothing (Gregson and Crewe, 2003; Jenß, 2005). In their research on secondhand cultures, Nicky Gregson and Louise Crewe (2003:148) find that consumers of 1960s retro style talk about the importance of wearing and displaying original items. As Heike Jenß also notes in her study of 1960s enthusiasts in Germany, original objects "rise into the rank of highly estimated acquisitions, original and rare," and the authenticity of the objects "is transferred to the self and the performance of a unique and authentic identity" (2005:194). Both studies recognize that obtaining original artifacts is an important part of cultural capital. However, they do not discuss this in terms of social class. For example, when considering the practices of 1960s enthusiasts, Jenß writes that "knowledge of the relevant fashion

history as well as the knowledge of good sources for obtaining original ar-
tefacts is essential for their retro-performances and in the sense of Pierre
Bourdieu, an important component of their (sub)cultural capital" (2005:182).
The use of the concepts of both subcultural and cultural capital by Jenß is
interesting, and it is as if she cannot decide which one to choose. Studies of
middle-class taste, particularly those that focus on domestic space, go some
way to clarifying this dilemma.

In research on household consumption in a southern English new town in
Britain, Dale Southerton (2001b) explored how different social classes designed and conceived of their kitchens. Drawing on Douglas Holt's (1998)
exploration of the concept of capital and the American middle class, Southerton found that members of the middle class are much more likely to individuate their consumption through authenticity and connoisseurship. The
middle-class interviewees in Southerton's study celebrated "original kitchens
for their perceived cultural authenticity and as a means of personal expression," in contrast to the working-class interviewees, who perceived kitchens
as having limited potential for individual creativity (Southerton, 2001b:168).

In her study of garden aesthetics and practices in West Yorkshire in Britain,
Lisa Taylor (2008) also found that the middle class valued authenticity. For
example, the middle-class gardeners in her study were not interested in using
sculptures purchased at garden centers but preferred antique items that gave
an authentic sense of history (Taylor, 2008:121). Thus, the privileging of the
original I have observed in the homes of retro enthusiasts is a wider middle-
class preoccupation.

Both Southerton (2001b) and Taylor (2008) also find that a valuing of the
original often emerges alongside a discussion of quality. They suggest that
the middle classes are more likely to talk about the quality of kitchens and
gardens in terms of rarity and origin, in contrast to the working classes, who
discuss quality as utility (e.g., modern and easy to maintain). For example,
a middle-class homeowner in Southerton's study highlights the quality of the
rare French oak used in the kitchen. Middle-class gardeners in Taylor's ethnography also describe purchasing plants from specialist garden centers as
a means of guaranteeing superior quality and as a form of connoisseurship
(2008:115). This mode of talking about quality was also evident in the responses of retro enthusiasts, who usually justified the value they placed on
original objects and buildings with comments regarding the superior craftsmanship of these artifacts. I was frequently given detailed descriptions of
these attributes, as the following quote demonstrates:

> The quality you would get with an older item, is actually something we couldn't
> afford new...for example, the chrome you can actually polish up, whereas if
> you bought affordable chrome now you couldn't....If you went to Habitat or

somewhere you would get a similar look, but it would be quite lightweight. I think it's just that the old craftsmanship is better. (Suzy, retro enthusiast, 2006)

Enthusiasts considered their secondhand retro items to be potentially longer lasting than their modern counterparts (at least those that they could afford). They talked about the inferiority of many of today's products, which they viewed as having "built-in obsolescence" and as more disposable than the furniture and decorative objects they were interested in. Although the majority of the secondhand items that enthusiasts collect were mass-produced, the material differences between the original objects and their new counterparts should not be dismissed. As suggested above, original retro objects have survived previous use and often are of superior quality.

However, when retro enthusiasts discussed originality and uniqueness, it was not always directly related to the age, rarity or superior quality of material objects. Styles were also thought of as original and unique. This meant that although enthusiasts preferred old and original items, they were not totally against purchasing the right sort of reproductions and newly designed pieces. Those enthusiasts with eclectic retro interiors occasionally purchased new retro items, and even those with more specific retro tastes were not completely committed to originals. For example, Mary and Peter were highly committed to 1930s and 1940s style, and most of their interior was furnished with original items. However, one of their display cabinets contained recently produced art deco china, of which it is relatively easy to find the originals. Mary and Peter were not embarrassed to tell me that the china was reproduction; in fact, they seemed proud that they could find something so original looking in the contemporary marketplace. Thus, while retro enthusiasts held on to a notion of originality in terms of the origin of designs, uniqueness and craftsmanship, they were more concerned with the stylistic qualities of objects and the ways they were acquired, assembled and talked about than with originality per se.[3]

In many ways this attitude to originality is inevitable. While style and aesthetics are paramount for all retro enthusiasts, homes are also places in which to live. The extent to which enthusiasts were settled in their homes affected their commitment to creating a retro interior. For example, Marianne imagined herself returning to the United States, where her family resides. This meant that she did not commit as much time to acquiring items and decorating her interior as other enthusiasts. Before buying objects Marianne would always consider the practicalities of moving with them. Thus, the majority of the retro items that she described were in storage in the United States. These factors meant that for Marianne the objects that made up "home" were spatially dispersed.

Yet most retro enthusiasts felt settled in Britain, and some thought they would remain in their properties for the rest of their lives. This meant that they were inclined to commit time and money to decorating their interiors and realizing their ideal homes. There were, however, other practices and life cir-cumstances that disrupted the creation of an ideal retro interior.

The spaces within the home are places for cooking, washing, sleeping and relaxing and need to be practical for these activities. Ideas about practicality are historically contingent because practicality is intimately linked to technol-ogy and has changed significantly over time. For example, a 1930s kitchen is significantly different from a new one, and its lack of time-saving technolo-gies is considered largely incompatible with modern lifestyles. Thus, for retro enthusiasts the choice between authentic-looking interiors and practicality is often a site of negotiation. Although enthusiasts preferred original retro ob-jects and aimed to create authentic retro interiors, people who gave up the ease of their everyday life for period style, such as having an outside toilet or living by candlelight, were viewed as "taking it too far." The following quote demonstrates how Tim and Suzy incorporated retro style into their kitchen while not compromising practicality:

> Our interest in retro even goes to when we buy new stuff, so we've got a 1950s style fridge or dualit toaster. . . . Kitchen appliances, you need them to work prop-erly and quite often the old ones don't. You have to draw the line somewhere. (Tim, retro enthusiast, 2006)

For all enthusiasts it was the kitchen that was the site of the most negotia-tion. As illustrated by the preceding quote, this is partly because of the high number of technological items kept in the kitchen, including fridges/freezers, cookers and washing machines, of which original retro versions are rare. It is also due to significant shifts in the use of the kitchen throughout the twenti-eth century. As Martin Hand and Elizabeth Shove (2004) argue, the kitchen has changed from a space designed for efficiency and isolated functionality in the 1920s to a space for eating, cooking, socializing and entertaining in recent times. Thus, a 1930s or 1940s kitchen is largely undesirable even to the most committed retro enthusiast.

> The kitchen, you've got to be quite practical about it as well because it depends what room you are in really. This room I wanted particularly '30s and '40s, um, the kitchen though, if you think about '30s and '40s kitchen appliances they were a bit basic and meagre. So, you know, the kitchen is all '50s. (Peter, retro enthusiast, 2006)

> We've got a dishwasher and a modern fridge freezer. We did um and ar about the fridge freezer. We thought we might be able to get modern parts and an old casing, um but we never came across anything that seemed right. Bosch have started to do a kind of retro style and we thought that it was a fairly good compro-mise. (Mary, retro enthusiast, 2006)

For Mary, a dishwasher was also an important addition to her otherwise 1950s kitchen because it helped her complete her domestic tasks while working full-time. The dishwasher did not jeopardize the overall aesthetic of the kitchen because it was hidden behind a retro-looking facade. For Peter, the compromise of a 1950s kitchen went against his general attitude toward 1950s style as "too mainstream." However, he justified his decision by discussing the practicality of different period kitchens and demonstrating his knowledge of the history of interior design. These compromises are further evidence of the relative flexibility of retro tastes so long as they are contextualized and talked about in appropriate ways.

Kitchens were not the only sites of negotiation; bathrooms were also often different from the rest of retro enthusiasts' interiors. For example, in Mary and Peter's house they had purchased a bathroom suite that was from the 1950s because an original or reproduction 1930s or 1940s bathroom suite was very difficult to find and was deemed too "cold." In Suzy and Tim's Victorian house they had created a more Victorian-looking bathroom partly because it was a relatively permanent fixture. Thus, although retro enthusiasts did not seem to think about the impact their retro tastes would have on the value of their properties (or at least they did not make this obvious to me), decisions about permanent features forced them to consider the wider desirability of their tastes.

Modern technologies and equipment, such as televisions, speakers and children's toys, also compromise the retro aesthetic. Surprisingly, there were a number of retro enthusiasts who said that their decision not to have children was partly influenced by changes they would have had to make to the style of their interior. Whether a commitment to retro style is the cause or the effect of these lifestyle choices, enthusiasts' feelings toward the impact of children on the organization and role of domestic space are astute. As Lydia Martens and colleagues note, household organization, style and design are all "compromised by the presence of kids' stuff and the functional requirements of (especially young) children" (2004:169). In fact, there was only one couple that had young children in this study, Andy and Louise. As documented in the previous chapter, Andy and Louise had more eclectic retro taste. They had also made a number of compromises regarding their choice of furniture; for example, they had bought a more comfortable and hard-wearing sofa than they would have otherwise purchased.

Even without children, the technologies and equipment associated with modern life were enough for retro enthusiasts to deal with. Therefore, for those interviewees who had the space, these items were often grouped in one room that was dedicated to watching television or using the computer. This room did not have a retro aesthetic and was not often shown to guests. It was, however, where many of the enthusiasts admitted to spending a significant amount of time. Those who did not have the space either lived with the contrasting styles or cleverly hid the objects in retro-looking cabinets or sideboards.

In most retro homes there were also rooms (usually dining rooms and lounges) that were specifically designed for entertaining and for the more overt display of retro objects. In this regard, retro dining rooms and lounges were not dissimilar to the front room or parlor in Victorian times (Logan, 2001). This allocation of space, with some rooms dedicated to display and aesthetics and others to more ordinary activities such as cooking and watching television, is evidence of the way in which everyday practices can disrupt displays of taste.

The attitudes toward originality and negotiations made over retro style seem slightly different from the theorizations of Gregson and Crewe (2003) and Jenß (2005) referred to above. While the practicalities of the home would always have influenced the extent to which original items could be valued, the views of retro enthusiasts also indicate a change in the importance of origin. As documented in Chapter 3, authenticity has been theorized as one of the most important values in the arts and consumer culture and is established through movement and traces of origin (e.g., Appadurai, 1986). However, Scott Lash and Celia Lury suggest that this regime of value is "being supplemented, if not surpassed by, a regime of value structured in terms of iconicity, or intensive qualities (rather than indexicality)" (2007:141). They note that in this new regime, value is not established "either in relation to price (as a mark of exclusivity) or origin (as a mark of authenticity), but in relation to information (that is, as a mark of distinctiveness)" (Lash and Lury, 2007:141). The discussions with retro enthusiasts indicate that this may be the case. However, iconicity, or style in the case of retro enthusiasts, also continues to be structured in terms of authenticity. As I explore below, value is established by appropriating authentic iconicity and using it to individuate interiors and identities.

THE "MASSES" AND INDIVIDUALITY

By demonstrating their appreciation of original artifacts, retro enthusiasts establish themselves and their taste as different from the "masses." In this respect, retro enthusiasts are similar to other middle-class consumers, who have been found to want to achieve distance from mass production and consumption (Southerton, 2001b). As Southerton notes,

> The uniformity associated with mass production and consumption has been met with great "fear" by the middle classes who associated it with the passive and uncritical acceptance of standardized goods which blunt the imagination and reduce consumption to a practice of uniformity and apathy. (Southerton, 2001b:167)

This attitude, as Skeggs (2004a:7) outlines, is partly due to the development and influence of the concept of the possessive individual, which has become central to the way the middle-class self accumulates value. Drawing on the theories of Celia Lury and Marilyn Strathern, Skeggs (2004a) suggests that the ability to own property in one's own person, to be an individual, was defined against the "mass." She argues that over time and through repetition the working classes have become "massified" (Skeggs, 1997:3).

The imagined inferiority of mass taste was evident in the talk of retro enthusiasts, particularly in their views of fashion and high street retailers. Many interviewees saw themselves as "genuinely interested" in eras and styles, as opposed to those simply following the latest fashion trend. For example, in the following quotes Tim suggests he is different from those who buy fashionable goods, and Marianne says that she is so out of touch with fashion that she doesn't even understand it.

> I don't think there is much point in going out and buying what you think happens to be the fashion at that moment. So I think we are genuinely interested in the look. (Tim, retro enthusiast, 2006)

> I think some of my friends probably think I have really bad taste or, yer, you know, I would look at a fashion magazine and think fashion is so blah, so boring, I don't get it, I don't understand why this dress this season, I don't understand why these things are in. My friend made a joke the other day about me, she was like "oh yeah if you had it your way, everyone would be like . . . the hoop skirt with a poodle on it would be back in." (Marianne, retro enthusiast, 2007)

Although enthusiasts considered themselves to be less engaged with fashion, many were very aware of fashion trends and were ready to predict them. For example, Mary said that she was "out of the loop" when it came to fashion. However, when discussing her new 1950s pink bathroom suite she mentioned that it was a good purchase because it would be in fashion in a few years' time. Thus, although retro enthusiasts thought of themselves as less engaged with changes in style, they were also acutely aware of them. As mentioned above, even the choice of decade of interest was subject to change. For example, Peter suggested that as 1950s styles had become more popular, he and his friends had moved on to different periods. Thus, an interest in retro style is one way of claiming a fashionable antifashion identity.

This ambivalence toward fashion is linked to retro enthusiasts' attitudes toward mass-produced furniture and its manufacturers. For many enthusiasts certain brands become associated with bad taste. Advertisements for furniture retailers, such as DFS or MFI, were the focus of many interviewees' objections.

What furniture wouldn't you buy?

Pine furniture. Most of things from Ikea. I detest with a passion far more furniture than I could actually give houseroom to. We look at MFI, there's loads of MFI and DFS sale adverts on, and I can't imagine what kind of a person buys that stuff. It's horrible, it makes my skin crawl. (Peter, retro enthusiast, 2006)

We were watching an advert for DFS and I was just going "that is horrible, that's even more horrible, and that's even more horrible than the last." I think that kind of mass produced un-individual stuff that is probably quite cheaply made and isn't built to last and you know in two or three years whoever buys that is going to be looking for something else, either because fashion dictates or the item itself has not worn well. (Mary, retro enthusiast, 2006)

Although the quality of the furniture sold by these retailers may well be inferior to original retro objects, these attitudes also differentiate enthusiasts from the masses. In the case of Peter, his distaste is so strong that he experiences a physical reaction to furniture he considers to be badly designed. He also says that he "cannot imagine the kind of person" who would buy that sort of furniture, therefore distancing himself from retailers and individuals with taste he considers inferior. The use of brands as a marker of distance and differentiation was also evident when Louise described her taste:

I'd like to think we were understated and we weren't ostentatious. What I'm trying to say is if you go out and buy a leather sofa it's flashy in the wrong way. The "price is right" type of person. Mums that buy three for a fiver at Asda. (Louise, retro enthusiast, 2006)

In all three quotes certain brands function as metaphors for the working class and are forms of symbolic violence. Distaste is not made obvious or communicated directly but put onto the type of person who would shop at DFS or Asda (budget retailers in Britain). This is a product of the majority of interviewees being very cautious about being thought of as snobs because these are the very people that the majority of retro enthusiasts would like to distance themselves from. To emphasize this point, after the discussion of the DFS adverts, MFI or Ikea, enthusiasts would often add, "Well, even at those shops you might find the odd good thing." Indeed, as suggested above, retro enthusiasts may find the "odd thing" in one of these shops, and its origin would not detract from its value. If anything it would add to enthusiasts' status because it would demonstrate their ability to find retro furniture in the most unlikely of places.

Similar attitudes were also evident in the way interviewees described the types of interiors they did not like. Although enthusiasts talked about bad types of revival, they were more reluctant to describe other types of bad taste.

Instead, they suggested that it was the level of effort and commitment to creating an interior that was important. For example, for Andy and Peter people with bad taste are those who furnish their whole house with Ikea furniture without making any "effort to choose the furniture themselves." This does two things: it links bad taste with those who might be duped by the promotional strategies of high street retailers, and it also associates good taste with subject, rather than object, unity. Peter Corrigan (1997) suggests that subject unity is created by the "imposition of the personal biography onto stylistic order" (Corrigan quoted in Southerton, 2001b:165–166). This is in contrast to object unity, whereby objects are matched according to brand, range or type. Southerton applied Corrigan's terms in his study of kitchen consumption. He found that middle-class respondents with high cultural capital tended to have no qualms about mixing and matching objects and styles, whereas working-class respondents were more likely to discuss their interiors in terms of object unity, for example, by matching objects in their kitchens according to sets or color patterns. Thus, although the valuing of stylistic unity may appear less hierarchical, these views of good and bad taste continue to communicate class differences.

The reference to effort is also interesting in Andy's and Peter's responses and was evident in other enthusiasts' discussions of bad taste. Although Marianne usually likes what others would consider bad taste, she thought that putting no effort into interior decoration would be less appealing. Mary also suggested that although she did not like 1970s or arts and crafts styles herself, she could appreciate these interiors because at least their owners "liked something different." In these responses, effort appears to be something that anyone could put into decorating their interior. In some respects this is true because effort does not require money or good taste. However, this depends on how effort is defined. It seems to me that there is as much, or even more, effort required in going to Ikea than in going to a retro boutique. For retro enthusiasts, effort is intimately linked to cultural capital and the display of individuality through the avoidance of mass taste. The theorists quoted above suggest that this is characteristic of the values of the middle class. To explore whether this is the case, I now consider the social position of retro enthusiasts in more detail.

IDENTIFYING RETRO ENTHUSIASTS

Using Southerton's (2001b) and Taylor's (2008) studies of domestic culture I have explored similarities between the tastes and values of retro enthusiasts and those of middle-class homemakers. However, the middle classes are internally differentiated. Retro enthusiasts' interiors, their preferences and their views of bad taste locate them even more precisely in social space. The majority of retro enthusiasts differentiate themselves from those who collect and display antiques, a practice associated with the upper middle class and older generations. Through their distaste for other types of revival, such as the styles of the pub and the country cottage, they distance themselves from "provincial" lower-middle-class taste. In their attitudes toward high street brands and fashion, they also consider themselves different from the working class.

These dispositions are similar to those that Bourdieu associated with the "new middle classes" in *Distinction* (2005 [1979]). In 1960s France, he suggested that the new bourgeoisie and the new petite bourgeoisie stood aloof from the "uptight" older dominant classes and marked themselves as different from the working class (Bourdieu, 2005 [1979]: 310–311, 362). He noted that the new bourgeoisie and new petite bourgeoisie worked in the creative and media industries and were the most developed in Paris. Bourdieu observed that these groups embraced "laidback" and aestheticized lifestyles, which included substituting "rustic" items for antiques and purchasing furniture from flea markets. Therefore, although Bourdieu does not refer to retro style in *Distinction,* the values he associates with the new middle classes are similar to those held by retro enthusiasts.

More recent studies of the middle class in Britain have identified similar groups. For example, Mike Savage, James Barlow and colleagues (1992) identify a section of the middle classes for which style and cultural capital are a key asset (in combination with economic, property and organizational assets). They classify this group as "postmodern" and observe that they are more likely to have high levels of educational achievement. Although Savage and colleagues recognize similar traits in the postmodern middle class to those that Bourdieu identified in the new bourgeoisie and new petite bourgeoisie, they suggest that "what were once practices of an 'alternative' middle-class minority resisting materialism . . . have now been adopted on a much larger scale by those with much greater economic resources" (1992:113). Thus, they argue that the 1960s counterculture "has been transformed into a 1990s-style post-modern cultural conformity" (Savage, Barlow *et al.,* 1992:113).

As shown in more detail in Appendix 1, the upbringings, occupations and educational backgrounds of the majority of retro enthusiasts interviewed in this study position them as part of the middle class. Of the twelve enthusiasts interviewed, eight had fathers who worked in professional occupations. These included lecturers, bank managers, engineers and psychologists. Half of the interviewees' mothers were housewives; of those in employment all apart from one had occupations categorized as professional. This is significantly different from the backgrounds of most of the retro retailers outlined in Chapter 5. Apart from three enthusiasts, who are discussed below in more detail, most described their backgrounds, home life and childhood as "comfortable." In fact, many viewed their own standard of living as similar to that of their parents.

There were also similarities between enthusiasts' occupations and those of their parents. Eleven out of twelve retro enthusiasts were categorized as professional. Occupations included a marketing consultant, a civil servant, a software house director and a graphic designer. These findings reinforce those of Savage, Barlow and colleagues (1992) who suggest that those with greater economic resources have adopted the values and aesthetics of the "alternative" middle class. However, the majority of enthusiasts were also employed in "softer" industries and had jobs that depended more on cultural capital than those of their parents. This may be a result of retro enthusiasts' specific skills and interests. It may also be a product of the increased importance of culture and aesthetics in the British economy, particularly in urban areas (du Gay and Pryke, 2002). In fact, all enthusiasts lived in cities well known for their cultural and artistic communities.

Nine out of twelve retro enthusiasts had the equivalent of a BA (Hons) qualification or higher, and this meant that their cultural capital had been authorized by educational institutions. However, while retro style has been linked to arts education in previous studies (McRobbie, 1989), only three out of the twelve interviewees had been to art college. This was lower than I expected and is perhaps the product of a relatively small sample. It may be a result of those with art school backgrounds being less likely to identify themselves as specifically interested in retro, a point I come back to below.

Educational qualifications were higher among retro enthusiasts than retro retailers. This is illustrative of the greater ease with which individuals from middle-class backgrounds can convert cultural resources into educational qualifications and into occupations with higher salaries. Levels of academic qualification are particularly relevant to the discussion of the three individuals who were not from middle-class backgrounds in this study: Chris, Suzy and Dave. Chris and Suzy both went to university and now work in middle-class occupations. Dave did not go to university and is a DJ. He supplements his income working as a painter and decorator.

In many ways the biographies and homes of these three individuals are the most interesting. They are evidence of the way in which the relationship between class background, education and taste is made more complex by a number of factors, including the expansion of higher education and the role of the media in the circulation of tastes. Thus, in the next part of this chapter, I discuss the ways in which the interiors and tastes of retro enthusiasts are internally differentiated and how, and indeed if, this relates to social, economic and cultural capital.

RETRO INTERIORS OR RETRO LIVES

While retro enthusiasts' homes were similar in the type of furniture they displayed, they were divided in the way they mixed objects and styles. The retro homes I encountered could be separated into two distinct groups: one that had a more eclectic mix of retro styles and one that demonstrated a highly committed interest to a specific period. This was made obvious not only by the style of enthusiasts' interiors but also by their own descriptions of their tastes.

The first group appropriated objects and styles from different decades, juxtaposed retro pieces with other styles of furniture and described their taste as eclectic. Although members of this group were linked by their eclecticism, this had two different manifestations. There were those who mixed retro styles with antiques (for example, Catherine and Thomas displayed art deco pieces of furniture alongside older items), and there were those who mixed retro styles with modern design (for example, Louise and Andy had a new and modern-looking kitchen).

Those people who mixed retro styles with modern design were younger and tended to have been involved in youth and music cultures in the 1970s and 1980s. These enthusiasts' homes were not unlike those displayed on the pages of high-end lifestyle magazines, such as *Elle Decoration*. In addition to being eclectic, these interiors had changed over time. For example, Andy and Louise told me that their furniture had gradually become "more sophisticated."

At the same time, however, all enthusiasts with eclectic interiors were keen to disassociate their tastes from fashionable interiors shown by retailers or in the media. They preferred to think of themselves as creating unique and desirable homes, and in this regard they emphasized subject unity more than those enthusiasts committed to one particular period. This "imposition of the personal biography onto the stylistic order" results in enthusiasts conceptualizing their tastes as distinct from the masses but also different from those of their acquaintances, friends and family (Southerton, 2001b:165).

In fact, the enthusiasts with eclectic interiors went out of their way to stress their unique style and even relished other people's disapproval of their taste. For example, Catherine laughed when she said that most people think the ceramic heads she collects are "weird," and Louise emphasized that she was the only one in her family who saw the fashionable potential in the belongings of her grandfather. Enthusiasts with eclectic interiors thought of their tastes as marginal and felt that only those with an aesthetically trained eye would understand their interior choices. Both Catherine and Louise said that on the odd occasion when friends and family did appreciate their tastes, it was because they had an interest in art. Of the five households with more eclectic interiors, three had been co-created by individuals who had been to art college.

Thus, it may be art education that gave Catherine, Marianne and Louise the capacity and the confidence to legitimate their own unique tastes and to describe themselves as completely different from those around them. Perhaps this also indicates why people involved in the arts may be less likely to categorize their taste as retro, preferring to think of it as completely individual.

Although no one in the two other eclectic households had been to art college, Suzy's and Sylvia's tastes seemed to have been influenced and partly legitimated by their occupations. Suzy's past experiences in retro retailing, in combination with her social mobility, contributed to her and her partner emphasizing the individuality of their tastes. For example, when showing me their 1950s cocktail bar, Suzy said proudly, "That's one of those things someone can really hate." This was reinforced by her reaction to the question about what their family and friends thought of their taste. With a large smile Suzy said, "They all think it is blinking odd."

Sylvia also mentioned that her taste for retro and eclectic display of furniture and decorative objects had been influenced by her job in arts marketing and was quite different from that of her friends. However, Chris, Sylvia's partner, is a prolific collector and collects objects according to brand and type. Chris goes to collecting fairs and car boot sales and has friends who have many of the same interests. The combination of an individual who prefers eclectic interiors and one who collects one type of object living in the same household creates a number of tensions, which are explored in more detail below.

The second group of retro enthusiasts were committed to one specific period or decade and had thoroughly retro lifestyles. For example, Mary and Peter described their taste as specifically 1930s and 1940s. They wore clothes from the period and wanted to give me an authentic 1930s and 1940s experience: they played 1930s music throughout my visit, and Peter made a fire rather than putting on the central heating. Dave, the other enthusiast committed to one period, described his taste very specifically as "1964 to 1973 syndrome." This meant that, like Mary and Peter, he had very few modern items in his home, and he wore retro clothes most of the time.

Peter and Mary and Dave all lived in homes designed and built in their eras of interest. This meant they were able to buy retro furniture and decorative objects that they were attracted to and not worry about whether they would fit with the style of their properties. For example, Peter and Mary had always wanted an art deco dining table, and their art deco house meant they had the perfect space to put it in. Dave lived in a block of flats designed in the 1960s, which until recently had its original kitchen.[4] Whether an interest in retro leads to the purchase of an architecturally retro house, or the house encourages this interest, is difficult to determine. In the case of Peter and Mary, the interest led to the house because they "scoured the county" for an art deco property, and when they found one, they approached the owners even though the house was not for sale. Whether cause or effect, I found that similarities between the architectural style of a property and its interior were representative of a high level of commitment to retro style. In Peter and Mary's house and in Dave's flat, retro objects from different periods were hidden away, if acquired at all.

The commitment that Peter, Mary and Dave demonstrate toward one particular style is part of their involvement in style and music cultures. This was obvious when they talked about other people's reactions to their tastes.

> Yeah, I think people think it's quite unusual and I think they think it's unusual in a positive way, but you definitely feel that you are not in the mainstream. Um, for example people at work will say "I'm going to DFS to get a new sofa" and they are as excited about that as we were about finding this suite, but you do feel that you are out of the mainstream. But then you meet people who are into the same sort of thing and you will have like an hour long conversation about Bakerlite or Vitralite or Lucite jewellery or something like that and you realize there is a strata of society who are interested in that sort of stuff. (Mary, retro enthusiast, 2006)

Thus, although Peter, Mary and Dave talk about their taste as being different from that of their families and the majority of society, they have similar taste to their friends. They think of themselves as belonging to groups of unique but similar individuals, who have retro lifestyles as well as retro interiors. Because of this they put less emphasis on individuality than the enthusiasts discussed above. While they use their own biographies to legitimate their styles (the way Dave does this is particularly interesting and is explored in more detail below), their adherence to a style code or particular era also seems to represent object as well as subject unity (Southerton, 2001b:165–166). Although there are many possible reasons for an extreme commitment to one particular style, Peter, Mary and Dave did not go to art college and seem to have less of a general interest in art and design. Thus, although it is difficult to come to any conclusion with such a small sample, it may be that highly committed retro lifestyles are a cause and effect of lower levels of cultural capital. As Matt Hills suggests, "Alternative forms of cultural resources are likely to appeal to those who either lack official cultural capital, or those who have yet to convert high levels of cultural and educational capital into economic capital" (2002:59). For those with less cultural capital, involvement in retro groups and scenes helps to mark tastes as legitimate. High levels of commitment also define these enthusiasts' tastes as distinctively retro rather than old-fashioned.

Thus, I would suggest that it is involvement with three contexts that make an interest in retro more likely and that enable enthusiasts to change old objects into retro ones. These are arts education, retro retailing and retro scenes. The first two are related to institutions (education and the arts) and to business. Retro scenes, however, are less institutionalized; therefore, knowledge gained from involvement in them generates less external reward. For example, Mary and Peter's knowledge of the manufacturing process of their 1950s English Rose kitchen is highly specialist and less likely to be convertible into economic capital than a broad knowledge of fashion and design—unless lifestyles like Peter and Mary's are appropriated and legitimated by the media, the effects of which I now consider.

OLD WORKING-CLASS OBJECTS AND OLD WORKING-CLASS IDENTITIES

Earlier in this chapter I suggested that retro enthusiasts' attitudes toward bad taste demonstrate their valuing of connoisseurship, originality and authenticity, which have their origins in the discourses of modernism. However, I also found that retro enthusiasts use these notions relatively fluidly, and the majority attempt to avoid notions of high culture, which are associated with bourgeois snobbery. The appropriation and revaluing of pieces of furniture and decorative objects that are considered old-fashioned or were previously associated with the working class are manifestations of the latter sensibility, and it is this aspect of retro style I want to focus on now.

In Chapters 1 and 2 of this book, I observed that a key facet of retro style was the transformation of objects that were previously considered old-fashioned, popular and kitsch into fashionable and high art objects. Many of these types of furniture and decorative pieces were present in retro enthusiasts' homes. Cocktail bars, Midwinter china, 1960s brightly colored glass, 1930s plaster heads and 1970s tiled coffee tables are among the objects that fit into this category. In their first lives these pieces were associated with lower-middle-class and working-class décor and were viewed as kitsch and in bad taste (Gillilan, 2003). Enthusiasts were well aware of these associations, and this was part of their attraction. For example, when discussing his cocktail bar and matching drinks display, Tim said, "Well, isn't this tacky!"

The appropriation and redefinition of these objects and styles by middle-class retro enthusiasts could be argued to be evidence of cultural omnivorousness. Cultural omnivores are individuals who consume a wide range of cultural forms. The concept is most frequently associated with Richard Peterson and Roger Kern, who argued that "the aesthetics of elite status are being redefined as the appreciation of all distinctive leisure activities and creative forms along with the appreciation of the classic fine arts" (Peterson and Kern, 1996:252). The change that Peterson and Kern observed in the middle classes is partly a result of the strategies of cultural intermediaries and outside intellectuals who legitimized the celebration of popular and marginal tastes (Featherstone, 1991). As Featherstone argues, it was not a question of this group "promoting a particular style, but rather catering for and promoting a general interest in style itself, the nostalgia for past styles, the interest in the latest style" (1991:93). However, unlike Featherstone, who was much more skeptical about the egalitarian nature of this change (1991:84), some theorists of cultural omnivorousness have suggested that cultural omnivores represent a democratization of taste and greater tolerance (Bryson, 1997; Peterson and Kern, 1996).

Others have questioned these conclusions and argued that omnivorousness reinforces middle-class distinctions (Brooks, 2000; Erickson, 1996; Skeggs, 2004a). For example, as outlined in Chapter 5, Skeggs observes that middle-class status relies on knowledge of other cultures and the "display of access to the culture and resources of others" (2004a:148). She suggests that it is increasingly working-class cultures, rather than foreign cultures, that are plundered to demonstrate and reinforce cultural capital (Skeggs, 2004a:144).

In agreement, I would question whether the appropriation of pieces of furniture and decorative objects previously associated with the working class represents a democratization of taste. As evidenced by the hierarchy of acquisition in Chapter 5 and the discussions above, the ability to redefine retro objects previously categorized as old-fashioned or associated with the working classes is partly dependent on their contextualization in relatively clutterless gallery-like spaces and the way in which they are discussed in terms of authenticity and connoisseurship. It is also partly contingent on the ability of the objects' owners to mark their tastes and their identities as individual and as distinct from the masses. Thus, I would agree with Holt's (1997) criticisms of empirical studies of cultural omnivorousness as blind to processes of distinction because they focus too much on cultural forms (what is consumed) without considering cultural practice (how they are consumed).

Lury (1998) has argued for an approach to consumption in which processes of accumulation are even more central. She suggests that rather than what or even how things are consumed, value and status increasingly lie in the trying on and taking off of cultural resources. Using the example of photography, she argues that the terms of self-possession originally encouraged by liberal democratic societies are being "renegotiated in a process of experimentation" (1998:1). Lury suggests that defining characteristics that were viewed as fixed, such as consciousness, memory and embodiment, are increasingly sites of strategic decision making, technique or experimentation. She calls this "prosthetic culture" (1998:2). For example, in a discussion of the advertising strategies of Bennetton, Lury (2006) argues that race has been reworked from biological or natural essence to become a matter of choice. She suggests that race is founded in culture and is used as a "medium of difference" available to us all (2006:263). Biology and nature have not been used to explain and legitimate class differences to the same degree as they have for race; however, choice has become increasingly central to the discussion of class (Skeggs, 2004a:138–139). The identity of the middle classes has become one defined by "compulsory individuality" and the freedom to choose (Cronin, 2000:279; Strathern, 1992). Like race in Lury's discussion of Bennetton's advertising campaigns, class was also conceptualized by some retro enthusiasts as an identity to be played with.

Of the twelve enthusiasts interviewed, six identified themselves as working class or as having working-class "roots," although three were from middle-class backgrounds. While this discrepancy could be due to a lack of confidence in handling class labels and understanding sociological terms, I also think that it demonstrates flexibility in the way that enthusiasts think about class. By mentioning their "working-classness" enthusiasts claim an "ordinary" identity. For example, interviewees spoke fondly and proudly about their associations with parents or family members who are, or were, working class. While these experiences inevitably influence interviewees' own positions and tastes, they also establish their ordinariness. For example, in the following quote from Andy he briefly mentions his own middle-class status but then quickly goes on to talk about the background of his father in more detail.

> I suppose I'm typically middle class. My Dad's traditionally working class, he's from Manchester, which doesn't mean he's working class, but he's from a fairly working-class background. (Andy, retro enthusiast, 2006)

These findings echo Mike Savage, Gaynor Bagnall and Brian Longhurst's research, in which they suggest that "a common theme in people's perspectives on class is their desire to be 'ordinary' and not to appear 'above' others" (2000:117). They argue that this indicates a "strong populist critique of high culture," which is seen as a violation of "ordinariness" and does not allow people to "be themselves" (2000:118). At the same time, by mentioning their working-class connections, enthusiasts claim authentic and different identities. Both these themes were apparent in Mary's response when I asked about her own class position.

> I think I see myself as a class that doesn't even exist anymore. I see myself as that '40s, '50s housewife who wears high heels round the home. Somebody said to me I ought to have a finishing school. I don't know modern class wise. I don't like to think of my self as middle class because it's a bit Daily Mail readerish, I'd rather be one thing or the other than be in the middle really. So I suppose I would call myself working class. (Mary, retro enthusiast, 2006)

For Mary, claiming a working-class identity is about not being viewed as conservative or pretentious. It is about being different and not being "in the middle." It is also nostalgic about the identity of the 1940s and 1950s house-wife. This imagined identity is particularly interesting in terms of gender and is discussed in more detail in the next chapter.

While Mary's response may well indicate a desire to be antihierarchical, fantasies regarding working-class identity and the valuing of objects previously associated with the working class usually come from a position of distance. As Skeggs notes, when objects are valued precisely because they are tacky, "the person who is doing the naming is usually of significance" (2004a:107). Naming something as tacky demonstrates knowledge of the prior negative significance of the object or identity, without one's taste or identity being marked as in bad taste or as working class. In the cases explored here, the identities and objects that are appropriated are temporally and spatially distant from the retro enthusiasts themselves. The majority do not come from working-class backgrounds; for those who did and now occupy middle-class positions (Chris and Suzy) retro styles are relatively "safe." This is because retro styles are different from the current working-class tastes from which many enthusiasts are keen to disassociate themselves. Thus, it could be argued, as Skeggs (2004a) does, that the plundering of working-class culture is not just a demonstration of authenticity and cultural capital by factions of the middle classes but contributes to the maintenance of class difference. While some of the styles, tastes and affects of the working class are fetishized and valued when attached to the middle-class self, others are beyond appropriation and continue to be denigrated.[5] However, because retro styles are also temporally distant, it may mean that those from working-class backgrounds can participate in the practices related to the creation of a retro interior and capitalize on the cultural capital that an interest in retro creates.

To reflect on this question I focus on one retro enthusiast in this study, Dave. When I conducted my research, Dave was working as a DJ and a painter and decorator. Although he was slightly uneasy with categorizations, he described himself as working class.

> Ah, I hate class. I think, obviously I suppose I'm working class, but the thing is when there are lots of working class people like myself, as you grow older you can educate yourself, self-education really, from life. (Dave, retro enthusiast, 2007)

As Dave implies when talking about his "self-education from life," it is his involvement in, and passion for, the northern soul scene that has given him an interest in, and in-depth knowledge of, retro style and the social and cultural history of the 1960s and 1970s. Partly because of his knowledge of and commitment to northern soul, Dave has been on television programs, in short films and has been used as a model in advertisements. The media interest in Dave is also due to his style, identity and the way he talks about his life.

In the interview, it seemed as though he had regularly spoken to journalists and academics about his life story, style and domestic interior. All the enthusiasts I interviewed enjoyed talking about their homes. However, Dave, like the tastemakers I interviewed, was extremely comfortable with this process, and his answers were often given in sound bites perfect for a lifestyle magazine article. He was also keen to emphasize his working-class roots and talked in great detail about his childhood in the 1960s. In a recent documentary about Dave and northern soul, his first line is:

> Most people onto this scene, were always, yer they were, your bog standard working-class people. As regards to where the actual people who made the music actually came from, again that becomes an obvious thing as well, they were just people from the absolute depths, people from the gutter. (Dave, retro enthusiast, 2008)

The camera then pans to a photograph in Dave's flat. He also described the photograph to me in the interview I conducted with him. When showing me it, he said,

> For me this is the most beautiful photo in the world. The photo is by an artist called Shirley Baker and it's from 1965 and it's actually set in Hulme, here, and it's my favourite photo in the world. That sense of, it's real inner city life, and it's absolute deprivation. We were children at that time, where all of us had to find, we had to find our own things because we had nothing. It was based around a rope swing or conkers or marbles in the street. We had to find our own sense of something. (Dave, retro enthusiast, 2007)

Dave's description of the interior of his flat, like this quote, is peppered with nostalgic talk for working-class life. I don't doubt that many people involved in the northern soul scene are from working-class backgrounds. Neither do I want to question Dave's pride in his identity. However, the amount of emphasis that Dave places on his working-class roots and his experiences of the northern soul scene seems to suggest he is aware of their cultural value. As I argued in Chapter 4, cultural resources gained in music and youth cultures have become more widely accepted as cool and legitimated by the market and media. Thus, Dave's cultural resources have been recognized and legitimated as cultural capital. However, like for the retro retailers I explored in Chapter 5, cultural capital legitimated by the market or the media is more difficult to convert into material reward than cultural capital legitimated by the education system. In addition, Dave may be less able to play with identity than his middle-class counterparts because he is marked *as* authentically working class, rather than being in a position to appropriate some of its attractive and exchangeable qualities. Thus, while cultural capital may be more fluid and valorized by the market and the media, it is in combination with social and economic capital that cultural capital makes class.

RETRO STYLE AND AN EVERYDAY AESTHETICS

The appeal of past working-class objects and identities, as well as that of retro style more generally, should not only be thought of as following the logic of exchange. While the metaphor of capital is usual for exploring contemporary class relations as I have done here, it does not (and cannot) capture all of social and material life. As I suggested earlier in the book, lifestyle choices are also "ethical and sensual responses to the world" (Highmore, 2011:11). In the last part of this chapter I briefly explore some of these experiences and sentiments. Of course, in the right hands and in the appropriate context anything can become capital, particularly because that which is the most illusive is frequently the most desirable.

In retro enthusiasts' responses to questions regarding class and taste there was a strong sense that they did not want to criticize other people or their choices. While cultural distinction was communicated by talk of good and bad brands, the desire not to be above others should not be dismissed. As Andrew Sayer has suggested, "People may be, or want to be, respectful, considerate and warm to individuals from other classes," but these feelings have often gone unrecognized in social and cultural theory (2005:1). By discussing the moral significance of class, Sayer highlights the importance of mutual respect, benevolence and compassion, as well as disgust, contempt and shame when examining class relations. Perhaps, then, in retro enthusiasts' attitudes toward class and taste there is a desire to be less hierarchical, even if the consumption of retro style is a middle-class practice. Therefore, while retro style may not go beyond class boundaries in the way McRobbie (1989) theorized, the legacy of its radical beginnings in the 1960s counterculture may still inform enthusiasts' attitudes and make them more open to critical discourses about class relations.

The appeal of past working-class identities and objects is also due to the cultural associations they embody. While retro enthusiasts are temporally and spatially distant from the cultures from which they appropriate, their responses contain visions of past working-class culture. These times are imagined as simpler and less focused on the acquisition of branded goods. In their own practices Peter and Mary recreated this sensibility by reusing as much as they could; once they had found the perfect item, they claimed to keep it in their home for longer than most people. Past lives were also thought of as more social, with family members seeing each other more and having more time to spend together. In Andy and Louise's home the retro dining table was the place where they sat down to eat together as they had "done as kids." The feelings of having more time that were associated with the past were also talked about in terms of dress. Peter and Mary spoke of their dismay at the fact that nowadays people would wear the same clothes to clean the car, go to work and go to the theater, and they compared this to the formal glamour of past periods. In their everyday practices they tried to mark out activities by dressing up or down. In the design of retro homes many enthusiasts also attempt to contain the ways that modern technologies impact on their lives. As discussed above, many enthusiasts had separate rooms for watching television and using the computer.

While visions of past working-class life as more social, more leisurely and simpler may well be more of a romantic fiction than a reality, they represent a longing for conditions that retro enthusiasts find to be lacking in contemporary life. Rather than being read as a retreat into the past and into the home, this nostalgia could be interpreted more positively. As Michael Pickering and Emily Keightley argue, rather than unproductive melancholia, nostalgia can be seen as a "desire for engagement with difference, with aspiration and critique, and with the identification of ways of living lacking in modernity" (2006:921). In this respect a longing for the past can be thought of as a resource for the future. I return to consider this point in relation to gender in the next chapter.

A desire for sociality is part of retro enthusiasts' love of original artifacts. When talking about the secondhand objects they owned, interviewees would frequently refer to patina. While the patina that is added to new retro objects in the manufacturing process may look similar, retro enthusiasts feel that it does not have all the same qualities or authentic iconicity. Patina on secondhand objects is created over time and by different people, and it is these qualities that make retro enthusiasts feel connected with previous users. Thus, through collecting and acquiring original objects enthusiasts are connecting with the material world as well as previous users. As Highmore (2011) suggests, possession is not only about owning property; things also possess us. The homes enthusiasts live in, as well as the objects they possess, change their practices. Highmore writes that

> to be possessed by things (rather than simply possessing them) interrupts the endless cycle of newness and obsolescence. To enter into the lure of a things intransigent status is to be in part possessed by the thing-ness of things and to lose the I-ness of self" (2011:81).

By this Highmore means that practices of acquisition and collecting can be understood as an attempt to dissolve the self into its nonhuman environment rather than to represent, or accrue objects to, the self. Due to its ubiquity collecting may well be illustrative of this argument. While collecting is part of consumer society (Belk, 1995), less commodified objects, such as conkers, shells and lucky charms, were collected prior to the industrial revolution. For example, collections of interesting rocks, fossils and shells have even been found in Cro-Magnon caves (Pomian, 1990).

In the case of retro style, collecting is also interesting because it often disrupts the dominant aesthetics of good taste. The homes of people who collect can become crowded and cluttered; it is for this reason that some retro enthusiasts stop collecting. For example, Jan and Dave no longer purchased new pieces because of the lack of space in their homes. They were keen that the furniture and decorative objects they had already bought should be exhibited and should have enough space to be admired. They both said that they were tempted by new objects but managed to "control themselves." Chris, however, was not deterred by lack of space because he was not as motivated by display as the other enthusiasts. Chris collected Midwinter pottery and glass bottles, among other items. Much to his partner Sylvia's dismay, Chris had lots of items around the house, in boxes in the loft and in sheds (one of which he purchased specifically to accommodate his growing collection). The difference between the ways that Sylvia and Chris thought about retro objects is illustrated by this quote:

> Chris is different, he hoards everything and what I keep on saying is that I would rather he would trim his collection down and have the most beautiful collection and cabinets to display things. But for me, again, maybe that's my background in museums and galleries, it is about displaying things. Whereas for Chris we've got boxes and boxes of Midwinter in the loft and I just think it is sad, either not to use them, which I would love to use them on a daily basis, some of the dinner services and things like this, um, but Chris wouldn't dare, you can't touch them, but then you can't see them either, so I think it is sad. (Sylvia, retro enthusiast, 2006)

Even when the objects were put in display cases that had been purchased by Sylvia, Chris's collecting practices, such as leaving the sale price on objects, compromised the look of the display. For Chris, the process of collecting was almost as important as the aesthetics of the objects themselves. He enjoyed finding the correct item to complete a set as well as packing and unpacking the objects he had acquired. This makes the type of collecting that Chris was involved in less exchangeable. Compared to the other enthusiasts his activities do not reflect or add to such high levels of cultural capital. This is not to suggest that the practices of the other retro enthusiasts always constitute, reflect or add to cultural capital either. They, like Chris, also have affective, practical and emotional relationships with their retro objects.

CONCLUSION

This chapter has concentrated on retro enthusiasts, their tastes and domestic interiors. I began by documenting the types of retro objects commonly found in enthusiasts' homes. I found that the inspiration for retro interiors usually came from the decades between 1930 and 1970, with art deco and 1960s styles being the most popular. Retro interiors usually included a number of items that had previously been associated with working-class and popular tastes, such as brightly colored glass, cocktail bars and tiled coffee tables. Enthusiasts were well aware of these associations, and this was part of the reason the items were valued.

I also observed that a number of statement pieces of furniture were common in retro enthusiasts' homes. These included jukeboxes, radiograms, cocktail cabinets and sideboards. In addition, display cases and shelving were important because they helped to create gallery-like spaces where retro pieces could be exhibited and admired. This aesthetic differentiated retro enthusiasts' tastes from other interiors associated with revival such as the pub or the country cottage. Drawing on these observations, I suggested that ideal retro homes were material manifestations of the aestheticization of everyday life.

I also documented how a number of factors limit the creation of an ideal retro interior. For instance, life circumstances may mean that homes are temporary or too small for large retro collections. New technologies used for domestic tasks and leisure activities also compromise the look of the interior. In addition, children affect the organization and role of domestic space. Nevertheless, most retro enthusiasts find solutions to these issues that do not compromise the aesthetic of their homes. Sometimes this makes the interiors and practices of retro enthusiasts significantly different from those of the majority of homemakers; for example, retro enthusiasts are much less likely to "do comfort."

Yet retro enthusiasts conceptualized their tastes in terms of originality, individuality and quality in a similar way to the rest of the middle class. This was unsurprising because, unlike retro retailers, the majority of retro enthusiasts were from middle-class backgrounds and most had higher education qualifications. Retro enthusiasts individuated their interiors through authenticity and connoisseurship and frequently talked about quality in terms of rarity and origin. They also conceptualized their own tastes in opposition to a homogeneous mass of consumers, a sensibility found to be common among the middle class (Southerton, 2001b:167). Such views were most overt among those who had been educated in art colleges and who thought of their tastes as distinctive from those of their friends and family. This type of enthusiast was also more likely to have an eclectic retro interior, similar to the ones found in lifestyle magazines such as *Elle Decoration*.

Among most enthusiasts, the aversion to the masses manifested itself in distaste toward high street retailers and people who "followed fashion," and I suggested that this was a form of symbolic violence. I argued that instead of making definite statements about bad taste, enthusiasts discussed value in terms of the authentic iconicity of brands and past styles. Rather than being communicated through the consumption of original objects, good taste was established by appropriating objects with authentic stylistic characteristics. I observed that some retro enthusiasts even thought of their class identities in these terms. I went on to argue that a preference for authentic working-class styles and identities was premised on social distance: on being able to appropriate without being marked as old-fashioned or working class.

However, three of the enthusiasts were from working-class backgrounds. Two had gained educational qualifications that had legitimated their knowledge and given them cultural and economic capital (through their occupations). As discussed in Chapter 4, one of these enthusiasts had also been involved in the selling or retailing of retro style. One other enthusiast was from a working-class background and continued to lead a less privileged lifestyle. I argued that because of the wider valuing of knowledge associated with youth subcultures, his cultural resources had become cultural capital. However, I suggested that the extent to which this cultural capital could be converted into economic capital was limited. This is partly because those in working-class positions are less able to play with their identities. They are marked as authentically working class rather than being able to appropriate its desirable and exchangeable qualities.

Throughout the chapter, however, it is clear that a taste for retro style is about more than the accumulation of capital. Retro objects symbolize important emotional relationships, and through patina they link enthusiasts with previous users. The views of retro enthusiasts also indicate a desire to be antihierarchical, even if distinctions continued to be played out through taste. In addition, retro enthusiasts' practices indicate a desire to connect to the nonhuman environment as well as to live differently. I consider some of these issues in the final chapters of the book.

8

Retro Femininities and Domestic Labor

In the late 1980s Angela McRobbie suggested that the consumption of retro styles allowed women to play with "the norms, conventions and expectations of femininity" (1989, reprinted in 1994:148). She argued that pastiche was not necessarily depthless or meaningless. This perspective was informed by feminist critiques of modernist discourse that problematized the way interest in decoration had been viewed as superficial and questioned why superficiality had become equated with the feminine. In this chapter I explore this argument by analyzing the tastes and practices of retro enthusiasts. As the title of the chapter suggests, I include a discussion of domestic labor and draw on feminist theorizations of the activities that go on in the home. I use the concept of domestic labor in a broad sense to include homemaking as well as housework, physical as well as emotional labor. I combine an analysis of lifestyle media and responses from online forums with my ethnographic work to look more widely at how retro aesthetics are used to reinforce or to question normative gender roles.

I begin the chapter by discussing previous academic work that explores gender and modernist design and consider the activities of retro enthusiasts in relation to this body of knowledge. This includes an analysis of the gendering of interior decoration and furniture choices. These findings highlight the ways in which retro interiors are co-constructed, and thus I go on to explore how couples' relationships are central to the creation of the home. I consider enthusiasts' shopping and DIY (do-it-yourself) practices and the relevance of these practices to theories of capital as well as ideas regarding the home as a heterosexualized space.

In the analysis of enthusiasts' practices and their relationships, fantasies about past lives and identities emerge. In the second half of the chapter I explore these fantasies and their implications in terms of the division of domestic labor and gender relations. I focus specifically on femininity rather than masculinity because visions of past masculine identities, particularly the working-class hero, have been written about more extensively (e.g., Gregson and Crewe, 2003; Rutherford, 1992). I use the term *retro femininities* both to make connections between enthusiasts' love for retro and their gendered practices as well as to suggest that past gender identities are used as a resource and reworked in new contexts. In my view the concept of retro femininities is preferable to a term like *traditional femininity* that suggests stasis. I consider what the desire for retro femininities can tell us about women's lives in the present. I conclude the chapter by exploring what an analysis of the allure of past gender identities can offer a feminist politics.

GENDER, MODERNISM AND RETRO HOMES

The gendering of modernism and modernist design has been widely theorized (e.g., Attfield, 2007; Kirkham, 1996; Sparke, 1995). While I do not have the space to discuss all of these ideas here, I briefly outline modernist attitudes toward function, decoration and materials because, as Deborah Leslie and Suzanne Reimer suggest, these discourses "continue to enliven contemporary stories about domestic furniture" (2003:294). As discussed in the previous chapter, modernist aesthetics also influence the design of retro enthusiasts' domestic interiors.

Early modernist design (1914–1929) was committed to social and political reform based on the tenets of collectivism, standardization and social egalitarianism (Sparke, 2004:85). It was thought that one of the ways an egalitarian society could be achieved was through mass production and the use of new materials such as steel, plastic and fiberglass. Belief in the progressive possibilities of mechanization and technology also influenced other aspects of the design. Tied to the rational philosophy of "form follows function," discourses of modernism called for surface ornament to be expelled. For example, as Leslie and Reimer note, Le Corbusier viewed decoration as "pretense" and as "stuck on to disguise faults" (2003:296). This view extended to color as well as form, with modernist architects such as Le Corbusier favoring the "honesty" of black and white. This design manifesto was particularly evident in modernist attitudes toward the domestic interior. As Penny Sparke suggests, "Interior decoration lay completely outside the limits of modernism. Rooted in historicism and aimed at an elite and aspirational audience it betrayed most of modernism's rules and was looked upon with distaste by most modernists." After 1930, as Sparke suggests, the "object" of the modern movement, the machine aesthetic, spread throughout the world. In this process the modernist aesthetic became somewhat detached from the democratic beliefs it had engendered (2004:85).

As highlighted in the discussion of the history of retro in Chapter 4, even the early modernist movement was far from democratic. As Sparke has suggested, modernism related exclusively to male, white, middle-class values (2004:94). The "ordinary" domestic tastes of the public were to be swept away, and, in the case of social housing, modernist tastes were imposed on one class by another. Ornament was seen as "meaningless embellishment" and became thoroughly associated with bad taste (Negrin, 2006:223). When ornament was used, it was associated with the feminine (Sparke, 1995). Women frequently came under attack for their lack of taste, and the eclectic accumulation of bric-a-brac was viewed as a sign of feminine weakness. Aesthetic preferences for frills, unnecessary display and glitter were also marginalized. As Leslie and Reimer suggest, "Notions of craft, decoration, and ephemerality seen to be a part of mass culture, and coded as feminine, have long served as a binary Other to a functional and rational modernist project" (2003:298).

However, the masculinism of modernism is not as straightforward as it seems (Wolff, 2000). Femininity was part of modernist subjectivity, and the gendering of modernist design is often contradictory and ambiguous. For example, the work of furniture designers Charles and Ray Eames validates the "the pre-industrial, personal and the hand-made [characteristics associated with feminine tastes] as well as the industrial, the uniform and the mass-produced" (Kirkham, 1998:28). In addition, Margaret Maile Petty (2012) highlights the centrality of the "soft" architecture of curtains, upholstery and electric lighting in postwar domestic interiors, even if these elements were not necessarily valued by modernist architects or critics. However, despite the mixed provenance of modernist objects and the various ways that people lived in modernist interiors, modern design was frequently conceptualized as masculine.

In their study of the legacy of modernism Leslie and Reimer (2003) suggest that the gendering of the modern continues in recent times. They find that aesthetic preferences for chintz, frills and glitter continue to be coded as feminine and that women are encouraged to embrace modernist design to distance themselves from "traditional and oppressive constructions of femininity" (2003:313). Leslie and Reimer suggest that while both men and women may consume modernist furniture and create modernist interiors, there continues to be an implicit gendering behind these practices. This is illustrated by distinctions made between "hard" and "soft" as well as "warm" and "cold" interiors; public and private space in the home; and decoration and design.

These findings were replicated in retro enthusiasts' attitudes toward furniture and interior decoration. As documented in the previous chapter, the majority of male and female retro enthusiasts valued clean lines over clutter, cool colors over bright patterns, and minimalism over comfort. More than in the past,[1] and perhaps more than other homemakers, male retro enthusiasts were also central to the decoration of the home and were part of decisions about the appropriate furniture, paint colors and soft furnishings. For example, Tim spoke about the fabric their 1950s suite had been refurbished in. At first glance these findings seem to indicate that interior decoration is no longer coded as feminine and that modernist design has become gender neutral.

However, as in Leslie and Reimer's study, the gendering of domestic tastes and practices also persists in retro enthusiasts' homes, albeit in subtle ways. For example, women in the study were more likely to speak about spaces conceptualized as private, such as bathrooms and bedrooms, and had greater influence over the design of these rooms. For example, Suzy described the style of the bathroom as more "shabby chic" than the rest of the house. The bathroom had been refurbished using a reclaimed bath, basin and toilet. The floor had been sanded and whitewashed, and a large French ornate mirror had been hung on the wall. While Suzy had said to me that she "didn't do comfort," the room had a much warmer feel than the rest of the house. Tim admitted that this was "not his style," but he didn't really mind. Another female enthusiast, Mary, also spoke about the style of her and her partner Peter's bedroom. Mary was particularly fond of her dressing table, where she was able to do her 1940s-style hair and makeup. It is interesting that male retro enthusiasts were less involved in designing bedrooms and bathrooms, particularly when they were outspoken about their tastes in other spaces, including kitchens. This finding reinforces Leslie and Reimer's (2003:307) suggestion that modernism and masculinity remain associated with public spaces in the home and, conversely, that the private and the feminine continue to serve as modernism's Other. It is also indicative of changes in the use and meaning of the kitchen over time: from a private space for culinary and domestic work to a public space integral to the home and social life (Hand and Shove, 2004).

Occasionally, objects more likely to be associated with feminine tastes did enter into public spaces within retro enthusiasts' homes. Frequently, these were items that were viewed as kitsch and were chosen by women. For example, Louise showed me a 1950s-style domino clock that was indicative of the style of Louise and Andy's previous flat. Andy wanted to "get rid" of the clock because it was "too kitsch," but Louise was particularly fond of it. Mary also spoke of her penchant for kitsch "1950s bits," but these had been banished to a shelf above the computer in a small room off the lounge. Thus, in this respect at least, the aesthetic preferences of retro enthusiasts continue to be gendered because feminine tastes are thought of as frivolous in comparison to "good" modernist design.

In addition, as Leslie and Reimer suggest, "the gender politics of (neo) modernism cannot be read off straightforwardly from the emergence of more minimalist styles" (2003:312). The practicalities of living in such spaces also need exploring because the domestic work required for the maintenance of minimalist spaces can often reproduce normative gender roles. While retro enthusiasts did not speak about the amount of cleaning that their homes created, the furniture that retro enthusiasts chose to talk about was indicative of gendered practices within the home. Female retro enthusiasts valued more "practical" retro furniture such as sideboards, coffee tables and dressing tables. They emphasized the usefulness of these pieces of furniture in comparison to those made more recently. Dressing tables and sideboards were especially valuable because they contained other retro objects such as makeup compacts, ceramics and cutlery, and because they concealed the paraphernalia of contemporary living. For example, Louise mentioned that her 1960s sideboard was useful for hiding the children's things and her work papers. This was in contrast to male retro enthusiasts, who were more likely to talk about the statement pieces discussed in the previous chapter. Although the majority of male retro enthusiasts did some of the housework, the valuing of statement pieces may be illustrative of the type of engagement that men have with domestic space, an engagement based around leisure rather than everyday domestic labor. I return to this point below.

While domestic tastes and practices continue to be gendered, the gender politics of the revival of modernist aesthetics are different the second time around. Unlike modernism in the early twentieth century, the recent valuing of modernist styles is usually accompanied by a taste for eclecticism that juxtaposes old with new. Rather than being a sign of feminine weakness, appropriate eclecticism connotes good taste. This is evidence of the influence of postmodern design, which, as Sparke suggests, has allowed "feminine taste to be legitimized" (1995:10). In this study at least, both women and men valued this "softer version" of modernism (Grimshaw, 2004). In addition, men's participation in homemaking may be a sign of greater flexibility in terms of gender norms. This is evidence of a feminization of the modernist aesthetic and a masculinization of women's tastes, as well as an indication of changes in terms of what is expected of men and women in the home. Therefore, it is not only in the workplace that gender-related properties are no longer stuck to the person (Adkins, 2000). In the home as well as the workplace, feminine and masculine qualities are resources drawn on to perform certain activities regardless of the individual's biological sex. Whether normative feminine traits can be used as a form of cultural capital is, of course, dependent on whom they are attached to. For example, in Tim's case, the ability to talk about soft furnishings confirmed his knowledge of design history and aesthetics. As the example of kitsch indicates, aesthetic preferences coded as feminine may be valuable capital only when they are attached to male bodies. As I discuss below, women with bright kitsch tastes seem more likely to be criticized in the media. Thus, as Lisa Adkins (2000) suggests, gender is both detraditionalized (men and women can appropriate masculine and feminine qualities) and retraditionalized (women continue not to have access to the full terms of individuality as defined by the possessive self as an ideal) in the contemporary context. Adkins argues that "this eerily echoes the classic sexual contract of modernity" (2000:265). Old ways of doing and thinking about gender continue in the home and are also evident in enthusiasts' DIY practices, which I outline below. By exploring these practices I am able to consider whether the accompaniment to conventional divisions of masculinity and femininity, heteronormativity, is also produced in the making of retro homes.

HOMEMAKING, COUPLE CAPITAL AND HETERONORMATIVITY

As evidenced by the findings above concerning tastes for modernist styles, homemaking is a collective process, and decorating decisions are often undertaken by households or couples rather than by individuals. This is one of the reasons why interviewees who had partners presumed I would want to talk to them together. The collective decision-making process involved in creating an interior has not often been reflected in methodological approaches to consumption. For example, studies like *Distinction* (Bourdieu, 2005 [1979]) conceptualize taste as "an individualistic process, undertaken by a single...actor" (Reimer and Leslie, 2004:189). More recent research about the home has questioned this assumption and has drawn attention to the way cohabiting couples "create shared identities through joint decision-making about household provisioning" (Gorman-Murray, 2006:150; Reimer and Leslie, 2004; Silva, 2006b). This research found that decorating decisions were negotiated between partners, and collective identities were produced, even if these were fractured according to the differing desires and practices of individuals. In this part of the chapter I consider this work in relation to two practices: DIY home improvement and shopping.

From the early twentieth century on, DIY home improvement was promoted as a central part of homemaking in Britain. Renovating and decorating houses using one's own labor was particularly encouraged in the postwar period and was often depicted as a leisure activity for couples. For example, the front covers of the magazine *Practical Householder* from the 1950s frequently show young couples, rather than individuals, renovating their homes. These depictions are highly gendered, with women usually taking auxiliary roles such as holding ladders or paint pots and men undertaking more practical tasks. While the gendering of DIY may well have changed, a point I explore below, DIY home improvement continues to be central to ideas about the domestic interior. Indeed, as a number of theorists have suggested, DIY is part of the recent obsession with the home and generates significant economic activity (Allon, 2008).

As Helen Powell (2009) argues, however, there is not necessarily a correlation between the increased interest in home renovation and actual DIY practices. In a detailed study of retail sales, leisure time activities and attitudinal statements from 2002 to 2008, Powell (2009) argues that there has been a decline in DIY in Britain. She suggests that the value of leisure time has increased in a society that is "time poor," which makes DIY compete with more attractive leisure pursuits. Therefore, those with higher incomes may choose to employ a tradesperson to carry out DIY activities. Powell also suggests that due to the fragmentation of the extended family and the prioritization of entertainment over instruction in lifestyle media, individuals often lack the necessary skills to complete DIY tasks.

Retro enthusiasts do not seem to be in the majority in this regard. Although some of the enthusiasts in my study employed builders and carpenters for larger jobs, most of them decorated their own interiors and renovated retro objects. They also committed significantly more time to DIY renovation projects than the majority of homeowners. This was obvious in enthusiasts' interiors. For example, in Dave's flat intricate 1960s- and 1970s-style paint effects covered the walls.[2]

Decorating also involved renovating original retro pieces, which, because of their age, frequently needed work before they were ready to display. This meant that furniture needed veneering or polishing, pictures reframing, sofas and chairs reupholstering and lights and electrical equipment rewiring. While in many homes these tasks would not be necessary or would be the job of tradespeople, some retro enthusiasts had acquired these skills. For example, all the light fittings in Tim and Suzy's home were 1950s, 1960s and 1970s originals, which Tim had refurbished and rewired himself.

When retro enthusiasts were not able to find original retro pieces they also sometimes constructed replicas. The following quote from Peter explains how he made and sourced materials for his art deco front door.

> This may seem an odd thing to say, but one of my favourite things is the front door. Purely because of the story, which is, as I said we found the original architects drawings to the house, and when we moved in there was just a horrible single glass pane door, which we knew was wrong and the architect's drawings had a different door on it. So this is a modern door, but it does represent the kind of trouble that I will go to recreate what I know will be the correct thing. I got the bar made from one of these places . . . what this is normally is, you know, when you go to the pub and you get the foot rails, you know the type of thing. . . . There is a company down in Kent that makes those, so I phoned them up and asked them if they would do this and they said "yeah, yeah" so we put it on the door. Originally this [pointing at the window in the door] would have been Vitalight, black glass, well you can't get that anymore so it's just black acrylic and it looks just the ticket, but it's all new. (Peter, retro enthusiast, 2006)

As the quote from Peter indicates, the process of undertaking DIY projects is enjoyable for retro enthusiasts. Amateur making, of which DIY renovation is part, is enjoyable because it offers a space to be "singleminded" and concentrate on one thing (A. Jackson, 2010:20). It also encourages spontaneity, "a way of working that uses the materials and tools at hand," which is gratifying because it "involves decision-making processes that are heuristic, iterative, and intuitive" (A. Jackson, 2010:20).

Female retro enthusiasts also enjoyed DIY renovation, and some gave examples of curtains and cushions they had made from 1940s, 1950s and 1960s fabrics. Louise showed me some of the fabric she had collected and was "meaning to do something with." Thus, while most female enthusiasts had been involved in renovation in their homes, they chose to speak about "softer" DIY tasks. In contrast, male retro enthusiasts tended to speak about and take on the majority of the more physical DIY tasks in the home. Thus, the DIY practices of retro enthusiasts, at least the ones in this study, conform to relatively traditional gender roles.

I would suggest that the gendering of DIY practices is partly due to the knowledge needed to undertake such activities. For example, Peter, who had made his front door, suggested that his practical and technical skills were passed down from his father, who was an engineer. He had put these skills into practice at vintage car rallies as well as in his home. While enthusiasts may be able to learn practical skills and share knowledge through their participation in retro communities and through adult education, it seems that the majority of practical competencies were learned when young. At the very least, a feeling of "being capable" passed on through families can shape future practice. As Elizabeth Shove, Matt Watson and colleagues (2007:64) suggest, previously perceived success in practical skills and DIY defines the possibilities of future practice. So success in building a set of 1940s-style shelves may inspire an enthusiast to create a front door. This may be one of the reasons why practical skills and knowledge continue to be gendered. There is nothing to stop a female retro enthusiast from learning carpentry skills to make an art deco front door, or a male retro enthusiast from making curtains, but she/he might be less inclined to if she/he has not been taught these skills or been made to feel capable of them. This is evidence of the way traditional gender roles are passed on through families and could be argued to confirm Pierre Bourdieu's theorization of the family as a central site of gender normalization and naturalization (Skeggs, 2004b:21).

At the same time, however, family structures and practices are multifarious, they are "co-ordinated by localized dynamics," and individuals "undergo multiple socializations along the lifecourse" (Silva, 2010:5, 2006b). For example, if all family members have little practical knowledge, the most adept individual would often be required to take on practical tasks regardless of gender. In addition, as Reimer and Leslie emphasize, "shared households do not always and everywhere and at all stages of the life course consist of heterosexual couples," and this can alter how domestic labor is distributed and what types of knowledge and skills are acquired to complete domestic tasks (Reimer and Leslie, 2004:202).

Although DIY practices in retro homes were distributed among couples, the finished product was viewed as a collective effort. The joint creation of the home was even more evident in retro enthusiasts' shopping practices. Within the popular imagination as well as in academic research, shopping has been associated with femininity. As a number of theorists have suggested, this is one of the reasons that until relatively recently shopping and consumption have been thought of as frivolous and unworthy of academic study (see Falk and Campbell, 1997). The association of shopping with femininity continues, not least because in Britain it is women who do the majority of the household provisioning (Key Note Media, 2008).

However, in the homes of retro enthusiasts, shopping, particularly for furniture and decorative objects, was a shared activity. Before discussing the role of shopping in retro enthusiasts' relationships, I want to explore enthusiasts' shopping practices in general because they are different from those of the majority of consumers, myself included. Enthusiasts emphasized that they never went out with the purposeful intent of buying something but rather that particular shops and pieces of furniture might "catch their eye." The majority of the items in retro enthusiasts' homes were found when browsing markets and shops or while engaged in activities with a different purpose altogether, such as eating out, or while on holiday. The spontaneity of shopping for retro is partly shaped by the limited availability of original retro goods. It also demonstrates how the consumption of retro objects is not usually driven by necessity. The majority of enthusiasts' homes already have the furniture, decorative objects and technologies deemed necessary for a comfortable life, like beds, ovens and radiators. As Suzy admits, they "don't actually 'need' anything. It's just things [they]...come across and think, ohh, that would be nice." This attitude toward shopping is made possible by having the necessary disposable income, credit or earning potential, as Suzy went on to illustrate:

> We don't go out thinking we want a table, we just come across it. Then we think whether we can afford the table. We decide we can't afford it, and then we buy it anyway! (Suzy, retro enthusiast, 2006)

Retro enthusiasts were keen to differentiate their shopping practices from those of other consumers who "just bought things." They were able to wait, both practically and mentally, for "perfect" objects, as these quotes from Peter and Mary demonstrate:

> If we decide we need a bed we can't just go out and buy a bed like normal people would do, just go to MFI or Ikea and think "oh yeah that one will do." Ok it will be

in the back of our minds that we need a new bed, but it might be three, four, five years before we see the one that we want and we might happen upon it in the most strangest of places and think we've got to have that bed. Then we work out the logistics of getting it home from Newcastle or wherever it is you happen to be when you see it…you know it is a different philosophy. (Peter, retro enthusiast, 2006)

Sometimes, you think, oh gosh, you know it would be really nice to like the stuff that is normal taste, and it would be easy, but it's just really, really satisfying when you are looking for the one, not even when you are looking for the one thing, when you see the one thing, and you just think that is absolutely, absolutely right. (Mary, retro enthusiast, 2006)

Mary and Peter may wait a number of years to find the perfect retro object. While Mary recognizes that this causes certain problems (such as interiors being unfinished, living without certain "necessary" objects and a constant search for retro objects that is embedded in their everyday lives), it is a practice they both enjoy. For Mary and Peter, and to varying extents the other retro enthusiasts I interviewed, the delay of satisfaction involved in finding the perfect object is rewarding.

The way in which retro enthusiasts delay satisfaction and value old items over new means that their shopping practices can be likened to anticonsumerist discourses that critique "fast living" (Binkley, 2008:613). For example, Wendy Parkins and Geoffrey Craig suggest that for those involved in the slow food movement slowness is an attempt to live in a "meaningful, sustainable, thoughtful and pleasurable way" that is often at odds with the values of contemporary modernity (2006:ix). Thus, the practices of highly committed retro enthusiasts could be viewed as resistant to consumerist discourses, much like the slow food movement. Waiting for perfect pieces of retro furniture also uses fewer environmental resources, because once pieces are found retro enthusiasts seem less likely to dispose of them. Therefore, the practices of some retro enthusiasts may be evidence of the "alternative hedonism" that Kate Soper (2008) has called for. Soper argues that the environmental impacts of consumerism are likely go unchecked without a seductive alternative or "alternative hedonism" that emphasizes the pleasures of consuming in less environmentally damaging ways. I return to the appeal of practices that are different from everyday experiences of time further on in the chapter.

As evidenced by the quotes about shopping above, all enthusiasts living with their partners used "we" when talking about their shopping practices, and men spoke just as enthusiastically and emotionally about the items they had purchased as women did. Shopping is associated with pleasure partly because it is experienced as a collective activity. As Daniel Miller suggests, even when done on one's own, shopping is "as much about others in the family as it is about the shopper, especially for women" (1998:17). Miller goes on to suggest that through shopping women both give themselves to the loving social relationships in which they are involved as well as validate their place within these relationships. Thus, shopping is as much about others as it is about individualistic needs or wants. In the case of retro enthusiasts, shopping is even more intensely about love because the couples often purchase furniture and decorative objects together. As evidenced in the previous chapter, objects acquired together become symbols of, and agents in, important emotional relationships.

Retro enthusiasts' shopping practices are also a product of their social position. As Jo Littler suggests, the practice of deliberately consuming less or delaying satisfaction through choice is "by definition an option practiced by those with enough resources and cultural capital to be able to consume in the first place" (2008:107). Although Mary and Peter's shopping practices compromised the comfort and practicality of their interior for extended periods of time (e.g., living without a proper bed until they found the perfect one), they had the knowledge that if it "got too much," they would have been able to buy new furniture.

These practices can also be interpreted as a form of distinction making and distancing from other consumers with no patience and restraint. Historically, as Mica Nava (2000) suggests, the irrational impulses of consumption have been perceived as feminine, and it is particularly interesting that male retro enthusiasts were the most likely to describe their decision-making processes when shopping as rational and considered. Sally Munt has argued that with the decline of Britain's manufacturing industry in recent years the working class has become feminized and by implication "discursively associated with 'waste', typified by the profligate spender" (2000:8). Thus, retro enthusiasts' shopping practices can also be viewed as a way of distancing themselves from the working class.

The shared project of homemaking and related shopping practices also exemplify the way cultural and economic capital are created and strengthened by (conjugal) partnerships. Two salaries mean a greater likelihood of buying a house and thus committing more time and energy to the design of its interior. This reflects and produces cultural capital. The joint creation of a retro interior is also more powerful in terms of the legitimation of taste. Both partners are able to help, encourage and justify the taste of the other. This finding would seem to confirm Bourdieu's suggestion that partnerships develop partly based on affinities of cultural consumption. Bourdieu writes that taste for each other is "a way of loving one's own destiny in someone else and so of feeling loved in one's own destiny" (2005 [1979]:243).

However, this view of partnership is questionable for a number of reasons. As Elizabeth Silva argues, this conception of love is "reminiscent of a notion of the *habitus* as destiny, and of the determination of relations of friendship and partnership" (2006b:184). It assumes that individuals are unable to identify with people and things outside the social space they inhabit. This is problematic because, as Silva suggests, identity and identification are "not only found within roots, but are also located in relations" (2006b:184). Individuals can often appreciate people and things outside their own sphere of reference, even if they do not like or agree with what they stand for. This can occur at a micro as well as a macro level. For example, while retro enthusiasts mostly represented their homes as jointly produced, interior decoration was also a site of contestation. As documented in the previous chapter, Sylvia did not have the same passion for collecting as Chris and found his practices very difficult to live with because they made it hard for her to display objects in the way that she wanted. Louise also suggested that Andy was much more particular about period authenticity than she was, and sometimes this was frustrating when she wanted to "get rooms looking nice" in a shorter time frame.

Bourdieu's view of elective affinities of partnership is also linked to a number of problematic assumptions in terms of the family, gender and sexuality. While Bourdieu suggests that the family is a social construction, he normalizes his own conception of the family and the relations within it (Silva, 2004). As Silva writes, Bourdieu's conception of habitus suggests that early childhood experiences of one's mother's and father's bodies as well as the sexual division of labor "guarantees a 'natural' acquisition" of gender dispositions (2004:84). Bourdieu suggests that the normalization of gender roles within the family is so ubiquitous that it is impossible to escape masculine domination: women misrecognize their subordination, and gay and lesbian couples replicate normative gender roles.

As many feminist theorists have suggested, this view of gender (as partly biologically determined and so ingrained as to seem natural) does not allow for how gender is challenged in everyday relations and experiences (see Adkins and Skeggs, 2004). Using Bourdieu's model it is difficult to explain changes in family forms as well as the various gender roles undertaken in specific domestic contexts. As documented above, in retro enthusiasts' homes men take a very active role in decisions about interior decoration. Men can use femininity as a resource, and this can generate capital. This finding challenges Bourdieu's theorization that it is women (as aesthetic objects and the converters of cultural capital into symbolic capital) who naturally take charge of everything concerned with aesthetics in the division of domestic labor. For Bourdieu, even outside of the home, "the domestic world is superimposed upon the woman, and her role remains essentially the aesthetic one" (Silva, 2004:84). As I suggested in Chapter 3, this fails to consider the ways in which women also accumulate capital. Capital is both an individual resource available to men and women as well as a household resource. For the reasons I outlined above, (conjugal) partnership can make the whole (household capital) greater than the sum of its parts (individual capital). This is not to suggest that all households replicate the gender and sexual relations in Bourdieu's conception of the family or that one type of family form is better than another. Rather, it is to argue that through (conjugal) partnership the exchange value of taste can be maximized. This is partly because discourses of home as a shared family identity, most commonly the nuclear family, have carried strong weight in the West (Gorman-Murray, 2006; Reimer and Leslie, 2004). Therefore, the ways in which retro enthusiasts produce and describe their interiors reflect not only class difference but also heteronormativity.

The joint accrual of capital raises an interesting point in terms of theories of possessive individualism. As suggested in Chapter 3, theorists such as Marilyn Strathern (1992) and Celia Lury (1998) have argued that the possessive self has been renegotiated and involves "prosthesis"—the taking on and off of cultural resources. Strathern argues that this middle-class form of distinction making is about creating perspectives and communicating them as knowledge. Exchange value, then, is about relationships rather than equivalence. These findings confirm this point. It is through relationships (in this case conjugal partnerships) that the exchange value of individual taste is enhanced.

RETRO FEMININITIES, THE HOUSEWIFE AND FEMINISM

The fantasies that retro enthusiasts have about past identities also raise questions about whether their lifestyles and views are retrogressive in terms of gender and sexuality. For example, as a quote in the previous chapter demonstrates, Mary identified with the 1950s housewife and valued the practices associated with this vision of domesticity. While no other female retro enthusiasts were as explicit about their identification, many spoke fondly about domestic practices such as sewing and baking and were attracted to retro domestic technologies such as Aga cookers, Kenwood mixers, 1960s sewing machines and melamine bowls.

This finding is indicative of a wider increase in the value of domestic practices associated with the mid-century housewife within popular culture. For example, in recent years lifestyle programs in Britain have highlighted the advantages of the homemade and the pleasures of being a "domestic goddess"; museums and galleries have held exhibitions about "make do and mend" and domestic crafts; and membership in the Women's Institute, baking groups and knitting circles has increased significantly. By linking retro enthusiasts' fantasies with wider trends I do not mean to suggest that interest in past domesticities is ubiquitous or restricted to women. Rather, retro femininities are one of the multiple forms of femininity "in circulation and in competition in current times" (Hollows, 2003:181).

The gender and sexual politics raised by a turn to retro femininities are particularly apparent in a short documentary entitled *Time Warp Wives* (2008) that was aired on Channel 4 in Britain. The documentary focuses on the lives of four female retro enthusiasts and claims to represent their desire to live in the past. It begins with a number of scenes audiences would recognize as distinctly modern. This includes shots of people commuting to work, a police car and a woman looking stressed. In the background a news bulletin states that twenty-five knife crimes occurred in London in one day; there is a warning about the state of the economy and a prediction that 300,000 jobs are at risk. The narrator suggests,

> In twenty-first century Britain the stresses of modern living can be unbearable. To escape, many of us exercise to excess, drink one too many glasses of wine or live for our next holiday. But some people have a much more extreme solution. They have retreated into the past.

The documentary cuts to images of female retro enthusiasts baking and serving tea in their homes. The narrator says that for these women "it is not just about vintage clothes and vintage houses, they have vintage values to match." The documentary shows Joanne, the woman who is the main focus of the documentary, baking in her kitchen (Figure 8.1). The first thing the audience hears Joanne saying is:

> I'm happy to stay at home and be an old-fashioned housewife. I suppose it fills me with a happy wifely glow when Kevin comes in and says oh these are delicious, oh that cake is fabulous.

The audience then sees Joanne making breakfast in bed for Kevin, baking a cake, sewing and scrubbing the floor— all activities associated with housewifery. The viewer is told that Joanne finds housework "fulfilling" and that gender roles are strictly defined in her household. Joanne says that she does the "womanly jobs," such as taking care of Kevin, and he does things like cleaning the cars and repairing anything that needs fixing.

The documentary goes on to show the lives of three other women. The viewer gets to see the old technologies that the women display in their homes, such as the 1930s, 1940s and 1950s ovens, kettles, fridges and vacuum cleaners. The program continues to frame the women's interest in the past as a longing for vintage values as well as vintage clothes and domestic interiors. It particularly emphasizes the women's fantasies about housewives, and the narrator continually suggests that the participants value a time when

Figure 8.1   Joanne in her kitchen (2008). © Associated Newspapers Ltd.

a "women's place was in the home." The documentary also implies that these women live in relative isolation, socializing only with other "time warp wives." The overall message of the program is that retro enthusiasts crave a conservative lifestyle that is retrogressive in terms of gender norms. It is implied that because the women in the program get satisfaction from housework and homemaking they are reasserting traditional forms of femininity.

By emphasizing and critiquing female retro enthusiasts' retreat into the home, the documentary rehearses an opposition between the feminist and the housewife that is partly a legacy of past feminisms. As Stacey Gillis and Joanne Hollows suggest, the housewife has often operated as the feminist's Other (2009:1). Gillis and Hollows argue that while many "second-wave feminists clearly sympathized with the position of the housewife," the home was frequently viewed as a prison from which women should escape (2009:1). In the work of writers such as Betty Friedan and Ann Oakley, housework is conceptualized as denying women a sense of identity, and public space (rather than the home) is viewed as the site where satisfaction and achievement can be obtained. For example, in *The Feminine Mystique* Friedan (1983) critiqued media discourses that showed women as fulfilled by marriage and housewifery. She suggested that women were encouraged to pursue their feminine potential through housework and that the myth of the happy housewife caused fatigue and a loss of identity. Friedan hoped that women would realize their manipulation and challenge their oppression in the home. Equally, while Oakley's ethnographic research aimed to add complexity to the conflicting stereotypes of the housewife as either an oppressed worker or a happy homemaker (1974:41), she continued to view housework as opposed to "human self-actualization" (1974:222). In her book *Housewife* Oakley claimed that

> an affirmation of contentment with the housewife role is actually a form of antifeminism, whatever the gender of the person who displays it. Declared contentment with a subordinate status—which the housewife role undoubtedly is—is the rationalization of inferior status. (1974: 233)

The arguments about the oppression of women found in these texts were valid in contexts in which many women felt trapped in the home and had no access to pensions, health insurance or credit (except through their husbands). The stories told by these texts, from oppression in the private sphere to liberation in the public sphere, also united women in the fight for gender equality. These feminist works also provided narratives in which "women could understand themselves as modern individuals and find the means for their self-actualization in the world of work" (Johnstone and Lloyd, 2004:154).

However, by suggesting that women could only find fulfillment outside of the home,

> feminism confirmed the very way in which home and everyday life had been understood in modernist thought and hence the way it banished women to the edges of modernity. This contradiction was solved by disavowing the housewife, casting her out, and positioning her in relation to the feminist as symptomatic of a failure to engage with the project of modern individuality. (Johnstone and Lloyd, 2004:154)

In a similar way to how Bourdieu theorizes masculine domination, in these feminist texts those who display contentment with the role of the housewife are conceptualized as having internalized the views of the dominant and thus misrecognize their own subordination. This argument is problematic because, as Skeggs (2004c) has argued, it ignores the contradictions of masculinity and femininity and reproduces a distinction between the public and the private. She writes that "women can often easily produce a perfect critique of masculine traits and dispositions, yet this does not lead to resistance or change as Bourdieu would predict" (2004c:26). Just as a critique of masculine domination does not always lead to resistance or a feminist identity, identification with the housewife and enjoyment of housework are not necessarily an antifeminist position. Indeed, Leslie Johnstone and Justine Lloyd have argued that it was the figure of the housewife that made the feminist subject possible (2004:152).

There has been a counterhistory of feminist work that takes a similar position to that of Johnstone and Lloyd (2004), Gillis and Hollows (2009) and Skeggs (2004c), in the sense that it recognizes the complexities of gender relations and domestic life (e.g., Probyn, 1990; Lopata, 1971; Rubin, 1976; Young, 1997). However, the idea that the housewife is antithetical to the feminist continues in feminist writing and seems to be the position most associated with popular feminist discourse. For example, Gillis and Hollows observe how Susan Faludi (1993) argues that the backlash against feminism attempts to turn the clock back to prefeminist times by renaturalizing the association between women and the home. From this perspective there is little that the home or past domesticities can offer feminism.

This was the view of the majority of feminist bloggers regarding the *Time Warp Wives* documentary. The blogs describe Joanne and the other women as unhinged for the energies they invest in their homes and families and as superficial for the time they spend on cultivating their lifestyles. The enthusiasts' visions of the past are criticized as wholly inaccurate, and their practices interpreted as sexist and homophobic. While I understand this reaction and recognize the many inequalities that women continue to experience, these critiques continue to view the home as a prison from which women need to escape. This is surely a rather ahistorical account when the majority of women in Britain are now employed in paid work outside of the domestic sphere (e.g., Harris, 2004). As Joanne Hollows has asked, "How can women now leave home when they have never been there?" (2006:104).

All the female retro enthusiasts filmed in the documentary were employed in paid work, and so were all those I interviewed in my ethnography. For example, Joanne had three jobs: she worked in the shop of a National Trust property, as a waitress at events held at a stately home and as a 1940s-style singer. In response to the critiques of her practices she stated,

> My friends all know that I run around all the time doing so many things, travelling all over the country, always busy. I don't just stay home cleaning my floor! If I have a day off, I love to bake, keep my house nice and have tea ready for Kevin, but there is definitely more to me than that! (Joanne, retro enthusiast, 2008)

The enthusiasts in the documentary felt they had been misrepresented. On the forums they reflected on the process in which they were asked to take part. They suggested that they wanted to be involved because the producer had said that "the women were strong characters." Joanne writes,

> We were all strong women, as were the women of the time, especially wartime women who kept the home fires burning, etc! I was promised lots of coverage for "Lola" [Joanne's stage name], and so we agreed to do it. (Joanne, retro enthusiast, 2008)

Joanne and the other women in the documentary were disappointed because they saw themselves as strong independent working women, not subservient to, or dependent on, their partners. Thus, while the women would probably not consider themselves to be feminists, their attitudes and practices are "a product of a historical period informed by feminism" (Hollows, 2003:181).

Another woman on the forum reflected on the questions that she had been asked when she was approached to participate in the program. The producer had asked her whether she used any old technologies in her home such as a mangle. She writes,

> I played with my great-gran's mangle and flat irons as a child (she was a laun-dress), which was enough to convince me not to use them now I've got a fast spin setting on my washing machine!!! (though if they'd got there before she died in 1961, they could've interviewed her . . . !). ("vintagelover," retro enthusiast, 2008)

Like "vintagelover," all the retro enthusiasts I interviewed had also chosen to include new domestic technologies in their homes and were fully aware that they selected specific objects from the past. For example, as documented in the previous chapter, in her 1950s-style kitchen Mary had incorporated a dish-washer, washing machine and fridge freezer. While these appliances were hid-den behind retro-looking facades so as not to jeopardize the overall aesthetic, they were chosen partly because they are more efficient than older technolo-gies. As Silva (2010) finds in her study of domestic life and the family, techno-logical advances have enabled domestic chores to be completed in less time. Silva also notes how, in some households, technologies have distributed do-mestic labor among family members. For example, freezers and microwaves have made cooking possible for individuals with less culinary knowledge.

There have been other changes that have meant that retro enthusiasts' lives are different from those of the mid-twentieth-century housewives they fantasize about. While all the enthusiasts that I interviewed and those in the documentary were heterosexual,[3] an interest in retro style is not limited to this group. For example, on a blog designed to "celebrate the beauty within all gen-der expressions," a contributor posts pictures of herself in her kitchen dressed as a 1950s housewife. She entitles the photos "Getting my lesbian femme 50's housewife on while making Sunday dinner, such fun!:)." In this statement the contributor both identifies with the housewife and transgresses typical as-sociations because her desire for women rather than men is revealed. Thus, while the exchange value of the coproduction of retro interiors may reflect heteronormativity, fantasizing about, or performing, past identities does not necessarily reproduce sexist or homophobic views. Of course, there is a differ-ence between ironically performing this identity once in a while and living as a 1950s housewife most of the time. Nevertheless, in both cases past objects and identities are being reworked in new ways. In light of these complexities the turn to retro femininities cannot simply be labeled as conservative traditionalism or dismissed as false consciousness. It is for this reason that the appeal of retro femininities calls for deeper analysis.

THE ALLURE OF RETRO FEMININITIES

Retro enthusiasts' fantasies about mid-century housewives always seemed to be accompanied by glamour, whichever period they were interested in. The "make do and mend" housewife of austerity Britain, the 1950s housewife of Hollywood and the 1970s housewife from *Abigail's Party*–style suburbia are all imagined as having both more glamorous and simpler lives than the modern-day woman. As Carol Dyhouse notes, "Glamour has almost always been linked with artifice and with performance, and is generally seen as constituting a form of sophisticated—and often sexual—allure" (2011:1). Glamour became a buzzword in the twentieth century and is most associated with American cinema between the 1930s and the 1950s (Dyhouse, 2011:1). Retro enthusiasts' imaginings draw on media representations from the period, particularly Hollywood films and advertising. Objects associated with the mid-twentieth-century housewife were also thought of as glamorous. These included hostess trolleys, retro fridges, cocktail glasses and dressing tables. Enthusiasts like Mary also connected items of clothing and makeup with the housewife, namely, high heels, tea dresses, housecoats and red lipstick. The association of some of these items with the 1950s pinup also adds to their (sexual) allure. In this regard, the rise in interest in the housewife may also be tied to an increase in the popularity of burlesque dancing (Willson, 2008), where past femininities become a resource for sexual fantasies.

Although none of the enthusiasts had been alive in the periods they fantasized about, they were all well aware that the reality of housewifery in the past was anything but glamorous. They were also aware that they had choices that women in the past did not, such as being able to work. In this respect, female retro enthusiasts are able to appropriate past domestic identities only because they are temporally and spatially distant from those positions. Just as the appropriation of working-class objects and identities as "cool" is available only to those who are not working class, the identity of the housewife is appealing only to those who have the choice to be one. Therefore, it could be suggested that retro femininities are attractive and available only to those in privileged positions.

The female enthusiasts in this study not only had a penchant for furniture and decorative objects but also had extensive collections of retro clothes, bags and shoes. Thus, in a similar way to how Hollows theorizes "downshifting," attraction to past domestic identities may involve "a profoundly classed and thoroughly commodified narrative that centers on choices for those who inhabit specific middle class femininities" (Hollows 2006:110–111). By implication, as McRobbie warns, we should be wary of celebrating an "entitlement to claim back femininity" because "this pro-capitalist femininity-focused repertoire plays directly into the hands of corporate consumer culture eager to tap into this market on the basis of young women's rising incomes" (2009:158).

However, the glamour of retro femininities cannot simply be thought about in terms of temporal and spatial distance and explained solely as a product of class distinction and commodification. Glamour is an affective experience that has its own satisfactions. The bright and shiny plastic of a melamine plate, the change in posture when an enthusiast puts on high heels and pushes a hostess trolley, the look of perfectly applied red lipstick and the change in outlook that wearing a 1950s dress to bake a cake can deliver should not be ignored. In her discussion of beauty Rita Felski argues that "to neglect the visual and the tactile, to overlook the seductive interplay of colour and pattern and form, is to risk losing sight of why beauty matters at all" (2006:277). The same can be said for glamour.

Part of the allure of glamour is its perfection and its effortlessness (Thrift, 2008). In the domestic interior, where everyday tasks often create messiness and clutter, these qualities are desirable. Indeed, this may be one of the reasons for the attraction that retro enthusiasts have toward mid-century modern furniture and decorative objects. As Alice Friedman (2010) has suggested, the design of mid-twentieth-century interiors, furniture and decorative objects in the United States reflected a fascination with glamour. Mid-twentieth-century items objectified luxury and sensuality, values that had become important in a growing consumer culture. While items designed in Britain in the same period use less luxurious materials, the connotations of glamour remain. Thus, the appeal of secondhand mid-twentieth-century items highlights that glamourousness is not necessarily linked to excessive or less sustainable types of consumption.

Not only are people attracted to glamorous objects because they desire perfection, but also because glamorous objects are resources for hope (Thrift, 2008). Glamorous objects hint at ideals that may never fully be realized but that can be glimpsed in the imaginary realm "as fleeting daydreams and fantasies, or as more comprehensively worked out paradises, utopias, and worlds to come" (Thrift, 2008:14). As Dyhouse (2011) suggests, glamour has often represented a refusal to be imprisoned by gender norms, a form of escape from the everyday demands placed on women. Thus, while the lifestyles of retro enthusiasts may be a product of specific middle-class femininities and linked with discourses of choice, they should not be dismissed. As Hollows (2006) has argued, analysis of choice is useful because it can highlight problems with living in the present as well as fantasies about living differently. In addition, histories associated with long-standing hegemonies such as that of the housewife "might, under certain conditions, serve as a resource for radical projects and for the constitution of agents to pursue those projects" (Bramall, 2011:84). Retro enthusiasts frame their interest as a form of resistance to everyday experiences of time. Thus, in order to explore what visions of the housewife may offer a feminist politics I consider retro enthusiasts' fantasies in relation to ethnographic research on domestic labor and time use.

DOMESTIC FANTASIES AND A FEMINIST POLITICS OF TIME

While sociocultural and technological changes have meant that retro enthusiasts' lives are different from those of the mid-twentieth-century housewives they identify with, retro enthusiasts continue to practice some of the same household chores as the women they fantasize about. Even if domestic labor was shared relatively equally in retro homes, female enthusiasts seemed to be the ones who took responsibility for domestic duties. Enthusiasts found balancing the demands of work and home life difficult. For example, Mary was critical of how people have to "rush around everywhere" in the modern world.

These findings are indicative of wider sentiments regarding the time pressures placed on individuals in everyday life (e.g., Parkins, 2004; Silva, 2010; Southerton, 2009). In her ethnographic study of the home Silva notes that for many families it has become "difficult to trace the boundaries between work and non-work time, time for care and time for leisure, as well as the uses of technologies for education, work, pleasure, relationships and so on" (2010:1). She argues that this means that there is a mismatch between inherited ways of doing gender in the home (that housework and childcare are female domains) and the external demands made of individuals, particularly in regard to paid work. The blurring of the boundaries between work and nonwork time also means that the temporal boundaries of events are less defined. As Dale Southerton argues, in the early twentieth century "temporal structures were held together by a combination of fixed institutional events and constraints surrounding practices of domestic life, paid work, consumption and network interactions which are much less defined in the contemporary period" (2009:61). Southerton suggests that his findings explain the paradox that people feel increasingly time pressured despite time-diary data consistently revealing that people have longer durations of free time today than did previous generations (2009:61–62). Feelings of time pressure do not affect only women, and it is interesting to note that men as well as women identified with the enthusiasts in the *Time Warp Wives* documentary.

For example, when commenting on the program online, "Jamie" suggested that he also longed to be a housewife baking for a V.E. Day party.

Despite time pressures being felt by all, however, Silva found that the boundaries between work and nonwork time, time for care and time for leisure, and so on, were more difficult to trace among women (2010:66). This may be one of the reasons why women of today say they feel the "time squeeze" much more than those from previous periods. It may also be one of the reasons that women are turning to past domestic femininities as an escape from, and comment on, the time pressures of contemporary life. As Wendy Parkins has argued, in "a context of conflicting time demands and disparate time cultures...lifestyle practices such as gardening and cooking, become newly significant as a means of creating or marking time as time for the self, outside of financial or familial responsibilities and duties" (2004:432). The glamour associated with visions of the housewife can also be interpreted as relief from the everyday and a means of escape from the demands of work and domesticity. Therefore, past femininities act as a resource for women to imagine different ways of living.

This argument echoes Hollows's analysis of Nigella Lawson, the television cook. In her analysis of the attractiveness of the "domestic goddess" Hollows suggests that

> the desire to temporarily inhabit a figure of femininity which appears stable, which is of another time (literal or mythical) in which things seem simpler and less contradictory than the present, can also appear to offer a sense of escape from the pressures of managing and ordering both everyday life and feminine selves. (2003:195)

Hollows goes on to argue that the domestic goddess advocated by Lawson negotiates the opposition between the feminist and the housewife "by being offered as a position that is only available in fantasy—in Nigella's words, 'not being a domestic goddess exactly, but feeling like one'" (2003:188). In a similar way, retro enthusiasts are aware that the housewife they imagine is a mythical vision of the past that is created in the present, as illustrated by their feelings about old-fashioned domestic technologies. The housewife they envisage is a housewife for whom cooking, cleaning, sewing and so on are pleasurable, visible and creative rather than invisible, monotonous, mundane drudgery. Retro enthusiasts such as those in the *Time Warp Wives* documentary are also making their care obvious and their domestic chores spectacular. In this respect, their fantasies and practices can be thought of as a form of political criticism where different social relations are imagined and lived (Young, 1996:151).

However, the possibility of making housework into something more enjoyable is available only to those who inhabit specific middle-class femininities.

It is also subject to more localized family dynamics and the practices that take place within the home. As Gillis and Hollows have argued, there is a significant difference between market-friendly domesticities such as baking cupcakes and other less desirable tasks such as cleaning the toilet after its use by other members of the family (2009:8). Thus, the fact that none of the women in the documentary and only one that I interviewed had children is highly significant. The main reason that enthusiasts gave for not having children was that they would be incompatible with their retro lifestyles. For example, Joanne suggested that children would "encroach on her time" and compromise the lifestyle that she had "built." Mary also spoke of the problems of "imposing" her retro tastes on children. Therefore, the majority of female retro enthusiasts are not engaged in the types of care demanded by motherhood. For many women this is the site where normative ways of doing gender are the most overt and where the time squeeze is most acutely felt (Bradley, 2007:125–128). Thus, while all women may be able to fantasize about retro femininities, it is only women without children who can afford the time to live them out.

Even for retro enthusiasts the enjoyment of domestic activities can be compromised by a lack of time. It is interesting that in the quote above it is in her days off from work that Joanne likes to bake and keep the house nice. Even on a day off, baking a cake can suddenly switch from being a leisurely and pleasurable activity to being much less enjoyable if it is necessary to feed guests and if it is squeezed in between other forms of work. Thus, the experience of time is complex, and the temporal organization of everyday life is influenced by the demands of both work and home life. These findings reinforce Lisa Adkins's suggestion that "women's relationship to their labour is no longer [solely] governed by a logic of male–female exchange in the private sphere"; instead, women are attributed with hypereconomic capacity, and labor is dispersed across socioeconomic contexts (2009:330). It is this change that the critique of the return to the housewife fails to acknowledge.

In view of these findings I would suggest that, somewhat paradoxically, it is feelings of having no time that attract female retro enthusiasts to retro femininities, and it is the privilege of having more time that allows them to play them out. Rather than dismissing these fantasies and their related practices because they represent conservative traditionalism or a site of privilege, we should explore the conditions that make retro femininities attractive as well as possible. Identification with the housewife should not be thought of as a step backward. Instead, visions of the housewife are a comment on the present moment and offer alternatives, however complex and problematic they are. The ways of fantasizing and acting out the past explored in this chapter reflect and produce the restructuring of time that Adkins has argued is central to a change in women's relationship to their labor. By implication, exploring the interest in retro femininities means thinking about the division of domestic labor and male–female exchange in the home but also considering how women's labor is dispersed across socioeconomic contexts. Thus, in light of the recent interest in domestic femininity, a feminism that is focused on the politics and pragmatics of time is all the more necessary.

CONCLUSION

I began this chapter by quoting McRobbie's (1989, reprinted in 1994) theorization of retro as a style that allows women to play with the norms and expectations of femininity. Throughout the chapter I have considered this question in relation to the homes and practices of retro enthusiasts. I began by exploring the gendering of modernism because modernist discourses continue to inform retro enthusiasts' attitudes toward their interiors. I found that a taste for mid-century modern furniture and interiors was common among both male and female retro enthusiasts. Men were just as likely as women to talk about interior decoration, paint colors and soft furnishings, interests typically coded as feminine. The revaluing of modernist styles also embraces eclecticism, a style that was seen as a sign of feminine weakness the first time around. While these changes could be interpreted as a neutralization of modernist design in terms of gender, I found that the gendering of domestic tastes and practices continued. Private spaces within the home such as bedrooms and bathrooms were viewed as feminine spaces; kitsch taste continued to be associated with women; and the valuing of specific items of furniture pointed to female enthusiasts performing a greater share of domestic duties in the home. I also found that DIY renovation practices conformed to relatively traditional gender roles. I suggested that feminine tastes and domestic practices can be valuable as capital only when attached to a legitimate identity, one that is more likely to be male and middle class. Thus, gender is both detraditionalized and retraditionalized in the contemporary context. These complexities are partly the combination of the legacy of the aesthetic values found in modernist discourses that denounced feminine taste with postmodernist discourses that legitimated it.

I went on to consider the creation of domestic interiors in relation to enthusiasts' DIY and shopping practices. I found that even if the design of interiors was contested and domestic practices were unevenly distributed, homes were represented as a joint effort made by (conjugal) partnerships. This finding reflects the emotional relationships that homes, interiors and decorative objects symbolize. It also led me to explore Bourdieu's theorization that partnerships are determined by elective affinities in terms of cultural capital. Drawing on the work of Silva (2004, 2010) I questioned Bourdieu's theorizations.

I recognized the limits to an approach that views individuals as attracted only to those with similar tastes and highlighted the role of women in the accrual of capital. I suggested that households and family structures vary and that the division of labor changes according to localized dynamics within these contexts. I argued that because of the prevalence of discourses that suggest the nuclear family is the best way to live, (conjugal) partnerships can produce greater amounts of cultural capital in terms of taste and that this reflects heteronormativity.

I also explored issues of gender and sexuality in relation to retro enthusiasts' fantasies about the mid-century housewife and associated domestic practices. I argued that retro enthusiasts' practices were an extreme version of a more general turn toward retro femininities in popular culture. To explore the issues that this interest raises, I analyzed the *Time Warp Wives* documentary and outlined the criticisms of the identities and practices of the female retro enthusiasts who took part. Enthusiasts were criticized for the amount of time they spent on homemaking, for the inaccuracy of their visions of the past and for their supposedly sexist and homophobic views. I argued that these criticisms were partly due to the influence of feminisms that viewed the housewife as antithetical to the feminist and that saw the home as a prison from which women should escape. I suggested that this perspective is problematic in a context in which the majority of women are employed in paid work. The criticisms were also overly simplistic because retro enthusiasts were very aware of the way they selected items from the past. They also saw themselves as strong women, not subservient to their male partners. In addition, identification with the housewife is not limited to women or those in heterosexual relationships. Indeed, I identified instances of how the adoption of the identity of the housewife can transgress gender norms.

I argued for an approach that focused on the allure of retro femininities and suggested that it was partly the glamour of these imaginings that made them desirable. Glamorous objects and identities connote perfection and effortlessness. They also hint at utopias that may never be realized in everyday life. Enthusiasts were imagining, and sometimes inhabiting, a place where housework could be pleasurable, visible and creative. Just as retro enthusiasts' shopping practices can be interpreted as a critique of consumerism, identification with the housewife can be seen as a radical comment on the demands placed on women in everyday life. In this respect, I agree with McRobbie's (1989, reprinted in 1994) suggestion that retro allows women to play with gender conventions. The identification with the twentieth-century housewife and the desire to reenact her domestic practices are particularly interesting because they include individuals who would not necessarily view themselves as transgressive or radical.

While fantasies of past domestic lives may be available to everyone, however, the ability to live them out is available only to those who inhabit specific middle-class femininities. Even then, the pleasures are restricted because of the dispersal of women's labor as well as the sexual division of labor in homes. A feminism that focuses on the politics and pragmatics of time could highlight these inequalities while possibly engaging individuals who may not ordinarily identify with the feminist project.

9

Conclusion

I began this book by outlining the changes in value of one particular retro item: flying ducks. I used this example because the history of these ceramic wall plaques exemplifies the processes, problems and questions I wanted to explore in this study. The change in value of flying ducks in the last thirty years demonstrates how items deemed old-fashioned and tasteless are valued as retro by certain individuals. It also illustrates how the meaning of retro items does not necessarily change for their original owners. Thus, the object biography of flying ducks highlights the importance of position and perspective in the making of retro style, and I have argued that a discussion of this process is lacking in previous academic accounts. To conclude, I return to theorizations of retro style and discuss them in relation to my own findings. I also flag issues that I could not cover in the book and propose some topics for future research.

In Chapter 2 I discussed the definitions and distinctions of retro style. I noted that some academic studies limited their analysis of retro to secondhand goods and others focused exclusively on reproduction items. Using examples of furniture and decorative objects, I argued that retro includes both types of items. I suggested that retro is an ambiguous categorization that varies according to the person doing the categorizing. This led me to propose that retro is an aesthetic, cultural and social judgment of value and that what makes the style is a combination of the characteristics of the material objects themselves; the practices of consumers, retailers and intermediaries; and their contexts.

Although retro is a rather vague style category, in Chapter 7 I documented commonalities between the periods that retro enthusiasts were interested in and the pieces of furniture and decorative objects they owned. The inspiration for retro interiors usually came from the decades between 1930 and 1980, and homes frequently contained items that had been mass-produced and were associated with working-class taste in their previous lives. Retro interiors were likely to include a number of statement pieces like sideboards, jukeboxes and cocktail bars, which were less common in other people's homes. Enthusiasts were also prone to minimalist-style interiors inspired by mid-century design. This included white or muted interior walls and an absence of wallpaper, carpet or curtains. In Chapters 7 and 8 I argued that retro enthusiasts' aesthetic values have their origins in both modernist and postmodernist design discourses.

Retro enthusiasts and retro retailers were also linked by the value they placed on authenticity, which was usually associated with the age, origin and quality of pieces of furniture and decorative objects. Although secondhand goods produced by famous designers were valued, those that were associated with popular tastes were seen as the most authentic. This finding reflects the process of "making authenticity" that James Clifford (1988) depicted in the art-culture system and that he used to describe the process of value creation in museums and art galleries. Therefore, retro objects and styles are not entirely decontextualized but are valued because of the authentic traces that make them desirable in new contexts. The process of making authenticity that retro retailers, enthusiasts and intermediaries are involved in means that they can be likened to curators, and their shops and homes to museums and galleries. Thus, as I argued in Chapter 7, retro interiors are material manifestations of the aestheticization of everyday life.

Retro retailers and traders were particularly adamant about the authenticity of secondhand retro objects. In Chapter 5 I documented how high street retailers also attempted to associate their products with the status of the authentic original, and I noted that the difference between original and reproduction was difficult to maintain. I observed that for retro enthusiasts value came from how and where objects were acquired as well as their age. I outlined a hierarchy of modes of acquisition in which singular and less commodified experiences and objects generated the highest value.

This hierarchy was made more complex by my findings in retro enthusiasts' homes, however. Rather than being entirely devoted to the origins of objects and particular retail spaces, retro enthusiasts valued and appropriated authentic iconicity. While an object found in a junk shop exudes more of this quality, retro objects and styles bought from high street retailers were not ruled out as long as styles were "appropriate." Furniture and decorative objects were purchased if they fitted with enthusiasts' tastes, which were usually shaped by interest in a specific period of design. As I noted in Chapter 7, sometimes this meant that enthusiasts were forced to choose between aesthetics and practicality.

One of the consequences of living modern lives in retro interiors was that enthusiasts could not be completely wedded to original retro items. For example, it was difficult for enthusiasts to find kitchen appliances unless they went to a high street retailer. Thus, it was the extent to which retro enthusiasts could impose their personal biography onto their stylistic order that was most important. Talking about unusual items, statement pieces and furniture found in extraordinary places made enthusiasts' identities appear more distinct. As I outlined in Chapter 7, an emphasis on individuality has been found to be a particularly middle-class way of talking about the home, and the majority of enthusiasts' descriptions of their tastes reflected their middle-class backgrounds and lifestyles. In this respect, my findings are different from those of Angela McRobbie, who suggested that retro style marked "increasing fluidity across old class lines" (1994:152). This is a point I return to below.

At the same time, however, much of the research in this book confirms, illustrates and develops the points McRobbie made in "Second-Hand Dresses and the Role of the Rag Market" (1989, reprinted in 1994). In the discussion of the history of retro in Chapter 4 I argued that the style emerged in the 1960s and that the aesthetic built on the traditions of revival, antique and the bohemian values of the European historical avant-garde. I proposed that retro represented a new structure of feeling that emphasized eclecticism, individuality and self-expression rather than cultural exclusivity.

Like McRobbie, I also found the history of retro style to be closely connected to the history of youth cultures. Young people were the first consumers to adopt retro clothing, and throughout the book I have suggested that this turn to retro included an appreciation of retro furniture and decorative objects. In Chapter 4 I noted how in the 1960s businesses and retailers used retro designs to speak to their young consumers in more authentic and rebellious ways. The dissemination of retro styles by the media in the early 1970s and late 1980s meant that the cultural resources that young people had gained from their participation in youth cultures became increasingly valuable in the symbolic economy. This is one of the reasons why retro retailers involved in youth cultures in the 1970s and 1980s were able to capitalize on their cultural resources. As McRobbie suggested, for some female "prosumers" their involvement in informal retail networks opened up pathways for economic independence, however short-lived these were.

Of course, the history outlined here is a British one, and retro is global as well as local. Unfortunately, the global histories of retro production and consumption were well beyond the scope of this book. Nevertheless, in the British context at least, the growth in the symbolic value of the cultural resources gained from participation in youth cultures is a reflection of the centrality of the media and the market in legitimating lifestyles. Perhaps, then, the presence of retro retailing and retro enthusiasts around the world[1] is partly a product of global mediascapes (Appadurai, 1996). The ways in which retro objects and styles circulate and the many perspectives from which they are valued in other countries would be an interesting topic to explore in more detail.

In a British context my findings regarding the role of the media in legitimating taste and the speed with which new styles are circulated could be viewed as evidence of a change in the way cultural capital is accumulated. In *Distinction* Pierre Bourdieu (2005 [1979]) identified cultural capital as objectified in objects, as inherited and as legitimated by education. He did not consider the capacity of the media to circulate and authorize the tastes, values and practices that reflect cultural capital. It was for this reason, as well as the mass production of retro styles by the high street and wider access to education, that McRobbie (1989) contested Bourdieu's theorizations regarding the correlation between lifestyle and social class.

I have found, however, that while retro retailers and enthusiasts may have cultural capital (retro knowledge that is valuable within the arts and consumer culture more generally), those without higher education qualifications and from working-class backgrounds found it harder to convert this into economic capital in the labor market. Thus, although it may appear that cultural capital is easier to acquire, the inequalities that Bourdieu documented remain.

Class differences also continue to be made through cultural distinction. Although the media circulate retro styles, good and bad retro interiors are defined by the individuality, eclecticism and effort that they represent. As suggested above, the possession of good taste and a desirable identity is dependent on talking about objects and styles in certain ways, as well as acquiring them and exhibiting them correctly—that is, displaying individuality.

In the discourses of possessive individualism discussed in Chapter 3, I documented how individuality is dependent on ownership of oneself and the articulation of a plausible history, as well as the ownership of objects. I noted how people who relate to themselves as property are constituted in opposition to others who are seen as the objects of value (colonial subjects, women and the working class). Drawing on a number of theorists, I suggested that discourses of possessive individualism continue in a consumer culture structured by the idea of the "self as project" (Cronin, 2000). In this context authenticity is viewed, rather contradictorily, as a quality of objects, persons or processes that is already established, as well as an ideal to be aimed at through the consumption of lifestyles.

The ways in which retro style is produced, consumed and represented are evidence of the continuation of the possessive self as ideal. As outlined above, retro enthusiasts and retailers value objects and retail spaces that are considered more authentic. Among most enthusiasts this was illustrated by distaste toward the "masses," who were conceptualized as buying goods from the high street and "following fashion." I found that instead of making definite statements about items and people that were associated with bad taste, enthusiasts discussed value in terms of the authentic iconicity of brands.

However, reproductions produced by high street retailers could be desirable if they were made legitimate by an appropriate context and identity. Thus, in order to appropriate, display and talk about old or mass-produced furniture as good taste, enthusiasts need a plausible preestablished identity that allows them to relate to the self as property. As the discussion of possessive individualism in Chapter 3 showed, only certain people have access to the status of the individual. Therefore, those who cannot authenticate the self in terms of a unique body are less able to possess desirable and exchangeable retro styles.

In a similar vein, only certain individuals are able to appropriate old working-class objects and identities, a practice that I have suggested is part of retro cultures. In Chapter 8 I observed that the ability to do this was dependent on distance. I argued that there was a difference between those who could appropriate working-class and old-fashioned qualities to enhance their exchangeable authentic selves and those who were marked as working class and old-fashioned. Therefore, although the choice of a retro lifestyle appears available to everyone, it depends on a particular subject position, often one that is middle class. This finding is more akin to McRobbie's recent discussion of the "new realms of injury and injustice" that individualization and lifestyle produce (2009:19) than to her earlier, rather optimistic discussion of retro style as "fluidity across old class lines" (1994:152).

The analysis of the renewed value of modernist aesthetics in Chapter 8 produced similar findings. I found that male retro enthusiasts were just as likely as women to talk about domestic practices and aesthetics that were typically coded as feminine. Women also spoke about their love for clean lines and minimalism. I argued that rather than representing a neutralization of the modernist aesthetic in terms of gender, these findings were illustrative of how gender can be used as a resource. In asserting their "masculine tastes" women distance themselves from oppressive constructions of femininity, and men are able to appropriate "feminine tastes" without being marked as superficial or frivolous. This illustrates that women are capital-accumulating subjects and that gender can be used as capital. It also demonstrates that the categorization of "feminine" aesthetics as good taste is dependent on the person to whom they are attached. In Chapter 8 I also documented how homemaking practices were conceptualized as joint activities undertaken by couples. I argued that (conjugal) partnership created greater amounts of cultural capital than the sum of the individual capital of those in the relationship. I proposed that the role of conjugal partnerships in enhancing the exchange value of individual taste both reflected heteronormativity and confirmed that it is actually through relationships, rather than equivalence, that exchange value is created.

In its appropriation of authentic qualities, the consumption of retro style is a fetishized defetishization of commodities and identities. Retro enthusiasts are temporally and spatially distant from those they appropriate from, and through exchange the social features of people, goods and experiences can be altered. For example, the media interest in retro enthusiasts from working-class backgrounds as "cool" illustrates the way in which working-class cultures are defined as exchangeable while the everyday experiences of working-class people are often invisible (Skeggs, 2004a:184). In Chapter 4 I observed that the fetishization of past lives was most apparent when consumers did not come into contact with the previous contexts or people from which they appropriated. For example, the processes that underpin sales on eBay work to obscure chains of production and consumption and the affective relations of exchange experienced in other informal retail spaces.

The value that retro enthusiasts placed on old gender identities, particularly the mid-twentieth-century housewife, is more difficult to explain in terms of temporal or spatial distance. While women's lives have changed since the mid-twentieth century, particularly in regard to paid employment, female retro enthusiasts are still involved in, or at least take responsibility for, many of the same domestic practices. I did not find this to be some form of misrecognition of masculine power; instead, enthusiasts were well aware of these contradictions. I also observed how the appropriation of the identity of the mid-twentieth-century housewife was not limited to women or those in heterosexual relationships and could be performed ironically to transgress gender norms. These findings reinforce McRobbie's suggestion that retro allows individuals to play with the "norms, conventions and expectations of femininity" (1994:148).

In Chapter 8 I argued that even when identification with the mid-twentieth-century housewife was a serious commitment, the past was being reworked in new ways that were not necessarily recreating old gender norms. I suggested that part of the allure of retro femininities was the glamour associated with past objects and identities. Drawing on Joanne Hollows (2006), I argued that enthusiasts' fantasies about retro femininities were partly a comment on the time pressures placed on women in everyday life. I went on to suggest that, somewhat paradoxically, it was feelings of having no time that attracted female retro enthusiasts to retro femininities, and the privilege of having more time that allowed them to play them out. Having analyzed the allure of retro femininities I proposed that a feminism that explored the politics and pragmatics of time was all the more necessary.

The desire to engage in practices that would claim back or puncture through everyday experiences of time was common among all retro enthusiasts, not only those who identified with the mid-twentieth-century housewife. In Chapter 8 I explored the practices of retro enthusiasts that could be interpreted as a critical commentary on the transience of modern life. I documented how retro enthusiasts often waited for long periods of time for the perfect objects and how enthusiasts' shopping practices could be likened to anticonsumerist critiques of "fast living." I also documented how mid-century modern items are attractive because they are seen as glamorous; thus, I argued that sustainable consumption and glamour are not opposing trends. I also recognized how the design of retro objects encourages practices to be completed in a more leisurely manner. For example, playing a vinyl record on a radiogram was a more enjoyable activity for many enthusiasts than pressing a button on an iPod. I observed the satisfaction that enthusiasts got from renovating old objects and "bringing them back to life." These intimate relations with objects go beyond exchange value and the accumulation of capital.

The limits of theoretical models that focus on the accumulation of capital were clear also when I analyzed practices of collecting and DIY (do-it-yourself). In Chapter 7 I argued that enthusiasts and collectors enjoyed the sensual pleasures involved in packing, searching for and ordering their objects and I speculated on the extent to which collecting can involve "losing the I-ness of self" (Highmore, 2011:81). This idea would be an interesting starting point for a future study of the practices of collecting.

In Chapter 8 I also documented the satisfactions involved in DIY practices such as rewiring lights, repairing sideboards and reupholstering furniture. I argued that these practices were enjoyable because they involved creative and intuitive decision-making processes, as well as creating a space where individuals could concentrate on one task. These practices are pleasurable because they are different from those experienced in the workplace or in a market system deemed "lacking in corporeal pleasure and expressive embodiment" (Binkley, 2009:106).

Collectors' and enthusiasts' relationships with each other and their objects also went beyond the accrual of exchange value. In Chapter 7 I documented how retro objects were symbolic of emotional ties with friends and relations and how retro furniture facilitated practices that were thought of as more sociable. In Chapter 5 I also observed the cultures of inclusion and sharing of knowledge in communities linked by retro niche media. This was particularly pronounced on the Midwinter website because collectors were not so concerned with the individuality of their tastes. In informal retail networks like jumble sales and Freecycle I also suggested that there was greater potential for altruism and less exploitative social relations.

Therefore, while there has been a popularization of the retro aesthetic, the search for authenticity also involves practices that are less dependent on commodified relations of exchange and are less environmentally destructive. A taste for retro represents a desire for deep and meaningful social relations between people and things and uses the past to imagine possible ways of living in the future. However, it is clear from the discussion in the preceding chapters that certain material and symbolic representations of the past have also become highly desirable commodities that can add to exchange value. By producing, consuming and representing retro style, retailers, enthusiasts and intermediaries are making and unmaking the value of themselves and others. Thus, while retro cultures can involve socially and environmentally progressive practices, any project that attempts to build on the valuing of authenticity needs to be mindful of reinforcing middle-class distinction and increasing social divisions.

Appendixes

APPENDIX 1

The ethnographic research and textual data that form the basis of this study were gathered between 2006 and 2010. The interviews with four tastemakers, six retro retailers and twelve retro enthusiasts took place over a seven-month period from September 2006 to March 2007. In this period retro retailers were also observed in their shops and enthusiasts in their homes. I adopted a "purposive" approach to sampling whereby participants were intentionally selected because their interest related to the purpose of the research (Patton, 1990). This allowed me to see how class and gender manifested themselves within retro cultures rather than presupposing how they were spread through a stratified sample. Twelve of the respondents were women, and ten were men. Their ages varied from twenty-seven to sixty-four. One respondent was mixed race, and the rest were white. All were heterosexual.

As I detailed in Chapter 3, I have used an approach to class that focuses on the possession and accrual of capitals (economic, social, cultural and symbolic). However, I have also used a number of other means of determining class position. I agree with Beverley Skeggs when she suggests that an analysis of class "should...aim to capture the ambiguity produced though struggle and fuzzy boundaries, rather than to fix it in place in order to measure and know it" and that classifications of class tend to do the latter (2004a:5). However, in order to describe classed experiences, some form of classification seems necessary to clarify social stratification and material inequality and to discuss the misrecognition of cultural capital. Even studies that consider class as being made through culture usually classify individuals as working class or middle class through their income, occupation and parents' occupation and the area in which they live, prior to the discussion of their practices (e.g., Savage, 2000). Indeed, Rosemary Crompton suggests that a combination of more traditional measures of class with those that discuss the cultural construction and reproduction of class can most effectively "illuminate different parts of the whole" (2008:6). Therefore, in addition to exploring the cultural practices, attitudes and locations of retailers and enthusiasts of retro style, their occupations and those of their parents have been categorized using the Office of National Statistics Socio-Economic Classification (2005) shown in Table A.1.

There are problems with classifying a person's background according to her/his parents' occupation. Historically, in academic studies (e.g., Goldthorpe, 1983; Bourdieu, 2005 [1979]) and in government statistics (e.g., the

Table A.1 Office of National Statistics Socio-Economic Classification Categories (2005)

Social Class
Class 1. Higher managerial and professional occupations
Class 2. Lower managerial and professional occupations
Class 3. Intermediate occupations
Class 4. Small employers and own account workers
Class 5. Lower supervisory, technical occupations
Class 6. Semi-routine occupations
Class 7. Routine occupations
Class 8. Never worked or long-term unemployed
Not classified

Table A.2 Demographics of retro tastemakers

Name	Age	Occupation	Mother's occupation	Father's occupation	Educational qualifications
Tommy	64	Retired fashion retailer and entrepreneur	Housewife	Salesman	CSEs
Wayne	45	Designer	Housewife	Professional sportsman	Degree
Heather	28	Advertising	–	–	Degree
Kate	27	Advertising	–	–	Degree
Edward	47	Journalist and writer	–	–	Postgraduate

Registrar General's classifications), social origin and class background have been determined by the father's occupation. This is problematic because the labor of mothers (both paid and unpaid) goes unrecognized. For this reason, the occupations of interviewees' mothers and fathers are included in the table. In addition, there is inconsistency between the period in which the National Statistics Socio-Economic Classification was devised and the period when most of the interviewees' parents were engaged in paid work. To address this, the specific occupations of parents are also included in the table.

RETRO TASTEMAKERS AND RETAILERS

I conducted four interviews with tastemakers and six interviews with retro retailers (details can be found in Table A.2 and Table A.3). The interview with Tommy, included in the Table A.2, was a secondary resource available from the British Library Sound Archive (Roberts, 2005). The other interviewees were asked whether they would like to take part in an interview via email or in person at their shop or market stall. The interviews were conducted either in the workplace of the interviewee or in an informal setting, such as a café

Table A.3 Demographics of retro retailers

Name	Age	Occupation	Mother's occupation	Father's occupation	Educational qualifications	Housing
Cathy	38	Retailer (boutique)	Housewife	Shopkeeper (Class 4)	GCSE's	Owner-occupied
Eloisa	42	Retailer (boutique)	Nurse (Class 2)	Civil service administrator (Class 2)	Degree	Owner-occupied
Clare	34	Retailer (online shop and retro fairs)	Dinner Lady (Class 7)	Electrical engineer (Class 3)	GCSE's	Rented
Helen	39	Retailer (boutique)	Secretary (Class 3)	Electrician (Class 5)	Degree	Owner-occupied
Steve	48	Retailer (boutique)	Shopkeeper (Class 4)	–	None	Owner-occupied
Keith	30	Market trader	Office worker (Class 3)	Painter and decorator (Class 7)	GNVQ	Rented

or bar. The participants were asked to reflect on the history of their interest in retro style, in the context of both their work and their own personal history. The interviews were informal and quite often led to discussions of other related topics. This was advantageous because it introduced me to issues related to retro style that I had not previously considered, such as gentrification.

RETRO ENTHUSIASTS

Retro enthusiasts were interviewed and observed in their homes and were contacted through retailers, friends and the Internet. Although there are groups who are interested in retro style (often linked to specific periods, objects or music), the enthusiasts I interviewed did not know each other. Only three out of the twelve participants I interviewed were involved in retro groups or music cultures. I used the Internet to contact participants, and it enabled me to tap into virtual communities linked by taste, style or consumption patterns. By posting advertisements for interviewees on style forums such as www.modculture.com I was able to contact a large number of potential participants. This was not without its problems, however. The relative anonymity that the Internet provides for users made selecting participants difficult, especially in relation to my own personal safety.[1]

Although the majority of the participants did not know anyone else with a similar passion for retro, the consumption of the style for the home is by no means an individual pursuit. Due to the nature of the domestic environment, taste is negotiated with other members of the household. An unforeseen implication of this was that five of the eight interviews I conducted were with couples, sometimes with children present.

As outlined in Chapter 3, I began by talking to retro enthusiasts about their experiences and their tastes. The interviews were informal and quite often led to discussion of other related topics. I then asked them to give me a tour of their homes. Interviewees were largely comfortable with showing me their objects and enjoyed giving me a tour of their domestic interiors. Out of the eight interviews that I conducted, only one couple did not want me to video them directly. They allowed me to video their objects and the decoration of their home, however. This was the oldest couple, who were perhaps less comfortable with technology. Overall, the interviewees seemed to appreciate the need to record interiors visually and were keen to discuss and display their objects in this way. I decided to interview the participants and operate the camera myself. Although the video footage is shaky and interviewees are sometimes out of shot, I thought that two people (an interviewer and a camera operator) entering the home would have been too intrusive. In addition, the advantage of operating the camera myself was that I was able to record and analyze my own reactions and my position as a researcher in more detail.

Advances in technology made operating the camera and interviewing simultaneously an easier task. The video camera had a foldout mini-TV screen that allowed distance between my eye and the camera. This enabled me to view the screen and the scene being recorded and to obtain good eye contact with interviewees.[2] In video interviews, as Sarah Pink notes, "the camera becomes part of its user's identity and an aspect of the way he or she communicates with others" (2001:79). There was, however, often a noticeable change in the interviewees' manner when I pressed record compared to during the pre-interview chat. At the beginning of the interview, participants showed unease at being filmed, and they often avoided the lens. They also sometimes performed for or adopted a playful approach to the camera. For example, when I first started filming, Steve pointed to the fireplace in his 1940s-style house. He posed to the camera in a manner typical of 1940s and 1950s films and said, "I should have a pipe," laughed and said, "It's spiffing." This is an obvious reference to the camera and to his retro identity. The joke also masked the slight awkwardness that he felt being filmed.

After conducting the video interviews, I analyzed the film in two stages, focusing on both the content and the context of the video. The first stage, as Pink recommends, used "time coded log tables with information on camera angles and distances, spoken narrative and visual content" (2001:111). In the second stage, the interviews were analyzed by locating key markers and discursive themes. Demographic information of retro enthusiasts can be found in Table A.4, and pen portraits in Appendix 2.

Table A.4 Demographics of retro enthusiasts

Name	Age	Occupation	Mother's occupation	Father's occupation	Educational qualifications	Housing
Dave	42	Painter and decorator/DJ (Class 7/2)	Bus driver (Class 7)	Crane operator (Class 6)	GCSE's	Rented
Catherine	66	Artist/knitwear designer (Class 2)	Housewife	Farmer/landowner (Class 1)	Degree	Owner-occupied
Thomas	62	Management trainer (Class 2)	Heath visitor (Class 2)	–	Postgraduate	Owner-occupied
Tim	53	Civil servant (Class 1)	Housewife	Barrister's clerk (Class 1)	A-Levels	Owner-occupied
Suzy	47	Retail manager (Class 2)	Housewife	Baker (Class 5)	Degree	Owner-occupied
Marianne	27	Artist/publishing assistant (Class 2)	Therapist (Class 2)	Psychologist (Class 1)	Postgraduate	Rented
Louise	39	Graphic designer (Class 2)	Computer programmer (Class 2)	Project manager (Class 1)	Degree	Owner-occupied
Andy	37	Production manager (Class 2)	Pharmacist (Class 1)	Lecturer (Class 1)	A-Levels	Owner-occupied
Sylvia	40	Marketing consultant (Class 1)	Housewife	Engineer (Class 1)	Postgraduate	Owner-occupied
Chris	42	Treasurer (Class 1)	Housewife	Forestry manager (Class 3)	Postgraduate	Owner-occupied
Mary	45	District nurse (Class 2)	Administrator (Class 2)	Bank manager (Class 1)	Professional qualification	Owner-occupied
Peter	38	Software house director (Class 1)	Housewife	Engineer (Class 2)	Degree	Owner-occupied

MEDIA AND ARCHIVAL RESEARCH

In addition to ethnographic research, I have carried out media and archival searches identifying visual and textual references to retro style from 1964 to 2009. These included searches of national newspapers (the *Sunday Times*, the *Guardian* and the *Independent*), women's magazines and magazines about home decoration (*Women and Home, New Woman, Ideal Home, Elle Decoration* and *Wallpaper*) and national television programs (Channel 4 and BBC news and home lifestyle programs, such as *Changing Rooms, Grand Designs* and *To Buy or Not to Buy*). I also identified and analyzed texts specifically addressed to enthusiasts of retro style or with a retro aesthetic. This included national television programs (*20th Century Roadshow*), Internet websites (www.ebay. com, www.retroselect.com and various retro collectors' and retailers' web pages), promotional material and catalogs (from Habitat, Ikea and various retro retailers) and photographs of street markets, shop fronts and interiors (retro shops and markets in London).

Although these sources seem disparate, the texts that I have selected are linked by their references to, or use of, retro style. The visual and written content of these texts has been analyzed first for obvious references to retro style. This analysis involves as much focus on the context and categorization of objects and styles through written clarifications as on visual appearance. Second, texts have been analyzed to identify the "preferred meanings" that are communicated. This draws on Stuart Hall's (1980) notion of the way that discourses are encoded in texts. For example, retro interiors are frequently represented as aspirational in the media and are described as "retreats" and unique "havens." The encoding/decoding model proposed by Hall was one of the first communication models to explore the possible discrepancy between the meanings that were produced/encoded in media products and those that were consumed/decoded. Since then it has often been criticized as simplistic, because it views texts in isolation, is entrenched in the idea of transmission and suggests a single act of reading (see Morley, 1992). As Purnima Manekar notes, meaning "is frequently contested by viewers who are historical subjects living in particular discursive formations rather than positioned by a single text" (1999:8). Media texts are products that emerge from and circulate within discursive strategies, and the discourses that texts produce "flow in and out of constructions of identity, self, private and public, national, local and global" (Gray, 2003:142). Thus, the approach I have taken to the media is similar to the one I have taken to objects themselves. It is an approach that considers texts and the discourses they produce in relation to all of the other processes in the cultural circuit discussed in Chapter 2.

OTHER MATERIAL

I have drawn on a number of informal discussions I have had with jumble sale organizers, Women's Institute members and charity shop volunteers in the southeast of England in 2005.

In Chapter 8 I have also drawn on a number of online responses to the *Time Warp Wives* documentary. While these comments are widely accessible, I have used pseudonyms and have not revealed the specific blogs where these comments can be found. Although they may still be traceable, I have done as much as I can to protect the privacy of these individuals.

APPENDIX 2

RETRO RETAILERS

Cathy, age 38. A retro retailer who owns a small boutique on a street adjacent to a well-known market in London. Her store had been open for two years. She sells mass-produced original retro furniture and decorative objects, mainly from the 1950s and 1960s. She sources and sells objects herself and lives above the shop.

Eloisa, age 35. A retro retailer who rents a boutique on a shopping street in London. She sells original retro furniture, decorative objects and prints from a range of decades including the 1940s. She originally trained as a set designer. The shop had been open for two years, and Eloisa employs two members of staff.

Clare, age 34. A retailer who sells mid-century modern items online and at retro fairs. She has been trading for a couple of years. She went to college to do a secretarial course and then worked for a football fanzine. Now she also works as a freelance journalist.

Helen, age 39. Rents and runs a retro shop with her partner in London. She sells original and reproduction items, including many smaller items such as cocktail glasses, magazines and toys. The shop had been open for eleven years, and Helen employs one member of staff.

Steve, aged 48. Rents a shop on a street in London. He sells 1950s, 1960s and 1970s furniture and lights. The shop had been open for ten years, and Steve employs one member of staff. His career started as a runner for an antique dealer.

Keith, age 30. A retro trader who occasionally has a pitch in a London market. He sells smaller retro items including ceramics, lamps, books and so on.

RETRO ENTHUSIASTS

Dave,   age 43. Painter and decorator and DJ. Dave lives with a flatmate in a small flat in a large 1960s tower block in the north of England. He is interested in 1960s style and heavily involved in the mod scene. He wears 1960s clothes all of the time.

Catherine,   age 66. Artist/knitwear designer. Catherine lives in a two-bedroom house in London with her partner, Thomas (below), although she wants to move because the house is too small. She is interested in art deco and kitsch. In general Catherine tends to make more of the decorating decisions around the home than her partner, Thomas.

Thomas,   age 62. Management trainer. Thomas lives with Catherine (above). He likes the clean lines of art deco and modernism. He buys more reproduction furniture than his partner Catherine.

Tim,   age 53. Civil servant. Tim lives in a large four-story house in the southeast with his partner, Suzy (below). He likes a range of modernist retro styles. He has a high level of practical skill and enjoys renovation.

Suzy,   age 47. Retail manager. Suzy lives with Tim (above). She has a more "shabby-chic" aesthetic than Tim. Because Suzy works as a manager of a large number of charity shops she often changes the retro items in her home.

Marianne,   age 27. Artist and publishing assistant. Marianne is American and has lived in London for ten years. She rents a flat that she shares with two other people. She is interested in 1950s and 1960s design and likes kitsch.

Louise,   age 39. Graphic designer and illustrator. Louise lives in a three-bedroom house in London with her partner, Andy (below). She likes mid-century modern styles, particularly 1950s fabrics.

Andy,   age 42. Production manager. Andy lives with Louise (above) and their two children. He also likes mid-century modern styles and is very particular about the condition of retro goods.

Sylvia,   age 40. Marketing consultant. Sylvia lives in a two-bedroom house in London with her partner, Chris (below). She likes 1940s styles, although because of her partner's collecting she tends not to buy much herself.

Chris,   age 42. Company treasurer. Chris lives with Sylvia (above). He is a collector of Midwinter ceramics and other items including Victorian bottles and mining tokens.

Mary, age 45. District nurse. Mary lives in a three-bedroom art deco house in the southeast with her partner, Peter (below). Mary wears 1940s clothes most of the time and is involved in the "swing" scene.

Peter, age 38. Software house director. Peter lives with Mary (above). Peter also wears 1940s clothes when he can. He has a high level of practical skills. Peter also has a 1940s car.

APPENDIX 3

RETAILER INTERVIEW QUESTIONS

THE SHOP

- Can you describe what you do?
- How long has the shop been open?
- How did the business start? Why did you start?
- Why did you choose this area?
- How do you source your objects?
- What are your customers like? What kinds of things are popular with them?
- How do you feel about the term *retro*?
- How do you think the interest in retro or past popular culture has developed in Britain? Has it grown? Why do you think it has grown?

THE RETAILER

- Could you tell me a bit about your background?
- Do you remember when you first became interested in retro and twentieth-century design? Why did you become interested?
- Were you part of a subculture?
- Did you wear or use secondhand clothes/furniture?
- Were there any particular shops, people, specific media or cultural phenomena that influenced you?

ENTHUSIAST INTERVIEW QUESTIONS

THE ENTHUSIAST

- What job do you do?
- Where did you grow up?

- What did your parents do?
- Did you go to college or university? What did you study?
- Do you see yourself as part of a class? Is it different from your parents'?

RETRO STYLE

- Do you remember when you first became interested in retro and twentieth-century design?
- Why did you become interested?
- Were you part of a subculture?
- Did you wear or use secondhand clothes/furniture?
- Were there any shops, people, media or cultural phenomena that you liked or went to or that influenced you?

TASTE

- How would you describe your style?
- Is your ideal home the same as the one you have? How would you change it?
- Do your friends and neighbors have a similar style to you?
- What is your idea of bad taste? What would you hate to live with?

Notes

1. INTRODUCTION

1. Examples include advertisements for Harvey's furniture store (2008) and the branding and advertising for the website www.findaproperty.com (2012).

2. THE DEFINITIONS AND DISTINCTIONS OF RETRO STYLE

1. Discussion of the epistemological importance of social position has a long history within critical theory (Darling-Wolf, 2004; Nava, 1992).
2. This is a reflexive project that I would argue Bourdieu did not fulfill in *Distinction* (2005 [1979]).
3. However, as Mica Nava notes, "how to disentangle the specific [our positions, biographies and the research process] from the general [interpretations, methods, theories, histories] is a problem with no solution" (1992:6).
4. More detail about sampling methods can be found in Appendix 1.
5. The tastemakers were selected because of their interest in retro, their availability for interviews and their authority within the field.

3. RETRO STYLE AND THE CULTURAL POLITICS OF EVERYDAY LIFE

1. It is important to note, as Nigel Thrift does, that although the use of aesthetics by capitalism may seem all encompassing, "the system cannot work unless there are loopholes through which the new and quirky can make their way" (2008:21).
2. The term *classed* suggests that class inequalities are reproduced through the hierarchically differentiated nature of taste, which often functions below the level of consciousness and language (Bottero, 2004:990).
3. The descriptions in *Distinction* add richness and depth to Bourdieu's accounts. However, in the rest of the book Bourdieu (2005 [1979]) makes culture into units to be counted. For example, his use of correspondence analysis has been likened to the "top-line" data gathered from market research questionnaires (Miller, 1987:155).

4. A HISTORY OF THE RETRO AESTHETIC

1. The production of furniture made in traditional styles and fakes have a much longer history. As Walter Benjamin noted, "In principle a work of art has always been reproducible. Man-made artifacts could always be imitated by men. Replicas were made by pupils in practice of their craft, by masters for diffusing their works, and, finally, by third parties in the pursuit of gain" (1999 [1936]:217).
2. I Was Lord Kitchener's Valet opened on Portobello Road in 1964. See interview with director Robert Orbach (2006).
3. Kleptomania opened on Carnaby Street in 1965. See interview with founder Tommy Roberts (2005).
4. See interviews with Orbach (2006) and Roberts (2005).
5. Storm Thorgerson and Aubrey Powell (1999:113) suggest that Mick Swan, the designer of the album cover, looked down at the tin they used to roll joints and decided to copy it for the album.
6. Of course, the production and consumption of antiques and reproduction antiques also continued.
7. Another branch of Habitat opened in 1966 on Tottenham Court Road, and by the end of the decade six more branches had opened in Britain.
8. In the Habitat catalog in 2005, Habitat objects are placed in staged interiors with antiques and retro objects that cannot be bought at the shop.
9. Other films such as American Graffiti had depicted 1950s style although they had a smaller audience (Box Office Mojo, 2009).
10. All the retro stalls and shops used as examples in this study also opened after 1990.

5. RETAILING RETRO

1. Unfortunately there is no room for a detailed discussion of the consumption and production of retro style at charity shops and car boot sales in this chapter. However, unlike many of the spaces discussed in the book, charity shops and car boot sales have been the focus of detailed academic studies (e.g., Gregson and Crewe, 2003; Horne and Maddrell, 2002).
2. At one time, market stalls would have also fitted in this category; however, pitches in London have become increasingly hard to obtain and relatively expensive for the occasional seller. For example, a day pitch at Broadway Market costs £30 per day, and sellers have to participate in an informal interview process to get a stall.
3. High-end is the term many retro retailers and enthusiasts use to describe more expensive and exclusive shops.

4. Of course, branding and advertising aim to compensate for this discrepancy. See Leiss and colleagues (2005) for a more in-depth discussion.

5. See Greer (2001) for a highly stereotypical account of Essex girls and bad taste.

6. An exception to this trend seems to be objects designed for the Festival of Britain or associated with famous designers, such as Robin and Lucienne Day.

7. This definition has become slightly problematic as more occupations deal in symbolic goods and services. For a more detailed discussion see Negus (2002).

8. There is no doubt that youth and gender were also factors in marking Roberts as "cool."

9. Small shopkeepers have long been identified as lower middle class. See Benson and Ugolini (2003) for details.

10. This was conveyed to me in interviews with a member of the WI (Women's Institute) and a charity shop volunteer, conducted in 2005. See Appendix 1.

11. For example, the Wills Moody Jumble Sale is held in Euston and is "a gig and shopping all muddled up." Jumble sales are also regularly held in bars and pubs in East London, such as Jumble Boogie. Information about these sales and participation in them tends to be restricted to a small group of (usually middle-class) "creatives" and artists.

12. Although this process is relatively simple, it is prohibitive for some people who are not technologically competent or do not have the time or inclination to take photographs of objects and write marketing copy about them.

13. Although it is difficult to transport furniture from the United States, a number of transportation companies have been developed to help eBay buyers do this.

14. The practices of consumers of retro style are discussed more generally in Chapter 8.

15. Based on a search on eBay on January 11, 2008.

16. The narrative began "I found my ex-wife's wedding dress in the attic when I moved. She took the $4000 engagement ring, but left the dress." The dress eventually sold for $3,850. For detailed discussion see Hillis and colleagues (2006).

6. RETRO INTERIORS AND LIFESTYLE MEDIA

1. According to BBC News (2004) the program regularly attracted 10 million viewers.

2. Anna Ryder Richardson asked the women to build a sculpture from polystyrene balls. The two women complained that they could not be

asked to create art without a proper brief. They also queried how the money (£500) was being spent on the interior. The makeover was not completed.

3. Ironically, however, in the one episode when Handy Andy swapped roles with the designers the participants were extremely pleased with their interior.

4. The term *high-end* is also used by retro retailers and enthusiasts to describe lifestyle media targeted at more exclusive audiences.

5. The circulation of *Elle Decoration* was 60,056 in 2010 (*Elle Decoration*, 2010). The viewing figure of *Grand Designs* was roughly 6 million each week in 2008 (Barb, 2008).

6. Commitment to the consumption of originals and quality craftsmanship is also valued in *Elle Decoration*. For example, editorials are frequently focused on restoring mid-century modern or period properties.

7. Occasionally, in episodes of *Grand Designs* the participants seem to have more knowledge than Kevin McCloud. This was particularly evident in an episode in which an architect built a home near Waterloo station in London (2004, Season 4, Episode 7).

8. At the time I conducted this ethnography the British Terrestrial television programs based on the valuation of old objects were *Trash to Cash* (BBC), *Bargain Hunt* (BBC), *Car Booty* (BBC), *Cash in the Attic* (BBC) and *Dickenson's Real Deal* (ITV).

9. At the time of writing these included www.retroselect.com, www.retro wow.co.uk, www.retronaut.com, www.retrostyle.com and www.retrothing. com.

7. RETRO HOMES, TASTE AND CULTURAL DISTINCTION

1. Of course, as I also explored in Chapter 2, my own identity may have influenced which types of retro enthusiasts I encountered. More detailed information regarding the identities of these enthusiasts can be found in Appendixes 1 and 2.

2. Although children influenced these decisions, they did not seem to play such an influential role in this process.

3. This is different for collectors, whose values and practices are explored below.

4. Dave liked his old 1960s kitchen, but because it was dilapidated he felt unable to refuse when the council offered him a new one.

5. This is not to argue that the working class do not have successful ways of subverting middle-class taste (see Skeggs, 2004a:184).

8. RETRO FEMININITIES AND DOMESTIC LABOR

1. While men in the early and mid-twentieth century were encouraged to be involved in DIY, and the home was meant to represent a collective identity, decisions about color schemes and soft furnishings were more likely to be viewed as a woman's domain (Sparke, 1995).
2. Some of Dave's guests liked his style so much that they had asked him to reproduce it in their homes.
3. This may be due to the small sample or the limitations of the sample method.

9. CONCLUSION

1. Retro shops and scenes tend to be found in cosmopolitan metropolises. These include Mexico City, Rio de Janeiro, Shanghai and Johannesburg.

APPENDIXES

1. I made sure that I met my participants in a public place prior to the interview if I had made contact with them over the Internet.
2. I used a Sony DCR-HC23E Handycam.

References

Abercrombie, N., Hill, S. and Turner, B. S. (1986) *Sovereign Individuals of Capitalism.* Taylor and Francis, London.

Adams, O. (2008) "Ogdens' Nut Gone Flake Is Pop's Nuttiest Moment." *Guardian.* July 30. Available at http://blogs.guardian.co.uk/music/2008/07/ogdens_nut_gone_flake_is_pops.html. [Accessed August 3, 2008].

Adkins, L. (2000) "Objects of Innovation: Post-Occupational Reflexivity and Re-Traditionalisations of Gender" in Ahmed, S., Kilby, J., Lury, C., McNeil, M. and Skeggs, B. (eds.) *Transformations: Thinking through Feminism.* Routledge, London.

Adkins, L. (2009) "Feminism after Measure." *Feminist Theory.* 25(3), p323–339.

Adkins, L. and Skeggs, B. (2005) *Feminism after Bourdieu.* Blackwell, Oxford.

Allon, F. (2008) *Renovation Nation: Our Obsession with Home.* University of New South Wales Press, Sydney.

Anderson, J. (2002) "The History of Biba." *Sleazenation.* November. Available at http://www.bibacollection.co.uk/history.htm. [Accessed August 11, 2008].

Andrejevic, M. (2011) "The Affective Work That Economics Does." *Cultural Studies.* 25(4–5), p604–620.

Appadurai, A. (ed.) (1986) *The Social Life of Things.* Cambridge University Press, Cambridge.

Appadurai, A. (1996) *Modernity at Large: Cultural Dimensions of Globalization.* University of Minnesota Press, Minneapolis.

Aronczyk, M. and Powers, D. (2010) *Blowing Up the Brand: Critical Perspectives on Promotional Culture.* Peter Lang, New York.

Attfield, J. (2000) *Wild Things: The Material Culture of Everyday Life.* Berg, London.

Attfield, J. (2007) *Bringing Modernity Home: Essays on Popular Design and Material Culture.* Manchester University Press, Manchester.

Atton, C. (2002) *Alternative Media.* Sage, London.

Auslander, L. (1996) *Taste and Power: Furnishing Modern France.* University of California Press, Berkeley and Los Angeles.

Barb (2008) "Weekly Top Ten Programmes." Available at http://www.barb.co.uk/report/weeklyTopProgrammes. [Accessed August 11, 2008].

Baudrillard, J. (1994) *Simulacra and Simulation.* University of Michigan Press, Ann Arbor.

Bauman, Z. (2000) *Liquid Modernity.* Polity Press, Cambridge.

BBC News (2004) "R.I.P. Changing Rooms." Available at http://news.bbc. co.uk/2/hi/uk_news/magazine/4034503.stm. [Accessed June 2012].

BBC Press Release (2004) "Alan Titchmarsh Presents the 20th Century Road-show." Available at http://www.bbc.co.uk/pressoffice/pressreleases/ stories/2004/09_september/13/20thcentury.shtml. [Accessed June 19, 2008].

Beck, U. (1992) *Risk Society: Towards a New Modernity.* Sage, London.

Belk, R. (1995) *Collecting in a Consumer Society.* Routledge, London.

Bell, D. and Hollows, J. (eds.) (2005) *Ordinary Lifestyles: Popular Media, Consumption and Taste.* McGraw-Hill, Maidenhead.

Bell, D. and Hollows, J. (2005) "Introduction" in Bell, D. and Hollows, J. (eds.) *Ordinary Lifestyles: Popular Media, Consumption and Taste.* McGraw-Hill, Maidenhead.

Bell, D. and Hollows, J. (eds.) (2006) *Historicizing Lifestyle: Mediating Taste, Consumption and Identity from the 1900s to the 1970s.* Ashgate, London.

Benatouil, T. (1999) "A Tale of Two Sociologies." *European Journal of Social Theory.* 2(3), p379–396.

Benjamin, W. (1999 [1936]) *Illuminations.* Pimlico, London.

Benn, E. (1964?) Magazine and date unknown. Found in Habitat Press cuttings. Art and Design Archive. Box 2.

Bennett, T. and Joyce, P. (2010) *Material Powers: Cultural Studies, History and the Material Turn.* Taylor and Francis, London.

Benson, J. and Ugolini, L. (2003) *A Nation of Shopkeepers: Five Centuries of British Retailing.* I. B. Taurus, London.

Binkley, S. (2007) *Getting Loose: Lifestyle Consumption in the 1970s.* Duke University Press, Durham, NC.

Binkley, S. (2008) "Liquid Consumption." *Cultural Studies.* 22(5), p599–623.

Binkley, S. (2009) "The Bohemian Habitus: New Social Theory and Political Consumerism" in Soper, K., Thomas, L. and Ryle, M. (eds.) *The Politics and Pleasures of Consuming Differently.* Palgrave, London.

Binkley, S. and Littler, J. (2008) "Introduction, Cultural Studies and Anti-Consumerism: A Critical Encounter." *Cultural Studies.* 22(5), p519–530.

Biressi, A. and Nunn, H. (2007) *Reality TV: Realism and Revelation.* Wallflower Press, London.

Blanchard, T. (2003) "Building Sight." *The Observer.* November 2. Available at http://www.guardian.co.uk/theobserver/2003/nov/02/features. magazine47. [Accessed May 12, 2008].

Bloom, L. (2006) "The Contradictory Circulation of Fine Art and Antiques on eBay" in Hillis, K., Petit, M. and Epley, N. S. (eds.) *Everyday eBay: Culture, Collecting and Desire.* Routledge, London.

Boltanski, L. (2011) *On Critique: A Sociology of Emancipation.* Polity Press, Cambridge.

Boltanski, L. and Thevenot, L. (1999) "The Sociology of Critical Capacity." *European Journal of Social Theory.* 2(3), p359–577.

Bonner, F. (2003) *Ordinary Television: Analysing Popular TV.* Sage, London.

Booth, H. and Steiner, S. (2007) "Step Back in Time." *Guardian Weekend.* May 26, p86–93.

Botterill, J. (2007) "Cowboys, Outlaws and Artists: The Rhetoric of Authenticity and Contemporary Jeans and Sneaker Advertisements." *Journal of Consumer Culture.* 7(1), p105–125.

Bottero, W. (2004) "Class Identities and the Identity of Class." *Sociology.* 38(5), p985–1003.

Bourdieu, P. (1992) *Language and Symbolic Power.* Polity Press, London.

Bourdieu, P. (1998) "Social Space and Symbolic Space" republished in Robbins, D. (ed.) (2000) *Pierre Bourdieu.* Sage, London.

Bourdieu, P. (2001) *Masculine Domination.* Polity Press, Cambridge.

Bourdieu, P. (2005 [1979]) *Distinction: A Social Critique of the Judgement of Taste.* Routledge, London.

Bourdieu, P. and Wacquant, L. (1992) *An Invitation of Reflexive Sociology.* University of Chicago Press, Chicago.

Boyle, D. (2003) *Authenticity: Brands, Fakes, Spin and Lust for Real Life.* HarperCollins, London.

Boym, S. (2001) *The Future of Nostalgia.* Basic Books, New York.

Box Office Mojo (2009) "American Graffiti." Available at http://boxofficemojo.com/movies/?id=americangraffiti.htm. [Accessed May 12, 2009].

Bradley, H. (2007) *Gender.* Polity Press, Cambridge.

Bramall, R. (2011) "Dig for Victory! Anti-Consumerism, Austerity and New Historical Subjectivities." *Subjectivity.* 4(1), p68–86.

Briganti, C. and Mezei, K. (2012) *The Domestic Space Reader.* University of Toronto Press, Toronto.

"Brighter Than White, Whiter Than Clean." (1968) *Honey.* (March), p84.

Brooks, D. (2000) *Bobos in Paradise: The New Upper Class and How They Got There.* Simon and Schuster Paperbacks, New York.

Brown, G. (1992) *Domestic Individualism: Imagining the Self in Nineteenth Century America.* University of California Press, Berkeley and Los Angeles.

Brown, S. (2001) *Marketing: The Retro Revolution.* Sage, London.

Brunsdon, C. (2003) "Lifestyling Britain: The 8–9 Slot on British Television." *International Journal of Cultural Studies.* 6(5), p5–23.

Brunsdon, C. (2004) "Taste and Time on Television." *Screen.* 45(2), p115–129.

Bryson, B. (1997) "What about the Omnivorous? Musical Dislikes and Group Based Identity among Americans with Low Levels of Education." *Poetics.* 25, p141–156.

Burikova, Z. (2006) "The Embarrassment of Co-Presence: Au Pairs and Their Rooms." *Home Cultures.* 3(2), p99–122.

Busch, A. (2005) *The Uncommon Life of Common Objects.* Metropolis Books, New York.

Butler, J. (1997) *Gender Trouble.* Routledge, London.

Butler, T. with Robson, G. (2003) *London Calling: The Middle Classes and the Remaking of Inner London.* Berg, London.

Cahill, J. L. (2006) "Between the Archive and the Image-Repertoire: Amateur Commercial Still Life Photography on eBay" in Hillis, K., Petit, M. and Epley, N. S. (eds.) *Everyday eBay: Culture, Collecting and Desire.* Routledge, London.

Callon, M. (1991) "Actor-Network Theory: The Market Test" in Law, J. and Hassard, J. (eds.) *Actor Network Theory and After.* Blackwell, London.

Carr, R. (1970) "The Marks and Spencer of Instant Furniture?" *Guardian.* December 3, p11.

Carter, A. (1983) "The Recession Style." *New Society.* 63(1052), p25–26.

Chaney, D. (1996) *Lifestyles.* Routledge, London.

Chapman, P. (1964) "Someone Would Even Buy It for Himself." *Sunday Times Magazine.* January 4, p25.

Cieraad, I. and Porte, S. (2006) "Who's Afraid of Kitsch? The Impact of Taste Reforms in the Netherlands." *Home Cultures.* 3(3), p273–292.

Clarke, A. J. (2001) "The Aesthetics of Social Aspiration" in Miller, D. (ed.) *Home Possessions: Material Culture behind Closed Doors.* Berg, London.

Clifford, J. (1988) *The Predicament of Culture: Twentieth Century Ethnography, Literature and Art.* Harvard University Press, Cambridge, Massachusetts.

Cockburn, C. (2004) "The Circuit of Technology: Gender, Identity, Power" in Silverstone, R. and Hirsch, E. (eds.) *Consuming Technologies: Media and Information in Domestic Space.* Routledge, London.

Cohen, A. (2002) *The Perfect Store: Inside eBay.* Little and Brown, Boston.

Cohen, D. (2006) *Household Gods: The British and Their Possessions.* Yale University Press, London.

Cohen, L. (2008) "Antiques Roadshow Briefing: What Fiona Bruce Needs to Know." *The Times.* March 29. Available at http://entertainment.timesonline. co.uk/tol/arts_and_entertainment/tv_and_radio/article3625109.ece. [Accessed May 12, 2008].

Colin and Angela (2008) "Midwinter Pottery Directory." Available at http:// www.midwinterdirectory.co.uk/. [Accessed May 12, 2008].

Collard, F. (2003) "Historic Revivals, Commercial Enterprise and Public Confusion: Negotiating Taste, 1860–1890." *Journal of Design History.* 16(1), p35–48.

Corrigan, P. (1997) *The Sociology of Consumption: An Introduction.* Sage, London.

Couldry, N. (2003) "Media, Symbolic Power and the Limits of Bourdieu's Field Theory" in Gill, R., Pratt, A., Couldry, N. and Rantanen, T. (eds.) *MEDIA@LSE*

Electronic Working Papers. Available at http://www2.lse.ac.uk/media@lse/ research/mediaWorkingPapers/pdf/EWP02.pdf. [Downloaded September 22, 2008].

Crompton, R. (2008) *Class and Stratification.* Polity Press, London.

Cronin, A. (2000) "Consumerism and Compulsory Individuality: Women, Will and Potential" in Ahmed, S., Kilby, J., Lury, C., McNeil, M. and Skeggs, B. (eds.) *Tranformations: Thinking through Feminism.* Routledge, London.

Dant, T. (2005) *Materiality and Society.* Open University Press, Maidenhead.

Darling-Wolf, F. (2004) "On the Possibility of Communicating: Feminism and Social Position." *Journal of Communication Inquiry.* 28(1), p29–46.

De Certeau, M. (1984) *The Practice of Everyday Life.* University of California Press, Berkeley.

Deleuze, G. and Guattari, F. (1987) *A Thousand Plateaus: Capitalism and Schizophrenia.* Vol. 2. University of Minnesota Press, Minneapolis.

Denzin, N. (1989) *Interpretive Biography.* Sage, London.

Desjardin, M. (2006) "Ephemeral Culture/eBay Culture: Film Collectables and Fan Investments" in Hillis, K., Petit, M. and Epley, N. S. (eds.) *Everyday eBay: Culture, Collecting and Desire.* Routledge, London.

Duckett, M. (1968) "Conran's Own Habitat." *Telegraph Colour Supplement.* February 2, p26–30.

du Gay, P., Hall, S., Janes, L., MacKay, H. and Negus, K. (1997) *Doing Cultural Studies: The Story of the Sony Walkman.* Sage, London.

du Gay, P. and Nixon, S. (2002) "Who Needs Cultural Intermediaries?" *Cultural Studies.* 16(4), p495–500.

du Gay, P. and Pryke, M. (2002) *Cultural Economy.* Sage, London.

Duncombe, S. (1997) "Community: The Zine Scene" republished in Gelder, K. (ed.) (2005) *The Subcultures Reader.* Routledge, London.

Dunkley, C. (2005) *Essential Guide to London's Retro Shops.* New Holland, London.

Dunn, R. G. (2000) "Identity, Commodification and Consumer Culture" republished in Davis, J. E. (ed.) (2002) *Identity and Social Change.* Transition, New Brunswick, New Jersey.

Dyhouse, C. (2011) *Glamour: Women, History, Feminism.* Zed Books, London.

Elle Decoration (2010) "Media Information." Available at http://www.hf-uk. com/pdf/MediaPackElleDeco.pdf. [Accessed January 21, 2010].

Ellis, R. and Haywood, A. (2006) "Virtual_radiophile (163): eBay and the Changing Collecting Practices of the U.K. Vintage Radio Community" in Hillis, K., Petit, M. and Epley, N. S. (eds.) *Everyday eBay: Culture, Collecting and Desire.* Routledge, London.

Epley, N. S. (2006) "Of PEZ and Perfect Price: Sniping, Collecting Cultures and Democracy on eBay" in Hillis, K., Petit, M. and Epley, N. S. (eds.) *Everyday eBay: Culture, Collecting and Desire.* Routledge, London.

Erickson, B. (1996) "Culture, Class and Connections." *American Journal of Sociology.* 102(1), p217–251.

Falk, P. and Campbell, C. (1997) *The Shopping Experience.* Sage, London.

Faludi, S. (1993) *Backlash: The Undeclared War Against American Women.* Random House, New York.

Featherstone, M. (1991) *Consumer Culture and Postmodernism.* Sage, London.

Felski, R. (2006) "Because It Is Beautiful: New Feminist Perspective on Beauty." *Feminist Theory.* 7(2), p273–282.

Floch, J. M. (2000) *Visual Identities.* Continuum International, London.

Frank, T. (1997) *The Conquest of Cool: Business Culture, Counterculture and the Rise of Hip Consumerism.* University of Chicago Press, Chicago.

Franklin, A. (2002) "Consuming Design: Consuming Retro" in Miles, S., Anderson, A. and Meethan, K. (eds.) *The Changing Consumer.* Routledge, London.

Friedan, B. (1983) *The Feminine Mystique.* Penguin, Harmondsworth.

Friedman, A. (2010) *American Glamour and the Evolution of Modern Architecture.* Yale University Press, New Haven, Connecticut.

Giddens, A. (1991) *Modernity and Self Identity: Self and Society in the Late Modern Age.* Polity Press, London.

Gilbert, J. (2008) *Anticapitalism and Culture: Radical Theory and Popular Politics.* Berg, London.

Gill, A. A. (2005) "No Winners in the Waiting Game." *The Times.* April 24. [Accessed online May 10, 2007. Now unavailable].

Gillilan, L. (2003) *Kitsch Deluxe.* Mitchell Beazley, London.

Gillis, S. and Hollows, J. (2009) *Feminism, Domesticity and Popular Culture.* Routledge, London.

Goldsmith, S. (1983) "The Ready-Mades of Marcel Duchamp: The Ambiguities of an Aesthetic Revolution." *Journal of Aesthetics and Art Criticism.* 42(2), p197–208.

Goldthorpe, J. H. (1983) "Women and Class Analysis: In Defence of the Conventional View." *Sociology.* 26(3), p381–400.

Good, E. (1964) "What the Smart Chicks Are Buying." *The Sunday Times.* May 10, p43.

Gookin, D. and Birnback, R. (2005) *eBay® Photos That Sell: Taking Great Product Shots for eBay and Beyond.* John Wiley and Sons, London.

Gorman-Murray, A. (2006) "Gay and Lesbian Couples at Home: Identity Work in Domestic Space." *Home Cultures.* 3(2), p145–168.

Gray, A. (2003) *Research Practice for Cultural Studies: Ethnographic Methods and Lived Cultures.* Sage, London.

Greer, G. (2001) "Long Live the Essex Girl." *Guardian.* March 10: G2, p8.

Gregson, N. and Crewe, L. (1998) "Tales of the Unexpected: Exploring Car Boot Sales as Marginal Spaces of Contemporary Consumption." *Transactions of the Institute of British Geographers.* 23(1), p39–53.

Gregson, N. and Crewe, L. (2003) *Second-Hand Cultures.* Berg, Oxford.

Gregson, N., Crewe, L. and Brooks, K. (2003) "The Discursivities of Difference: Retro Retailers and the Ambiguities of the 'Alternative.'" *Journal of Consumer Culture.* 3(1), p61–82.

Grignon, C. and Passeron, J. C. (1989) *Le Savant et le Populaire.* Le Seuil, Paris.

Grimshaw, M. (2004) "Soft Modernism: The World of the Post-Theoretical Designer." *Ctheory.* Available at http://www.ctheory.net/articles.aspx?id= 418. [Accessed March 20, 2012].

Grossberg, L. (1997) *Bringing It All Back Home: Essays on Cultural Studies.* Duke University Press, Durham, NC.

Guardian website (2008) "Guardian Reader Profile." Available at http://www. adinfo-guardian.co.uk/the-guardian/gua-reader-profile.shtml.   [Accessed February 19, 2008].

Guffey, E. (2006) *Retro: The Culture of Revival.* Reaktion Books, London.

Guggenheim, M. and Potthast, J. (2012) "Symmetrical Twins: On the Relationship between Actor-Network Theory and the Sociology of Critical Capacities." *European Journal of Social Theory.*

Hall, S. (1980) "Encoding/Decoding" in Hall, S., Hobson, D., Lowe, A. and Willis, P. (eds.) *Culture, Media, Language.* Hutchinson, London.

Hall, S., Hobson, D., Lowe, A. and Willis, P. (eds.) (1980) *Culture, Media, Language.* Hutchinson, London.

Halnon, K. B. and Cohen, S. (2006) "Muscles, Motorcycles and Tattoos: Gentrification in a New Frontier." *Journal of Consumer Culture.* 6(1), p33–56.

Hand, M. and Shove, E. (2004) "Orchestrating Concepts: Kitchen Dynamics and Regime Change in Good Housekeeping and Ideal Home, 1922–2002." *Home Cultures.* 1(3), p235–256.

Haraway, D. (1988) "Situated Knowledge: The Science Question in Feminism and the Privilege of Partial Perspective." *Feminist Studies.* 14, p575–599.

Harding, S. (1987) *Feminism and Methodology.* Open University Press, Milton Keynes.

Harris, A. (2004) *Future Girl: Young Women in the Twenty-First Century.* Routledge, London.

Hearnden, J. and Norfolk, E. (eds.) (2006) *Miller's Antique Price Guide.* Mitchell Beazley, London.

Heath, J. and Potter, A. (2005) *The Rebel Sell: How the Counterculture Became Consumer Culture.* Capstone, Chicester.

Hebdige D. (1988) *Hiding in the Light: On Images and Things.* Routledge, London.

Heller, D. (ed.) (2007) *Makeover Television: Realities Remodelled.* I. B. Taurus, London.

Herrmann, G. M. (1997) "Gift or Commodity: What Changes Hands in the U.S. Garage Sale?" *American Ethnologist.* 24(4), p910–930.

Hewitt, J. (1987) "Good Design in the Market Place: The Rise of Habitat Man." *Oxford Art Journal.* 10(2), p28–42.

Highmore, B. (2011) *Ordinary Lives: Studies in the Everyday.* Routledge, London.

Hillis, K. (2006) "Auctioning the Authentic: eBay, Narrative Effect and the Superfluity of Memory" in Hillis, K., Petit, M. and Epley, N. S. (eds.) *Everyday eBay: Culture, Collecting and Desire.* Routledge, London.

Hillis, K., Petit, M. and Epley, N. S. (eds.) (2006) *Everyday eBay: Culture, Collecting and Desire.* Routledge, London.

Hillis, K., Petit, M. and Epley, N. S. (2006) "Introduction" in Hillis, K., Petit, M. and Epley, N. S. (eds.) *Everyday eBay: Culture, Collecting and Desire.* Routledge, London.

Hills, M. (2002) *Fan Cultures.* Routledge, London.

Hodkinson, P. (2005) "Communicating Goth: Online Media" in Gelder, K. (ed.) *The Subcultures Reader.* Routledge, London.

Holliday, R. (2005) "Home Truths?" in Bell, D. and Hollows, J. (eds.) *Ordinary Lifestyles: Popular Media, Consumption and Taste.* McGraw-Hill, Maidenhead.

Hollows, J. (2003) " 'Feeling like a Domestic Goddess' Post-Feminism and Cooking." *European Journal of Cultural Studies.* 6(2), p179–202.

Hollows, J. (2006) "Can I Go Home Yet? Feminism, Post-Feminism and Domesticity" in Hollows, J. and Moseley, R. (eds.) *Feminism in Popular Culture.* Berg, London.

Hollows, J. (2008) *Domestic Cultures.* Open University Press, Berkshire.

Holt, D. (1997) "Distinction in America? Recovering Bourdieu's Theory of Tastes from Its Critics." *Poetics.* 25, p93–120.

Holt, D. (1998) "Does Cultural Capital Structure American Consumption?" *Journal of Consumer Research.* 25, p1–25.

Horne, S. and Maddrell, A. (2002) *Charity Shops: Retailing, Consumption and Society.* Routledge, London.

Hurdley, R. (2006) "Dismantling Mantelpieces: Narrating Identities and Materialising Culture in the Home." *Sociology.* 40(4), p717–733.

Huyssen, A. (1986) *After the Great Divide: Modernism, Mass Culture and Postmodernism.* Macmillan, London.

Jackson, A. (2010) "Constructing at Home: The Experience of the Amateur Maker." *Journal of Design and Culture.* 2(1, March), p5–26.

Jackson, P., Lowe, M. and Miller, D. (eds.) (2000) *Commercial Cultures: Economies, Practices, Spaces.* Berg, London.

Jameson, F. (1985) "Postmodernism and Consumer Society" in Foster, H. (ed.) *Postmodern Culture.* Pluto Press, London.

Jameson, F. (1991) *Postmodernism, or, the Cultural Logic of Late Capitalism.* Verso, London.

Jenkins, K. (1995) *On What Is History?* Routledge, London.

Jenkinson, E. (2010) "What is the Future for Britain's Antiques Trade?" *The Independent.* June 10. Available at http://www.independent.co.uk/property/interiors/what-is-the-future-for-britainrsquos-antiques-trade-1996931.html [Accessed September 13, 2010].

Jenß, H. (2004) "Dressed in History: Retro Style and the Construction of Authenticity in Youth Culture." *Fashion Theory.* 8(4), p387–404.

Jenß, H. (2005) "Sixties Dress Only! The Consumption of the Past in a Retro Scene" in Palmer, A. and Clark, H. (eds.) *Old Clothes, New Looks: Second Hand Fashion.* Berg, New York.

Johnson, R. (1986) "What is Cultural Studies Anyway?" *Social Text.* 16(Winter), p38–80.

Johnstone, L. and Lloyd, J. (2004) *Sentenced to Everyday Life: Feminism and the Housewife.* Berg, Oxford.

Kennan, M. (2003) "Comment: Change Rooms at Your Peril." *The Sunday Times.* February. [Accessed online May 10, 2007. Now unavailable].

Key Note Media (2008) "Men's and Women's Buying Habits." Available at http://www.keynote.co.uk/media-centre/in-the-news/display/mens—womens-buying-habits/?articleId=61. [Accessed March 10, 2012].

Kirkham, P. (ed.) (1996) *The Gendered Object.* Manchester University Press, Manchester.

Kirkham, P. (1998) *Charles and Reay Eames: Designers of the Twentieth Century.* MIT Press, Cambridge, Massachusetts.

Kopytoff, I. (1986) "The Cultural Biography of Things: Commoditization as Process" in Appadurai, A. (ed.) *The Social Life of Things.* Cambridge University Press, Cambridge.

Korczynski, M. and Tyler, M. (2008) "The Contradictions of Consumption at the Point of Service Delivery." *Journal of Consumer Culture.* 8(3), p307–320.

Lash, S. and Lury, C. (2007) *Global Culture Industry.* Polity Press, London.

Latour, B. (1987) *Science in Action.* Open University Press, Milton Keynes.

Law, J. (1987) "Technology, Closure and Heterogeneous Engineering: The Case of the Portuguese Expansion" in Bijker, W. E., Hughes, T. P. and Pinch, T. J. (eds.) *The Social Construction of Technological Systems: New Directions in the Sociology and History of Technology.* MIT Press, Cambridge, Massachusetts.

Lawler, S. (2004) "Rules of Engagement: Habitus, Power and Resistance" in Adkins, L. and Skeggs, B. (eds.) *Feminism after Bourdieu.* Blackwell, Oxford.

Leiss, W., Kline, S., Jhally, S. and Botterill, J. (2005) *Social Communication in Advertising: Consumption in the Mediated Marketplace.* Routledge, Oxon.

Lemire, B. (1988) "Consumerism in Preindustrial and Early Industrial England: The Trade in Second Hand Clothes." *Journal of British Studies.* 27(1), p1–24.

Lemire, B. (2005) "Shifting Currency: The Culture and Economy of the Second Hand Trade in England, c.1600–1850" in Palmer, A. and Clark, H. (eds.) *Old Clothes, New Looks: Second Hand Fashion.* Berg, Oxford.

Leonard, M. (1997) "Paper Planes: Travelling the New Grrl Geographies" in Skelton, G. and Valentine, G. (eds.) *Cool Places: Geographies of Youth Culture.* Routledge, London.

Leslie, D. and Reimer, S. (2003) "Gender, Modern Design, and Home Consumption." *Environment and Planning D: Society and Space.* 21(3), p293–316.

Lewis, T. and Potter, E. (eds.) (2011) *Ethical Consumption: A Critical Introduction.* Routledge, London.

Lillie, J. (2006) "Immaterial Labor in the eBay Community: The Work of Consumption in the 'Network Society'" in Hillis, K., Petit, M. and Epley, N. S. (eds.) *Everyday eBay: Culture, Collecting and Desire.* Routledge, London.

Littler, J. (2008) *Radical Consumption in Contemporary Culture.* Open University Press, Berkshire.

Logan, T. (2001) *The Victorian Parlour: A Cultural Study.* Cambridge University Press, Cambridge.

Lopata, H. Z. (1971) *Occupation: Housewife.* Oxford University Press, Oxford.

Lovell, T. (2000) "Thinking Feminism with and against Bourdieu." *Feminist Theory.* 1(1), p11–32.

Lury, C. (1996) *Consumer Culture.* Polity Press, Cambridge.

Lury, C. (1998) *Prosthetic Culture: Photography, Memory and Identity.* Routledge, London.

Lury, C. (2006) "The United Colours of Diversity" in Manghani, S., Piper, A. and Simons, J. (eds.) *Images: A Reader.* Sage, London.

MacCarthy, F. (1966) "In Habitat." *Guardian.* October 5, p8.

MacCarthy, F. (2006) "How Do You Bring a Mid-20th-Century Home Back to Its Best without Living in a Time Warp?" *Elle Decoration.* August, p97–100.

MacPherson, C. B. (2007 [1962]) *The Political Theory of Possessive Individualism: Hobbes to Locke.* Oxford University Press, Oxford.

Maffesoli, M. (1988) "Jeux De Masques: Postmodern Tribalism." *Design Issues.* 4(1–2), p141–151.

Makovicky, N. (2007) "Closet and Cabinet: Clutter as Cosmology." *Home Cultures.* 4(3), p287–310.

Manekar, P. (1999) *Screening Culture, Viewing Politics: An Ethnography of Television, Womanhood and Nation in Postcolonial India.* Duke University Press, Durham, NC.

Marcus, D. (2004) *Happy Days and Wonder Years: The Fifties and Sixties in Contemporary Cultural Politics.* Rutgers University Press, New Brunswick, NJ.

Marsh, M. (1997) "Spirit of the Beehive." *Independent.* September 14.

Martens, L., Southerton, S. and Scott, S. (2004) "Bringing Children (and Parents) into the Sociology of Consumption: Towards a Theoretical and Empirical Agenda." *Journal of Consumer Culture.* 4(2), p155–182.

Massumi, B. (1987) "Foreword" in Deleuze, G. and Guattari, F. *A Thousand Plateaus: Capitalism and Schizophrenia.* Vol. 2. University of Minnesota Press, Minneapolis.

McCracken, G. (1988) *Culture and Consumption: New Approaches to the Symbolic Character of Consumer Goods.* Indiana University Press, Bloomington.

McKendrick, N., Brewer, J. and Plumb, J. (1982) *The Birth of a Consumer Society: The Commercialization of 18th Century England.* Indiana University Press, Bloomington.

McRobbie, A. (1989) "Second-Hand Dresses and the Role of the Rag Market" in McRobbie, A. (ed.) *Zoot Suits and Second Hand Dresses: An Anthology of Music and Fashion.* Macmillan, London.

McRobbie, A. (1994) *Postmodernism and Popular Culture.* Routledge, London.

McRobbie, A. (1998) *British Fashion Design: Rag Trade or Image Industry?* Routledge, London.

McRobbie, A. (2004) "'What Not to Wear' and Post-Feminist Symbolic Violence" in Adkins, L. and Skeggs, B. (eds.) *Feminism after Bourdieu.* Blackwell, Oxford.

McRobbie, A. (2009) *The Aftermath of Feminism: Gender, Culture and Social Change.* Sage, London.

Miller, D. (1987) *Material Culture and Mass Consumption.* Basil Blackwell, Oxford.

Miller, D. (1998) *A Theory of Shopping.* Cornell University Press, Ithaca, New York.

Miller, D. (ed.) (2001) *Home Possessions: Material Culture behind Closed Doors.* Berg, London.

Miller, D. (2008) *The Comfort of Things.* Polity Press, London.

Miller, D. (2012) Response in Baker, S. and Edwards, R. (eds.) (2012) "How Many Qualitative Interviews Is Enough." Discussion Paper. Available at http://eprints.ncrm.ac.uk/2273/ [Accessed March 25, 2012].

Molloy, M. and Larner, W. (2010) "Who Needs Cultural Intermediaries Indeed? Gendered Networks in the Designer Fashion Industry." *Journal of Cultural Economy.* 3(3), p361–377.

Morley, D. (1992) *Television, Audiences and Cultural Studies.* Routledge, London.

Morley, D. (2000) *Home Territories: Media, Mobility and Identity.* Routledge, London.

Moseley, R. (2000) "Makeover Takeover on British Television." *Screen.* 41(3), p299–314.

Munt, S. (2000) *Cultural Studies and the Working Class: Subject to Change.* Continuum International, London.

Myers, F. (2001) "Introduction" in *The Empire of Things: Regimes of Value and Material Culture.* School of American Research Press, Santa Fe, New Mexico.

National Readership Survey (2008) "Topline Readership." Available at http://www.nrs.co.uk/top_line_readership. [Accessed October 17, 2008].

Nava, M. (1992) *Changing Cultures: Feminism, Youth and Consumerism.* Sage, London.

Nava, M. (2000) "Modernity Tamed? Women Shoppers and the Rationalization of Consumption in the Inter-War Period" in Andrews, M. R. and Talbot, M. M. (eds.) *All the World and Her Husband: Women in Twentieth Century Consumer Culture.* Continuum International, London.

Negrin, L. (2006) "Ornament and the Feminine." *Feminist Theory.* 7(2), p219–235.

Negus, K. (2002) "The Work of Cultural Intermediaries and the Enduring Distance between Production and Consumption." *Cultural Studies.* 16(4), p501–515.

Nixon, S. (1997) "Designs on Masculinity: Menswear Retailing and the Role of Retail Design" in McRobbie, A. (ed.) *Back to Reality: Social Experience and Cultural Studies.* Manchester University Press, Manchester.

Oakley, A. (1974) *Housewife.* Penguin, London.

Ogundehin (2005) "Savvy Shopping, How to Save and When to Splurge: Beautiful Buys for Every Budget." *Elle Decoration.* (April), p22–34.

Oliver, P., Davis, I. and Bentley, I. (1981) *Dunroamin: The Suburban Semi and Its Enemies.* Barrie and Jenkins, London.

Orbach, R. (2006) "Interview." Available at: http://www.vam.ac.uk/collections/fashion/1960s/sixtiesfashion/interviews/orbach_interview/index.html [Accessed June 21, 2007].

Osterwold, T. (2003) *Pop Art.* Taschen, London.

Palmer, A. and Clark, H. (2005) *Old Clothes, New Looks: Second Hand Fashion.* Berg, London.

Palmer, G. (2004) "'The New You' Class and Transformation in Lifestyle Television" in Holmes, S. and Jermyn, D. (eds.) *Understanding Reality Television.* Routledge, London.

Parkins, W. (2004) "Out of Time: Fast Subjects and Slow Living." *Time & Society.* 13(2–3), p363–382.

Parkins, W. and Craig, G. (2006) *Slow Living.* Berg, Oxford.

Parr, M. (1992) *Sign of the Times: A Portrait of the Nation's Tastes.* Cornerhouse, London.

Pateman, C. (1988) *The Sexual Contract.* Polity Press, Cambridge.

Patton, M. Q. (1990) *Qualitative Evaluation and Research Methods.* Sage, London.

Peterson, R. A. and Kern, R. A. (1996) "Changing Highbrow Taste: From Snob to Omnivore." *American Sociological Review.* 61, p900–909.

Petty, M. M. (2012) "Curtains and the Soft Architecture of the American Postwar Domestic Interior." *Home Cultures.* 9(1), p39–56.

Pickering, M. and Keightley, E. (2006) "The Modalities of Nostalgia." *Current Sociology.* 54(6), p919–941.

Pile, J. (2005) *A History of Interior Design.* Laurence King, London.

Pink, S. (2001) *Doing Visual Ethnography: Images, Media and Representation in Research.* Sage, London.

Pink, S. (2004) *Home Truths: Gender, Domestic Objects and Everyday Life.* Berg, Oxford.

Pomian, K. (1990) *Collectors and Curiosities: Paris and Venice: 1500–1800.* Polity Press, Cambridge.

Potts, T. (2006) "Creating 'Modern Tendencies': The Symbolic Economics of Furnishing" in Bell, D. and Hollows, J. (eds.) *Historicizing Lifestyle: Mediating Taste, Consumption and Identity from the 1900s to the 1970s.* Ashgate, London.

Powell, H. (2009) "Time, Television and the Decline of DIY." *Home Cultures.* 8(1), p89–108.

Prince, D. (2007) *How to Sell Anything on eBay and Make a Fortune.* McGraw-Hill, London.

Probyn, E. (1990) "New Traditionalism and Post-Feminism: TV Does the Home." *Screen.* 31(2), p147–159.

Ramazanoğlu, C. with Holland, J. (2002) *Feminist Methodology: Challenges and Choices.* Sage, London.

Reimer, S. and Leslie, D. (2004) "Identity, Consumption, and the Home." *Home Cultures.* 1(2), p187–208.

Resnick, P. and Zeckhauser, R. (2002) "Trust among Strangers in Internet Transactions: Empirical Analysis of eBay's Reputation System." *The Economics of the Internet and E-Commerce.* Available at http://www-csag.ucsd.edu. [Accessed January 10, 2007].

Retroselect (2008) "BBC Antiques Programmes." Available at http://www.retroselect.com/Index/BBC%20Antiques%20Programmes.htm. [Accessed June 10, 2009].

Retrotogo (2012) "Modculture Media." Available at http://www.modculturemedia.com/retro_to_go/. [Accessed January 10, 2012].

Rheingold, H. (2005 [1994]) "Introduction to the Virtual Community" in Gelder, K. (ed.) *The Subcultures Reader.* Routledge, London.

Rigby, B. (2000) "Popular Culture as Barbaric Culture: The Sociology of Pierre Bourdieu" in Robbins, D. (ed.) *Pierre Bourdieu.* Vol. 3. Sage, London.

Roberts, T. (2005) Interview by Anne Dyke. British Library Sound Archive. C1046/12B [BL REF].

Rock, S. (1977) "Let the Good Times Roll." *19 Magazine.* October, p101.

Rolling Stone (2003) "Sgt. Pepper's Lonely Hearts Club Band." Available at http://www.rollingstone.com/news/story/6595610/1_sgt_peppers_lonely_hearts_club_band. [Accessed June 17, 2009].

Rubin, L. B. (1976) *Worlds of Pain: Life in the Working Class Family.* Basic Books, New York.

Rutherford, J. (1992) *Men's Silences: Predicaments in Masculinity.* Routledge, London.

Ryan, D. (1995) *The Daily Mail Ideal Home Exhibition and Suburban Modernity, 1908–1951.* PhD thesis. University of East London, London.

Samuel, R. (1994) *Theatres of Memory.* Vol. 1, *Past and Present in Contemporary Culture.* Verso, London.

Sassatelli, R. (2007) *Consumer Culture: History, Theory and Politics.* Sage, London.

Savage, M. (2000) *Class Analysis and Social Transformation.* Open University Press, Buckingham.

Savage, M., Bagnall, G. and Longhurst, B. (2000) "Individualization and Cultural Distinction" in Savage, M. *Class Analysis and Social Transformation.* Open University Press, Buckingham.

Savage, M., Barlow, J., Dickens, P. and Fielding, T. (1992) *Property, Bureaucracy and Culture.* Routledge, London.

Sayer, A. (2005) *The Moral Significance of Class.* Cambridge University Press, Cambridge.

Seigworth, G. and Gregg, M. (2010) *The Affect Theory Reader.* Duke University Press, Durham, NC.

Shove, E., Watson, M., Hand, M. and Ingram, J. (2007) *The Design of Everyday Life.* Berg, Oxford.

Showhome (2007) "About Showhome." Available at http://www.ourshowhome.com/. [Accessed June 17, 2007].

Silva, E. B. (2004) "Gender, Home and Family in Cultural Capital Theory." *British Journal of Sociology.* 56(1), p83–103.

Silva, E. B. (2006a) "Distinction through Visual Art." *Cultural Trends.* 15(2/3), p141–158.

Silva, E. B. (2006b) "Homologies of Social Space and Elective Affinities: Researching Cultural Capital." *Sociology.* 40(6), p117–189.

Silva, E. B. (2010) *Technology, Culture, Family: Influences on Home Life.* Palgrave Macmillan, Basingstoke.

Silverman, D. (2004) *Doing Qualitative Research.* Sage, London.

Sinclair, J. and Livingston, S. (2005) *eBay Photography the Smart Way: Creating Great Product Pictures That Will Attract Higher Bids and Sell Your Items Faster.* Amacom, New York.

Skeggs, B. (1997) *Formations of Class and Gender.* Sage, London.

Skeggs, B. (2004a) *Class, Self, Culture.* Routledge, London.

Skeggs, B. (2004b) "Exchange, Value and Affect: Bourdieu and 'the Self'" in Adkins, L. and Skeggs, B. (eds.) *Feminism after Bourdieu*. Blackwell, Oxford.

Skeggs, B. (2004c) "Introducing Pierre Bourdieu's Analysis of Class, Gender and Sexuality" in Adkins, L. and Skeggs, B. (eds.) *Feminism after Bourdieu*. Blackwell, Oxford.

Skeggs, B. (2004d) "The Re-Branding of Class: Propertising Culture" in Devine, F., Savage, M., Scott, J. and Crompton, R. (eds.) *Rethinking Class: Culture, Identities and Lifestyles*. Palgrave Macmillan, Hampshire.

Slater, D. (1997) *Consumer Culture and Modernity*. Polity Press, Cambridge.

Soper, K. (2008) "Alternative Hedonism, Cultural Theory and the Role of Aesthetic Revisioning." *Cultural Studies*. 22(5), p567–587.

Southerton, D. (2001a) "Consuming Kitchens: Taste, Context and Identity Formation." *Journal of Consumer Culture*. 1(2), p179–203.

Southerton, D. (2001b) "Ordinary and Distinctive Consumption; or a Kitchen Is a Kitchen Is a Kitchen" in Gronow, J. and Warde, A. (eds.) *Ordinary Consumption*. Routledge, London.

Southerton, D. (2009) "Temporal Rhythms" in Shove, E., Trentmann, F. and Wilk, R. (eds.) *Time, Consumption and Everyday: Practice, Materiality and Culture*. Berg, Oxford.

Sparke, P. (1995) *As Long as It's Pink: The Sexual Politics of Taste*. Harper Collins, London.

Sparke, P. (2004) *An Introduction to Design and Culture: 1900 to Present*. Routledge, London.

Sparke, P., Massey, A., Keeble, T. and Martin, B. (2009) *Designing the Modern Interior: From the Victorians to Today*. Berg, Oxford.

Spivak, G. (1990) *The Post-Colonial Critic: Interviews, Strategies, Dialogues*. Routledge, London.

Stallybrass, P. (1998) "Marx's Coat" in Spyer, P. (ed.) *Border Fetishisms: Material Objects in Unstable Spaces*. Routledge, London.

Stanley, L. (ed.) (1990) *Feminist Praxis: Research Theory and Epistemology in Feminist Sociology*. Routledge, London.

Star, S. L. (1991) "Power, Technology and the Phenomenology of Conventions: On Being Allergic to Onions" in Law, J. (ed.) *A Sociology of Monsters: Essays on Power, Technology and Domination*. Routledge, London.

Stobart, J. (2007) "In and Out of Fashion? Advertising Novel and Second-Hand Goods in Georgian England." *Business Links: Trade, Distribution and Networks,* CHORD Conference abstract. University of Wolverhampton, June 29–30. Available at http://home.wlv.ac.uk/~in6086/2007conf.html#js3. [Accessed December 12, 2008].

Storey, J. (2003) *Inventing Popular Culture: From Folklore to Globalization*. Wiley-Blackwell, London.

Strathern, M. (1992) *After Nature: English Kinship in the Late Twentieth Century.* Cambridge University Press, Cambridge.

Swartz, D. (1997) *Culture and Power: The Sociology of Pierre Bourdieu.* University of Chicago Press, Chicago.

Tate Website (2009) "Peter Blake." Available at http://www.tate.org.uk/servlet/ViewWork?cgroupid=999999961&workid=1029&searchid=9128. [Accessed June 28, 2009].

Taylor, L. (2002) "From Ways of Life to Lifestyle: The 'Ordinari-ization' of British Gardening Lifestyle Television." *European Journal of Communication.* 17(4), p479–493.

Taylor, L. (2005) "It Was Beautiful before You Changed It All: Class, Taste and the Transformative Aesthetics of the Garden Lifestyle Media" in Bell, D. and Hollows, J. (eds.) *Ordinary Lifestyles: Popular Media, Consumption and Taste.* McGraw-Hill, Maidenhead.

Taylor, L. (2008) *A Taste for Gardening: Classed and Gendered Practices.* Ashgate, Hampshire.

Thompson, M. (1979) *Rubbish Theory: The Creation and Destruction of Value.* Oxford University Press, Oxford.

Thorgerson, S. and Powell, A. (1999) *The 100 Best Album Covers: The Stories behind the Sleeves.* DK Publishing, London.

Thorne, C. (2003) "The Revolutionary Energy of the Outmoded." *October.* 104(Spring), p97–114.

Thornton, S. (1997) *Club Cultures.* Routledge, London.

Thrift, N. (2008) "The Material Practices of Glamour." *Journal of the Cultural Economy.* 1(1), p9–23.

Toffler, A. (1980) *The Third Wave.* Collins, London.

Toffler, A. and Toffler, H. (2006) *Revolutionary Wealth.* Alfred A. Knopf, New York.

Tomlinson, A. (ed.) (1990) *Consumption, Identity and Style: Marketing, Meanings and the Packaging of Pleasure.* Routledge, London.

Triggs, T. (2006) "Scissors and Glue: Punk Fanzines and the Creation of a DIY Aesthetic." *Journal of Design History.* 19(1), p69–81.

Turkle, S. (1995) *Life on Screen: Identity in the Age of the Internet.* Simon and Schuster, London.

Van Swol, L. M. (2006) "Return of the Town Square: Reputational Gossip and Trust on eBay" in Hillis, K., Petit, M. and Epley, N. S. (eds.) *Everyday eBay: Culture, Collecting and Desire.* Routledge, London.

Veblen, T. (1925) *The Theory of the Leisure Class.* Allen, London.

Wacquant, L. (2006) "Pierre Bourdieu" in Stones, R. (ed.) *Key Contemporary Thinkers.* Macmillan, London.

Warde, A. (2002) "Production, Consumption and 'Cultural Economy'" in du Gay, P. and Pryke, M. (eds.) *Cultural Economy.* Sage, London.

Warde, A. (2005) "Consumption and Theories of Practice." *Journal of Consumer Culture.* 5(2), p131–153.

Watson, M. and Shove, E. (2008) "Product, Competence, Project and Practice: DIY and the Dynamics of Craft Consumption." *Journal of Consumer Culture.* 8(1), p69–89.

Wernick, A. (1991) *Promotional Culture: Advertising, Ideology and Symbolic Expression.* Sage, London.

White, H. (1989) "New Historism: A Comment" in Veeser, H. A. (ed.) *The New Historicism.* Routledge, London.

Whitely, N. (1994) *Design for Society.* Reaktion Books, London.

Wilkes, N. (2006) "Inner Space." *Elle Decoration.* October, p172.

Willson, J. (2008) *The Happy Stripper: Pleasures and Politics of the New Burlesque.* I. B. Taurus, London.

Wilson, E. (1999) "The Bohemianisation of Mass Culture." *International Journal of Cultural Studies.* 2(1), p11–32.

Woodward, I. (2001) "Domestic Objects and the Taste Epiphany: A Resource for Consumption Methodology." *Journal of Material Culture.* 6(2), p115–136.

Woodward, I. (2009) "Material Culture and Narrative: Fusing Myth, Materiality and Meaning" in Vannini, P. (ed.) *Material Culture and Technology in Everyday Life: Ethnographic Approaches.* Peter Lang Publishing Inc., New York.

Wolfe, T. (1974) *Radical Chic and Mau-Mauing the Flak Catchers.* Bantam Books, New York.

Wolff, J. (2000) "The Feminine in Modern Art: Benjamin, Simmel and the Gender of Modernity." *Theory, Culture and Society.* 17(6), p33–53.

Wright, D. (2005) "Mediating Production and Consumption: Cultural Capital and 'Cultural Workers.'" *British Journal of Sociology.* 56(5), p105–120.

Young, I. M. (1997) *Intersecting Voices: Dilemmas of Gender, Political Philosophy, and Policy.* Princeton University Press, Princeton, New Jersey.

Zukin, S. (1988) *Loft Living: Culture and Capital in Urban Change.* Radius, London.

Zukin, S. (2004) *Point of Purchase: How Shopping Changed American Culture.* Routledge, London.

Index